TRIUMPH TR7
THE UNTOLD STORY

TRIUMPH TR7
THE UNTOLD STORY

DAVID KNOWLES

THE CROWOOD PRESS

First published in 2007 by
The Crowood Press Ltd
Ramsbury, Marlborough
Wiltshire SN8 2HR

www.crowood.com

British Library Cataloguing-in-Publication Data
A catalogue record for this book is available from the British Library.

ISBN 978 1 86126 891 4

Typeset by Bookcraft Ltd, Stroud, Gloucestershire
Printed and bound in Singapore by Craft Print International Ltd

Contents

Foreword

The TR7 project arrived like a bolt from the blue at a time when I was a relative youngster within the Austin Morris design set-up. We had been extremely busy at Longbridge, working on various Austin, Morris and MG projects, when we were asked to do a new Triumph sports car. Opportunities such as this do not come along very often. Many designers will sketch sports car designs from time to time, but to have the opportunity to work on a real sports car – and one destined for production – was a great experience. We drew it up in a short space of time, taking several design cues from my earlier Austin Zanda concept car, and styling the new Triumph very much with the North American market in mind. Then, almost as soon as we'd shown our full-size clay model, the project was relocated to Triumph's engineering section at Canley. We were left to consider a possible MG version, which would have shared the dimensional 'hard points' of the TR7 (as shown in some of my photos and sketches in this book), but it was never used. I might be responsible for the overall style of what became the TR7, but there were others after me who brought it to fruition. This book puts together pieces of the jigsaw for me. The TR7 was a fleeting introduction to sports cars which, although completed elsewhere, in the end was produced broadly as we'd envisaged it. We would possibly have done a few things differently, but the money wasn't available to perfect it completely. From reading this book, I have learned a great deal about the story of the TR7 after it left our studio at Longbridge. I am sure you will find the previously 'untold story' just as fascinating as I did.

Harris Mann
TR7 designer
Worcestershire
August 2007

Introduction

The Triumph TR7 is a British sports car that divides opinions like few others. There are those who passionately love its avant-garde style, comfortable cockpit, competent chassis and motor sport prowess. Equally there are those who despise the car, its looks and just about everything it stands for. Even some of those variously charged with bringing British Leyland's new 'corporate sports car' for the 1970s into the world, building it or selling it to the public, had mixed thoughts about their progeny, so the story of the TR7, the TR8 and their various still-born offshoots is hardly a simple tale of gestation, birth, life, death and mournful regret. But then if that had been the case, the story of what was, for many years, the last new mass-production British sports car (and which also remains, to date, the last sports car to bear the noble Triumph badge) and finally a British car that was arguably years ahead of the game, would have been so much more dull. If you regard all aspects of the TR7 through rose-tinted glasses, then parts of this book may not make comfortable reading. But if you are rational enough to accept that the path to greatness is often a tortuous journey, littered with wrong turns, and that it is often only the perspective of history that allows us to recognize the sparkle of greatness, then I hope you will not be disappointed.

1 Triumph TR Heritage

Although the origins of the 'Triumph' name go back to the 1880s, the process that led to the creation of Triumph vehicles more familiar to modern eyes only began during the closing months of the Second World War. When Sir John Black of the Standard Motor Company acquired the Triumph name in November 1944, he was buying little more than a moribund factory together with the 'rights and goodwill' associated with the name. While there had been some interesting pre-war Triumphs, their connection with the post-war cars amounted to little more than the badge.

Triumph Origins

Twenty-year-old Siegfried Bettmann left the Germany city of Nuremberg and arrived in London in 1883, determined to make his way in business. After working for others for two years, he opened S. Bettmann & Co., Import-Export Agency, in Coventry and started to import bicycles to sell under the Bettmann name. In 1886, however, he changed the company name to the Triumph Cycle Company; as he later explained: 'I gave it the name Triumph, which would be understood in all European languages.' The first Triumph motorcycle appeared in 1902. As the mania for powered two-wheelers took off, Bettmann expanded his business and the Triumph motorcycle soon became a significant success, building up a pedigree and reputation that survives to this day. He went on to become Mayor of Coventry in November 1913, although his political fortunes turned the following year

when he was forced to stand down because of his German origins.

Business continued to prosper, however, and Bettmann was still firmly in charge after the end of the First World War, during which Triumph had supplied more than 30,000 motorcycles to the Allied forces. The high regard in which they were held helped to foster demand for the 'Trusty Triumph' after hostilities had ceased. Since 1887 Bettmann had been in partnership with Mauritz Johann Schulte, an engineer from his hometown. Following the war Bettmann wanted to move into motor car production but Schulte would have none of it. Bettmann bought out his junior partner and the two parted company. The effective replacement for Schulte was Colonel Claude Holbrook, an English army officer who had overseen motorcycle procurement during the war. At first, Holbrook was unconvinced of the merits of moving into car making, but before long Bettmann acquired the assets of the Dawson Car Company and, in April 1923, the company introduced its first car, a 1.4-litre model called the Triumph 10/20. The car-making business took off, although the reputation of Triumph motorcycles meant that they remained an important part of the portfolio. In common with many other manufacturers, Triumph suffered acute financial problems during the so-called Great Depression but managed to stagger into the 1930s. The bicycle business was sold to raise money for the main business but this proved insufficient and, under pressure from Triumph's creditors, Bettmann was forced to cede control to Holbrook and retired from the company in 1933. Donald Healey, then an accomplished motor sports competitor who would later go on to found the company that bore his name, became the company's Experimental Manager in 1933.

Focusing on cars and the desperate need for cash meant that the Triumph motorcycle aspects of the business were sold off in 1936. Despite some exciting motor sports activities, however, the Triumph car business proved not to be viable, and so the Triumph Motor Company factory, equipment and goodwill were offered for sale in the summer of 1939. Thos. W. Ward of Sheffield purchased the company but the imminent onset of the Second World War put paid to any thought of producing cars. The Triumph works was one of the many casualties of the bombing of Coventry in November 1940: the factory dispatch bays later became the site of Coventry Cathedral's Chapel of Industry, believed to be the only case of a cathedral being built on a former factory. It would be only in the closing months of the conflict that Sir John Black offered salvation for the Triumph name.

The Standard Motor Company had been founded by Reginald Walter Maudslay, of the famous Maudslay engineering family, in 1903. By the mid-1920s Standard was similar in stature to Austin, but in common with many in the industry it suffered during the ensuing Depression. Success returned in the 1930s, however, when Captain John Black joined the company and helped mastermind significant growth: the famous 'Flying Standards', with their aerodynamic lines, proved popular throughout the pre-war decade. Black had ambitions to expand his business and tried to buy out one of his engine customers, William Lyons, whose SS Cars business would later become better known as Jaguar. Rebuffed by Lyons, Black looked elsewhere for a ready-made premium marque and finally found what he was looking for in 1944.

The first new-generation Triumphs of 1946 comprised a range of saloons and roadsters using Standard engines mounted in tubular steel chassis and clothed with coachwork by Mulliners of Birmingham. The 1776cc Triumph Roadster, although an open-top of reasonably sleek styling, with a bench seat and a rear 'dickey seat' for occasional use, was hardly a sports car. However, Black was determined to offer a competitor to Lord Nuffield's MG and, buoyed by success with the Roadster, gave his design team the go-ahead to create a Triumph sports car concept using Standard Vanguard components.

The Triumph TRX may have boasted hydraulic actuation of the roof and pop-up headlamps, advanced features for a British car in 1950, but the prototype was not well received and only three were built. (Norman Rose)

Standard Triumph's answer to the MG Midget was the 'Triumph Sports Car', which formed the beginning of the legendary TR line. The one-off 'TR1' is shown at Standard's Banner Lane factory after a road test session. (Norman Rose)

Three prototypes of the resulting 'TRX' were built in 1950, but although they had many clever features, they were heavy, ungainly and would have been expensive and finicky to build in production. By the following year Black was licking his wounds from a failed attempt to acquire the Morgan sports car concern. With the growing export success of the MG TD Midget, he was determined to create a modern contender in a market that secured not only much-needed dollars for the economy, but also significant profits for the participating manufacturers.

The result of these endeavours was a new concept known subsequently by historians and enthusiasts as the TR1, but exhibited at the 1952 Earl's Court Motor Show simply as the 'Triumph Sports Car'. The factory codename for this prototype (X516 in the prototype register) was 20TS – undoubtedly meaning 'two-litre Triumph Sports', since the eponymous Triumph Roadster could arguably have been thought of as the first of its line. The new car was quite a different animal from the old Triumph Roadster, however, and marked the very beginning of Triumph's legendary 'TR' sports car line.

The 'all-new' TR1 was nevertheless a motley collection of old Standard parts, including an old Flying Nine chassis wrapped in curvaceous new bodywork that was a modern interpretation of the classic sports car architecture, with the archetypal cutaway doors, cockpit set well back in the chassis and even an exposed spare wheel at the rear with access to the fuel filler cap through its centre. Triumph's stylist Walter Belgrove, who had also been responsible for the TRX, gave the new sports car simple lines without over-ornate fixtures and fittings or complex (and therefore expensive to form) panel shapes. Under the bonnet was a Standard Vanguard engine, with a capacity reduced slightly from 2088cc to 1991cc and fitted with twin 1½-inch SU carburettors.

The reception of this initial prototype by the press and visitors to Earl's Court was very positive. (Elsewhere at the same show, the former Triumph engineer Donald Healey concluded his deal with Austin's Leonard Lord to build the Austin Healey 100, while MG – now part of the Austin-Morris BMC combine – was pleading unsuccessfully for funding for a modern replacement for its essentially pre-war Midget line.)

During the following winter and spring the TR1 was evolved through engineering and testing development into the TR2, which was ready for production later in 1953, following an unveiling at the Geneva show in the spring.

The Classic Triumph TR: From TR2 to TR3B

The TR1 may have been a sensation at the 1952 Motor Show, but it was only the beginning of a revolution for Triumph; by the time that a production version appeared, it would be sufficiently different to be given the TR2 name, even though the TR1 had never made production. Conscious of the prominence of the Geneva Motor Show as an ideal spring platform to launch a new 'international' motor car, Standard Triumph unveiled the TR2 there in March 1953. The first production TR2s went down the Canley production

lines shortly after the summer factory closedown, although even by the turn of that first year, production rates were still very low.

At a price of just £555 (before tax) when the first cars were available to buy, the TR2 was something of a bargain – the MG TF Midget (new at the 1953 show) was £5 cheaper, but at the same time it was much more old-fashioned and slower than the new Triumph. The contemporary Austin Healey 100 was on offer for £725 (itself a price cut of £100 on the planned launch price), although the more 'exotic' sports cars tended to be well over the thousand pound mark. As sales took off, plans were put in hand to upgrade the TR2 and offer a fuller range of accessories. By late 1954 the second-generation TR2 was ready to appear, with different doors (shorter, allowing sills that ran straight through, thereby stiffening the body shell and allowing drivers to open the doors over the kerb) and

The first production iteration of the TR sports car was the TR2, seen here at a TR Drivers' Club rally in 2007.

Triumph in America

The years following the Second World War were marked by the rebuilding of Britain's national fortunes, with its economy ravaged by the expense of waging a costly war. Britain owed enormous sums to overseas allies, in particular the United States. It was incumbent upon business, with a nudge from government, to seek to redress the balance by bringing in foreign currency. One of the obvious means of doing this was through the production and export of high-value goods like cars, and the British car makers responded willingly, shipping large numbers of vehicles to 'Empire' countries like Australia and South Africa.

The Nuffield Organization's success with the MG sports car, however, had shown the potential of the United States as an export market. By the beginning of the 1950s a major proportion of the output of the MG factory at Abingdon was destined for North America. Over at Standard Triumph, most effort in the immediate post-war period had gone into the Standard Vanguard, a worthy but hardly exciting saloon model that, although it was reasonably well-received in Canada, sold poorly in the USA. Sir John Black had meanwhile come up with the Triumph Mayflower, a curious 'razor-edged' small car with what was, even for the time, a sort of 'retro' look that aped the much larger Rolls-Royces of the day. Sir John was convinced that this was what the Americans needed: the American customers thought otherwise, and the Mayflower was quietly withdrawn in 1953 after four years of dismal US sales. This then was part of the process that led to the creation of the TR2 and subsequent TR3. With sports cars, however, the United States was more than merely desirable to their success: it was unquestionably crucial.

In 1953 Standard Triumph sent out a young sales team led by Alan Bethell to set up a sales office in New York, from where they toured the USA in an attempt to persuade distributors and dealers to invest in franchises for a new car nobody had heard of. Initial results were disappointing: the eastern seaboard soon turned out to be the wrong place to have started, and before long the team transferred their attention to the west coast, where open sports cars are more readily usable year-round. They struck lucky with Dorothy Deen of Cal Sales, an enterprising young American businesswoman who was ready to invest $1.5 million. Her reward was a substantial Triumph franchise that extended across the USA west of the Mississippi. At a press conference at the Ambassador Hotel in Los Angeles, Black promised to unveil the Standard Triumph ranges at the January 1954 Los Angeles Auto Show, followed on the east coast by the April 1954 New York International Auto Show. Before long, TR2s were being shipped from Canley by lorry – with loads of six at a time – to Bristol docks and then out to the west coast on American Conference Lines freighters via the Panama Canal.

As sales and interest in the TR2 line grew, a further six distributors were signed up and they collectively dissuaded Standard Triumph from bringing in the everyday Standard saloon, or 'sedan', range (the word 'standard' meaning 'basic' in the USA rather than its home-market connotation of a 'high standard') and to focus primarily on the Triumph sports cars, but perhaps with a few small 'compact sedans' for good measure. By the time the Triumph sales team had established offices at a New York showroom on Broadway (at a rent of $8,000 per annum), sales were still modest but climbing rapidly. The arrival of the TR3, which was refined to meet US customer demand, with improved trim and colour ranges, helped sales to climb from below 1,000 to over 2,500; by 1959 TR3 sales had rocketed to 17,000. At around this time, the traditional 'Empire' export market of Australia was also coming under the threat of import sanctions that would seriously hamper direct exports to that market in the coming years in favour of local assembly. The importance of the United States to Triumph sports car production was consequently well and truly established.

improved brakes, although disc brakes still lay in the future.

In October 1955 the TR2 gave way to the TR3, featuring a modestly uprated engine, a new 'egg crate' radiator grille and the option of occasional 'plus two' seating. The new variant continued the TR sales success. The marque was given a further boost in October 1956 when, at last, front disc brakes were introduced – the first time on a series-production British car. These gave the TR3 the stopping power to match its performance.

Production output of the TR3 was double that of the TR2, as Triumph built sales in the all-important export markets, but this was not the end of the story, for even better things arrived in the autumn of 1957 with the introduction of the TR3A.

Although the name TR3A was attached by enthusiasts rather than the factory, it soon stuck, not least because it marked the first significant styling change. Just as BMC's MGA grille eventually succumbed to the stylist's scalpel, the TR3A differed from the TR3 by its wider

The TR3 was evolved from the TR2 in response to feedback from the North American market. (Norman Rose)

chrome-plated grille and slight recessing of the headlamps into the new front apron. Buoyed by good sales, Standard Triumph racked up production, only to be hit – in common with the rest of the motor industry – with the bleak recession of 1960. Many companies were hard hit and the still-independent Standard Triumph company became vulnerable to a takeover.

By that stage plans were in hand for a newer, more stylish version of the Triumph TR sports car, although there was one last gasp for the TR3 in 1962 in the form of the so-called 'TR3B', which was still only ever badged as the TR3. The TR3B was a response to North American dealers who were nervous of the change of direction that the next generation of TR was taking – a story that would be repeated some thirteen years later. Only 3,331 TR3Bs were built, and nowadays they have taken on almost mythical status, but the truth was that the styling of Triumph sports cars was heading in an exciting new direction.

By the time that the next step in the evolution of the 'TR' line was ready to be made, Standard Triumph would be emerging from the turmoil caused by decimated sales (the severe recession in the US market in 1960 and 1961 saw car sales plummet) and a change of company ownership,

largely owing to its fragile finances. The new owner, Leyland Motors, was best known as an ambitious manufacturer of commercial vehicles. Its Sales Director, Donald Stokes, had recently caught the public imagination through the sale of buses to the Marxist government of Cuba. Triumph as a car maker would come through this turbulent period, but some of the people in charge would not.

Lord Stokes, Sales Maestro

Donald Gresham Stokes was born in Plymouth on 22 March 1914. He studied at Blundell's School, where he apparently spent much of his time dreaming over car and aeroplane magazines, did extra science instead of the normal Latin, and was known to his peers as 'Motor blokes'. He then studied engineering at the Harris Institute of Technology, Preston. In those days, the pursuit of engineering as a profession was still somewhat unusual for a well-educated young man:

When I left school and wanted to go to Leyland – I'd always wanted to go there from the very beginning – I was told by my teachers that I was stupid; I was told 'what do you want to go and do that for? You can stay here and come and teach if you like – or you

Donald Stokes was the super-salesman who rose to become the head of British Leyland.

could go to university' – although not a lot of people went to university in those days – I'm talking about 1927–1928; they suggested I could also join the army or the navy or something like that – but very few people went into engineering.

Nevertheless, Stokes assumed a student apprenticeship at Leyland in 1930, and stayed loyal to the end:

> I was at Leyland Motors for fifty years. I went there originally as what was called a pupil apprentice – you had to pay to go; we spent six or so weeks in each department going all round, and then at the end of three years, if they liked you they offered you a job, and if they didn't they thrust you out into the world. But all the people who ever went there got good jobs, because it was very good basic training – very practical.

During the Second World War Stokes served as Lieutenant-Colonel in the Royal Electrical and Mechanical Engineers (REME): 'I was attached to and ran a Royal Marines unit – that was unusual in itself, because I was an Army officer – but then I got sent to just outside Caserta in Italy. From there, I then took part in the invasion

of Sicily.' All the time, Stokes's job at Leyland was held open for him, and he eventually returned in 1946:

> My job when I'd left had been manager of a department which made trolley buses – we made all the London trolley buses. After the war, I said 'there's no job left for me there!' and so they said 'well – what do you think we ought to do?' And so I said – with the impetuosity of youth and the sort of know-all attitude to business that you got in the army – 'well I could tell you – you've got to expand your horizons – it is no good just becoming a well-known Lancashire engineering firm – you ought to look after the world'. So Henry Spurrier, who was then the Managing Director, said 'well, you go and write something for me about what we should do'. And so I did that, and he said 'well, all right – you can have the job!' – and so they made me 'Export Development Manager'. They had an export manager who was a nice old boy with a long curly beard who had been there about a hundred years. I went all around the world and fixed up all their overseas business. You know, one thing led to another …

That is typical understatement, for Stokes's progression was rapid. By 1950 he had become Leyland's General Sales and Service Manager, and a Directorship followed in 1954. Stokes took a leading role in the successful 1961 bid to take over Standard Triumph. In 1963 Leyland's Deputy Chairman and Managing Director, Stanley Markland, resigned following a squabble over succession and the 49-year-old Stokes soon took his place. He was knighted in 1965, after three successive boom years for Leyland, and was raised to the peerage four years later, by which time he had masterminded the mergers with Rover and BMH to ultimately head up the British Leyland Motor Corporation. As Graham Turner related in his 1971 book *The Leyland Papers*, 'to [Stokes], selling involved a kind of psychological warfare and, since he was young and unknown, it also meant the successful projection of his own image – for which he had a special talent'. Stokes told Turner at the time: 'I always went for the top chaps … and I found that they didn't mind being seen by somebody they thought was up-and-coming'. It was Lord Stokes who saw the need for rationalization in the BLMC range, not least to tame the internecine battles between the competing sports cars, and it would be Stokes who made the choices that led to the Triumph TR7. By the time that the TR7 went on sale, British Leyland was a different animal and Stokes had been shunted into the largely honorary title of company President, a role he would fulfil until 1979, thereafter maintaining a link with Leyland Vehicles as a consultant for a further two years. At the time of writing he is living in retirement near Bournemouth with his wife, watching the affairs of the last vestiges of his empire with consternation.

Italian Style: The Triumph TR4 and TR4A

The Triumph TR4 of 1961 was just as much of a sensation as had been the TR1 of nine years

earlier, although in truth it should be said that most of the new-found beauty was skin-deep, for under the surface the new car, for all its exotic Michelotti styling, was mechanically much the same as the last of the TR3s.

The new car did benefit from a useful increase in width and much better 'creature comforts' for the driver and passenger (including wind-up door windows, face-level ventilation that was years ahead of the opposition, and an optional and very novel 'Surrey Top' hardtop – an idea similar in concept to the Porsche Targa of later years), and there was a new and much more up-to-date rack-and-pinion steering system to replace the antediluvian cam-and-lever system of the previous models – but the engine was the same 2138cc iron 4-cylinder that had seen service in the TR3B. One of the other key changes of significance to TR history was that the bodyshells for the TR4 were built at Triumph's new factory

Michelotti's TR4 married the basis of the TR chassis with a striking new body style.

Giovanni Michelotti, Italian Genius

Although the TR7 would, like the TR2 and TR3, be styled by a Briton, the man responsible for most of the models in between was an Italian, Giovanni Michelotti (the exception was the TR6, styled by Gerhart Giesecke of Karmann). Born in Turin on 6 April 1921, Michelotti worked for a number of design houses before establishing his own. His experience in the automotive field began with a job in the body-building section of Stabilimenti Farina in Turin in 1936. Thirteen years later, after the intervention of war, marriage and the arrival of two children, he set up his own design studio down the road, initially taking on work for other design houses such as Vignale, Bertone and Ghia. According to motoring writer and Michelotti fan Giles Chapman, Michelotti did much of his early design work on a single drawing board in his bedroom. His connection with Standard Triumph began in 1957, following a meeting with Harry Webster that was the start of a firm, lifelong friendship. Along with the majority of Triumphs built from then until the mid-1970s – including the Standard Vignale Vanguard, Triumph Herald and Vitesse, Triumph Italia, TR4 and TR5, Spitfire and GT6, 1300, 1500, Toledo, Dolomite, 2000/2500 and Stag – Michelotti worked on several makes of exotic sports car, as well as other mainstream but generally distinctive volume cars, including several BMWs. One of BMW's key design figures of the 1960s and '70s, Paul Bracq, believed that Michelotti's work on the BMW 1800 'saved the BMW factory'. In the early 1960s, as work increased, Michelotti moved his company to Orbassano, about 16km from Turin. In a tribute to his father, Michelotti's son Edgardo recalls that the Michelotti studios were run almost like a family affair:

> They used also to work on Sundays, but sometimes in the afternoons he would take all the staff to watch a football match … Torino team of course. Then they would come back again to the studio to carry on the work, always with an enthusiastic friendliness. When a prototype was completed, its delivery generated strong emotions, similar to the birth of a son. Then all the staff would spend a day at a simple restaurant to celebrate the successful delivery!

Bruce McWilliams first came to know Michelotti after the two met at Triumph's Canley studios in April 1967, when McWilliams became involved in a low-budget styling exercise that would seek to differentiate the TR250 from the basis of the TR4 from which it was so obviously derived. McWilliams found that Michelotti, far from being irritated at the involvement of the American, was charm and tact personified, and the two became good friends. As McWilliams noted in his tribute to Michelotti in the *TSOA Newsletter*: 'one could say that between the years of 1957 and 1966, Michelotti was the spirit behind the styling of almost all Triumph models, and their considerable acceptance underscored the skill of his many and diverse designs'.

Michelotti always had a reputation for hard work and being able to produce results to incredibly short timetables – his speed at creating usable sketches was legendary. In an interview for the Italian *Style Auto* magazine in 1968, Michelotti explained the genesis of the TR4: 'when in 1957 Triumph management asked me for a body design on their [TR3] chassis, they laid down one clear stylistic requirement: they wanted a strong, virile and "nervous" motor car. I remember that as an indicative comparison they chose the boxer – canine and human.' Hence the pugnacious appearance of the TR4, with its distinctive 'eyebrows' over the headlamps, the chunky square-set appearance: it was a look that would sustain TR sales from 1961 through to the early part of 1969. 'Micho was a remarkable character –and he used to chalk outlines on the floor, and tell his men to build the car to suit', Tony Lee recalls.

Sadly Michelotti's health suffered in the late 1970s, a consequence in part of his hands-on method in the studio, where he preferred to work directly with plaster of Paris rather than wood or clay. 'Harry Webster felt particularly bad about Micho's death', Tony Lee recalls. 'Harry had got Micho to set up with ovens to use the sort of beeswax and clay that we used in the UK, but in the hot climate in Italy he'd found that it wouldn't set – and so Micho had gone over to working with plaster of Paris, which he could scrape away at to get the shape he wanted.' In the end, the diminutive but effervescent Italian genius died of skin cancer on 23 January 1980, three months short of his sixtieth birthday. Giovanni Michelotti's last production car project was the Reliant Scimitar SS1, arguably not the best epitaph for such a talented man, but his studio contributed proposals for the Boxer and Broadside projects, which are covered later in the book.

Giovanni Michelotti.

at Speke, Liverpool, before being transported by road to Coventry for final assembly. It was the start of a long-running TR association with Speke.

Within four years of its launch the TR4 came in for a major overhaul in the form of the TR4A, which featured major alterations to the chassis allowing, for the first time, independent rear suspension in place of the previous live axle. Many Triumph enthusiasts have wondered why the TR4A was not simply badged as the TR5, since the major chassis change certainly would have justified this, but according to Triumph historian Graham Robson (employed by Triumph at the time) the reason was that 'the TR4 had established itself as a new breed of sports car, and the new model had to be seen as a development of it'. The US importers were less convinced of the benefits of the new independent set-up, which allowed Triumph to offer in the UK, uniquely for a mainstream British marque, an all-IRS range from Herald to 2000. As a result, the US market was offered a version of the TR4A with the old-style live axle set-up.

By 1967 the TR range had been in production for nearly fifteen years. Although there had been some major steps forward in terms of style, performance – from the old Standard Vanguard four – had slipped back in the league table. Triumph had already made a name for itself with the smooth, small 6-cylinder engines it offered in the Vitesse and 2000 ranges, and so it was natural that the next step would be to offer 6-cylinder power in the TR line. What would be the last 4-cylinder TR sports car for the next eight years ran down the Canley sports car line on 2 August 1967, followed by the first of a new generation of 6-cylinder TRs.

New Power for the Classic: The TR5 and TR250

The sturdy Standard Vanguard 4-cylinder engine had served well in three generations of TR sports car, but by the mid-1960s it was felt that the customer expected greater sophistication and refinement. The development of a 6-cylinder engine to replace the Vanguard unit is linked to Triumph's efforts to produce a contender in the growing 'executive' market for cars exemplified by the Rover 2000 and Triumph 2000: the initial 1.6-litre 6-cylinder of the Triumph Vitesse grew successively to 2 litres and ultimately 2.5 litres, the latter being the capacity deemed appropriate to supersede the 2.2-litre 4-cylinder of the Triumph TR4. However, although the new TR would benefit from a new powerplant, there were insufficient funds to develop the body or chassis beyond some rudimentary styling and equipment tweaks.

Bruce McWilliams took over responsibility for Triumph sales in North America following the merger between Leyland and Rover. In his view, the situation he inherited was something of a shambles: 'Annual sales, which had reached a high of 24,000, were headed to a projected 8,000. And there were roughly 5,000 TR4s in the warehouse as well as stocks of Triumph 2000s, 1300s and Heralds that, at current sales rates, would have lasted several years.' Part of the problem seemed to be, in McWilliams' opinion,

ageing and ill-suited models, and desperately bad sales and marketing policies. For example, when I discovered that a six-cylinder version of the TR4 would have no internal or external appearance differences, I went to work to create these, although little time or money was available. Still, within weeks, I developed a mock-up of the changes at the then Triumph headquarters in Teaneck, New Jersey, and then flew to the UK to demonstrate their nature to the people at Coventry. With virtually no time for their implementation, everyone gave them fullest support and, between April and October of 1967, they became part of the specification of what we had designated the TR250.

The TR250 was the name given to the US version of what elsewhere was known as the TR5; for the American market, the nose of the car succumbed to the contemporary fashion for 'racing stripes' and there were a handful of other cheap but reasonably effective attempts to make what many contemporary observers felt was something of the proverbial silk purse from a sow's ear. Even so, by this time the people at the top of what was by now known as the Leyland Motor Corporation had bigger issues on their mind: they were looking at a tie-up with the giant BMC colossus, makers of Triumph's deadly MG rivals.

Birth of a Colossus: The Creation of British Leyland

The car industry of the 1950s had been shaped by the events of the Second World War, with manufacturers in every nation having to respond in appropriate ways to the outcome of the conflict upon their national economies and, in some cases, according to the external economic assistance they received. Many British car makers had initially benefited from new plant and premises constructed as part of the war effort, but they also suffered from the legacies of outdated practices, poor rates of capital investment in new plant, outdated management techniques and fragile industrial relations.

Great engineering achievements, such as the BMC Mini, were achieved without the underpinning of sound financial principles and strategic planning. Just as the industry was having to develop, so the political environment was changing: successive governments during the 1960s attached enormous importance to the car industry as a means of economic governance through a whole variety of tax measures. As foreign car companies expanded rapidly, Britain seemed in danger of losing her status in the world league of car makers, and there was increasing political, economic and peer pressure for the car makers to consolidate their interests through mergers and acquisitions.

By far the biggest of these companies was the British Motor Corporation, creator of the Mini and overseen by Sir George Harriman, regarded by his contemporaries as something of

an avuncular statesman, gentlemanly and rather old-fashioned in his approach. BMC's factories, themselves a conglomeration of former Austin and Nuffield Corporation enterprises that had only been partially rationalized from an earlier merger in 1952, churned out large numbers of products with variable rates of efficiency. Biggest sellers were the ADO16 Austin/Morris 1100 and the Mini range, the latter claimed by some to be making either a loss or a minimal profit, depending on how one tried to unravel and interpret the complex intra-company accounting system.

Alongside the gigantic British Motor Corporation was the hardly less grandly titled but significantly smaller Leyland Motor Corporation. Whereas BMC was overseen by engineering-driven Harriman, Leyland's growing success in the marketplace was masterminded by ace salesman Donald Stokes, who not only knew how to shift product but also how to win influence and respect in the centres of political and financial power. Stokes was smooth but simultaneously as sharp as a tack; he and Harriman were as different as chalk and cheese.

From 1964 Britain entered into a new era of technology-focused socialist government under Prime Minister Harold Wilson (the 'Tony Blair' of his day). The new order increasingly saw businessmen like Stokes as the way forward, and quasi-patrician statesmen like Harriman as relics of the past.

Various government-sponsored talks within the motor industry were held to encourage consolidation, but they were generally entered into less than enthusiastically by most of the protagonists. However, a series of events in 1965–66 led to an escalation of such discussions. Firstly BMC's agreement to purchase Pressed Steel, the largest independent makers of car bodies in the UK, understandably concerned rival manufacturers who were dependent upon Pressed Steel for their car bodies. This was then followed by Rover Cars reaching an agreement with Leyland to join them and achieve some economies of scale through joint ownership of the Rover and Triumph marques. Also at this time, Jaguar, following talks with Leyland, decided instead to form an alliance with BMC and Pressed Steel, created a grouping called British Motor Holdings (BMH). Meanwhile the Rootes Group, whose various problems included misguided investment in the Hillman Imp and its troubled plant at Linwood, Scotland, looked increasingly in peril of being swallowed entirely by one of its key shareholders, the US-based Chrysler Corporation.

In December 1966 the Labour government's Minister of Technology, Anthony Wedgwood Benn, called Stokes and Harriman to meet him to discuss the growing crisis at Rootes. In his diaries, published long after he had come to be known as Tony Benn, he records:

> I put to them three simple questions. Do you want to see Chrysler take over Rootes? Do you think it is worth attempting a British solution – a regrouping that would include Rootes and British Motor [Corporation] and Leyland, in which there might be some government participation? Would you be prepared to bring about a merger between your two companies to try to absorb Rootes if the government were prepared to help?

Benn, however, states that there were 'tensions between Harriman and Stokes' and this overture came to nothing.

Neither Wedgwood Benn nor Wilson, however, lost his growing enthusiasm for the creation of a 'national' motor industry and they continued their lobbying. Less than a year later, on the evening of Sunday 15 October 1967, Wedgwood Benn joined Wilson, Harriman and Stokes at the Prime Minister's country retreat, Chequers, for a meal and discussion about the possibility of the two motor industry men working together. According to Benn, the Prime Minister wanted 'that subtle combination of a buccaneer and a statesman'. He did not have to spell out which was which. The process that followed somewhat resembled a wildlife scene where a fierce but relatively small predator circles an ailing elephant: both are wary of the other, but the eventual outcome is almost inevitable. Thus it was that by January 1968, what had started out as a merger became a takeover, even if there was an attempt to smudge the details for public consumption. By May 1968 the British Leyland Motor Corporation had come into being.

British Leyland Inc.: An American Marriage

In the USA, the merger between BMC and Jaguar was seen by those involved as a relatively painless exercise; there had, after all, been relatively little overlap between the two makers' car ranges, and so the opportunity to extend overall market penetration seemed to make a great deal of sense. With the BMH merger came a purpose-built office/warehouse in Leonia, New Jersey, and since BMC and Jaguar shared a number of common independent distributors, there was considerable impetus to make the union work.

From within the BMH camp, however, the merger with Triumph was viewed with some reservations. Bob Burden, who went on to flourish during the British Leyland era, saw operations close-up at both Triumph and BMC:

> I started in the car business with Triumph's advertising agency at the time, Doherty, Clifford, Steers and Shenfield, but later graduated to work for BMC … I've no idea how much, if anything, our management knew of the BMH-Leyland merger. I do know I was in early one Monday morning when word came through on the Telex. If I remember correctly, John White – our Chief Finance Officer at the time – was there also and we debated as to whether we should call Leyland Motors Sales to see if they had gotten the same message. I think we concluded to wait for our management to come in and make the call …

This was the start of a new chapter of 'integration', in the US operations as much as at home. The inverted commas are at the suggestion of Burden, who wryly observes:

> It always seems to me that the Brits had a theory that if you put two one-legged men together, you would create a two-legged man. What would really happen, of course, would be that they would fall all over each other. We were still in the process of putting BMC

and Jaguar together – and now there was a third one-
legged man …

Nevertheless, the process of reviewing, rational-
izing and adjusting got under way.

Some square pegs were pounded into round holes and
some pegs disappeared altogether [ironically, the
aforementioned John White was one of them]. However, with Graham Whitehead being named President
and Mike Dale eventually moving up to run Sales and
Marketing [rumour had it that Jo Eerdmans, the
former president of Jaguar Cars Inc., played a role in
those appointments], we who secretly wore our BMC
'prize pig' rosettes felt cautiously optimistic.

Burden readily admits that, although the
process seemed to go well from some viewpoints,
there was some resentment abroad:

Neither side had completely digested the earlier mergers – Standard Triumph with Rover and Jaguar with
BMC – hell, we still had a few Austin and Nuffield
loyalists – so this latest merger only added insult to
injury. Some of the resentment was petty as the Leyland people got shoehorned into 'our' building, and
offices became 'cubbies' and cubbies became 'bull
pens'. More of it was personal as careers were abrupt-
ly ended, changed direction or were dead-ended. Most
of all was the direction we saw the new company taking – the characterless 'kitchen cabinet' Leyland blue
(as described by our Creative Director, Marce May-
hew) replacing Jaguar green and MG red.

No less apprehensive about the merger were those
who came in from the Triumph organization. Mike
Cook was a Triumph man from the beginning:

My personal view, in the beginning, was that it might
work. I was familiar with the financial problems of
Rover and Triumph and the difficulty that Triumph
had in getting the TR6 project off the ground. 'Safety
in Numbers' seemed like a good approach to solving
the problems. Also, when I was hired by Graham
Whitehead to be Corporate Public Relations Manager, my whole thrust was to promote British Leyland
and its future.

Even as the British Leyland Motor Corporation
was coming into being, events in the United
States were taking place that would have a critical effect on cars sold in that market. With government and consumer lobby support, national
legislative bodies were assuming ever-increasing
roles in an effort to drive back the rise in deaths
and pollution arising from automotive safety and
emissions. While neither MG nor Triumph alone
was well equipped to tackle this dual onslaught,
the situation was really little better once the
two were nominally under the same hat, for the
management of the new organization felt it had
bigger fish to fry, in merging two very different
organizations and seeking to increase sales in the
home and continental European markets.

Triumph Engineering found itself having to
tackle the new safety and emissions requirements with very little outside assistance, although
the company did have some useful allies in the
right places. Triumph's US competition man Kas
Kastner, for example, confirms that:

the emissions difficulties had everyone and all engineering going mad. There was no money for car
development as the emissions side took it all. It was a
terrible, terrible period for the engineering staff. I was
involved in this country doing true industrial spying.
It was pretty cool, and we found out a lot … late night
meetings in shops and lawyers' offices and things like
that. Midnight phone call reports to the factory, all the
clandestine sneaking around was part of the work we
did in the Competition Department.

Indeed, Mike Dale, one of British Leyland's
senior marketing men in the United States, suggests that the knowledge of US tuning experts
like Kastner was often woefully overlooked or
dismissed by the British 'home team':

Some years before, Kas Kastner had told the company
how much power we were producing from a Triumph engine and he was heaped with much scorn.
Someone in the UK coined the phrase 'California air'
to describe Kas's horsepower figures and this really
ticked Kas off. He took an engine to the UK complete with his dyno charts and put it on a factory

dyno. It produced even more horsepower than Kas had claimed and that was the last we heard of our inept colonial efforts to produce horsepower!

Michelotti's TR5

In an ideal world, there is little doubt that Triumph would have liked to have made more sweeping changes to their TR sports cars than were possible given the constraints on time and money. The growing burden of United States emissions and safety legislation, which helped see a number of British cars dropped from US catalogues, also meant that engineering resources had to be focused on keeping the existing products in line with the law. Giovanni Michelotti was no less frustrated, for although he was prepared to work alongside Bruce McWilliams to create the TR250 style from that of the TR4, much better business and prestige came from working on a new style. Although Triumph would soon be in the market for a major facelift of the TR4 body, by the time they were ready Michelotti was busy working on other production car projects.

In the spring of 1967 the contract for what would become the TR6 therefore went to West Germany rather than Italy. In response Michelotti did what he always did best – created a prototype of his own for exhibition at one of the major European shows, no doubt with a hope that this could stimulate fresh business from Canley – perhaps for a 'TR6A' or even a 'TR7'! Taking a TR5 (and Triumph experimental chassis number X760) as his base, Michelotti lengthened the nose by 211mm (although the overall length was only up by 102mm since there was a slightly shorter rear overhang) and cleverly lowered the overall body appearance while actually maintaining the same scuttle height, engine bay clearance and wheelbase. This produced a sleek Italian interpretation of an English roadster, with a low upper door ledge capable of accommodating the traditional arm-resting qualities of the original sports cars. Twin circular headlamps, which, as Michelotti admitted, would have been too low to meet US legislative requirements, were framed in a full-width rectangular grille adorned with nothing other than chrome 'TR5 PI' badges, and below the grille aperture were slim chrome bumpers. The overall effect was very pretty, although arguably not particularly 'Triumph' in nature, and the prototype remained a one-off. It was shown at the Geneva Motor Show as the 'TR5 Ginevra' concept and still survives.

In an interview with the Italian magazine *Style Auto*, for its profile of the car in the spring 1968 issue, Michelotti said:

Michelotti TR5 Ginevra. (Michelotti)

Charles Spencer King

Although he has always been better known for his role in shaping many critically acclaimed Rovers, Charles Spencer King – 'Spen' to his colleagues – has also been involved with developing a number of Triumph models. King was born in 1925 and after school gained an apprenticeship at Rolls-Royce. Having family connections in Rover (his uncles were Maurice and Spencer Wilks) meant that he moved to the Solihull firm at the end of the Second World War and his early work there included the famous gas turbine-powered JET1 and T3 experimental Rover prototypes. King saw Rover grow throughout the 1950s and was intimately involved in the many innovative ideas explored at the time, including the 'Road Rover' – a concept that would eventually inspire the Range Rover of 1970 – and the highly advanced P6 Rover 2000 of 1963. In 1966 King oversaw the creation of the fascinating P6BS mid-engined Rover sports car prototype, which sadly never reached production.

The acquisition by BMC of Pressed Steel, Rover's source of bodyshells, helped precipitate the merger of Leyland and Rover interests; before long the merger of Leyland and BMC led to the formation of British Leyland. This in turn prompted a significant reshuffle of engineering talent, with a number of key Triumph personnel sent to Longbridge to oversee Austin Morris work. King found himself moved sideways to run Triumph. While there he oversaw the Triumph TR6, Stag and the 16-valve Dolomite Sprint cylinder head, as well as the beginnings of the replacement for the TR6 in the form of Project Bullet. In 1979 King became chairman of BL Technology and, with energy conservation and technological innovation in mind, he and his team developed a number of lightweight, aerodynamically efficient and technically advanced ECV (Energy Conservation Vehicle) experimental models. A few of the ideas found their way into subsequent BL vehicles but the majority of the innovative ideas were later taken up by other manufacturers. King finally retired from BL Ltd in 1985.

---

found himself moved to take on the hot seat of the Austin Morris part of the organization. In his place, Charles Spencer 'Spen' King, a long-serving Rover engineer who had contributed handsomely to the 1963 'P6' Rover 2000 and the project that became the Range Rover of 1970, found himself parachuted in to head up Triumph engineering.

King's first jobs at Triumph included bringing the Karmann-styled and -tooled TR6 to production the following year, picking up the threads of the similarly advanced Stag for launch in 1970, the introduction of the Triumph 2000 and 2500 Mark II in 1969, not to mention overseeing completion of what would become the Triumph Dolomite of 1971, the 'LT-77' (Leyland Triumph, 77mm) gearbox for the Rover SD1 and TR7, and further developments with the slant-four engine, including the four valve per cylinder 'Sprint' cylinder head, which arose from studies by Coventry Climax. It was clearly already quite a packed programme even without the added responsibility for a new sports car range.

Bruce McWilliams was by now the British Leyland Inc. Vice President in charge of Product Planning, and as such he was asked by Lord Stokes in 1970 to organize a fact-finding trip to the USA for senior UK staff:

> Sir Donald called to ask that I organize a sports car oriented briefing in California for Mike Carver [of British Leyland Central Planning] and Spen King. They immediately came over and we met in Los Angeles to embark on an energetic round of meetings with automobile writers, dealers, and others who could make a contribution on the probable future course of sports car design.

The US motoring press has always been influential and worthy of attention, particularly in the 'enthusiast' sector of the automobile market. McWilliams remembers the response:

> Perhaps the most useful meeting was a round-the-table discussion I had organized with the editorial staff of *Road & Track* magazine in Newport Beach. It was out of this meeting that the perception developed that we did not have to have anything exotic, such as a mid-engined car, but just something that was enormously competent, straightforward and attractive, essentially the very qualities that British sports cars had traditionally embodied.

Mike Carver also recalls the trip:

> At that time we went to the USA for two reasons,
> basically. We were tidying-up the sports car range and
> we were also looking at the Federal regulations that
> were coming – or at least the ones that looked as
> though they would prevent open cars. There was a
> great deal of sorting out to do with the whole sports
> car range – and we wanted to look into this – so Spen
> King and I joined Bruce McWilliams and we met
> dealers, racing people and journalists to discuss the
> sports car situation on the west coast of the USA. It
> wasn't a formally structured piece of market research
> – but then again, to try to get a 'representative sample'
> of US customers would have been hard – but then we
> were at least talking to people who knew what they
> were talking about.

Steve Redway, Editor of the TR Register's *TR
Action* magazine, points out there were other
issues too:

> The US felt that what was needed was a far simpler
> sportscar from Triumph, no more independent rear
> suspension, which all along was far too complicated
> for the good old boys of Detroit. The complications
> of fuel injection as seen in the TR6, whilst not mak-
> ing it to the US shores, wasn't wanted either. Four

*The Triumph Styling team is seen here in 1969 on the occasion
of a leaving party for François Talou: (left to right) John Ashford,
Norman Davies, Ray Innes, François Talou, Les Moore, Ray
Padmore, Eric Ingram, Brian Keane, Richard Hunt and Dave
Keepax. (John Ashford)*

cylinders and conventional carburetion was the order
of the day. What the US required was a comfortable
boulevard cruiser.

A slight counterpoint to this comes from TR7
Project Manager Mick Bunker, who feels that
the independent suspension is unfairly maligned:
'I think the semi-trailing arm suspension we
used on Triumphs was about the simplest suspension we could have used! The original [pure
Triumph] Bullet was to have used later-style
GT6 rear wishbone suspension, but of course we
changed to a live axle after Spen King's trip to
the USA.'

In Los Angeles, Carver recalls the lunch with
Road & Track:

> There were also people from a Triumph race team.
> Overall, they were not particularly biased towards Tri-
> umph – although Spen and I were quite surprised
> how in favour they were for Triumph and we were
> also very surprised that they were more in favour of a
> front engine rear-wheel-drive sports car rather than
> the then fashionable mid-engined layout.

McWilliams confirms the lack of enthusiasm for
an exotic specification: 'We were talking plain
old garden variety inexpensive mass-market MG
and/or Triumph sports cars.' Market research at
the time also forecast a severe falling-off of sales
of all the existing BLMC sports cars by 1975,
which helped give a timescale to the programme
for their replacement.

A side excursion to the Los Angeles expe-
dition was a meeting between Spen King and
McWilliams on the one side and Pete Brock
who, in conjunction with Kas Kastner, had
created a one-off special called the TR250K.
Kastner was Triumph's North American competitions manager while Brock had played an
important role with the Shelby Cobra, in particular the special Cobra competition coupé.
The TR250K had been created in 1968 on a
budget of $20,000 and featured prominently on
the April 1968 cover of *Car and Driver*, just as
the car made an ill-starred race debut at Sebring.
The TR250K had clearly excited Leon Mandel

at *Car and Driver*, for he wrote: 'it is so stunning it makes a Lamborghini look like a milk wagon … the wildest appeal to visceral response since mini skirts.'

In the view of its creators, the TR250K marked an exciting way forward for the Triumph sports car, and they were still keenly championing its cause two years on. However, according to McWilliams, although the car was beautifully designed and built, it could not be economically or practically turned into a production prospect.

Some in British Leyland had supported the modern 'European' mid-engine layout proposed for MG's ADO21; indeed Spen King, by this time at Triumph, had earlier masterminded the creation of the mid-engined Rover P6 BS sports car prototype. In his previous role at Rover's US office, McWilliams had enthusiastically supported the promotion of the exciting P6 BS and would have liked to have seen it form the basis of a production Rover sports car. With the BLMC merger, however, there was clearly much less of a case for yet another sports car line and, given the pressing need for rationalization, there was no longer room for lost causes.

Triumph in the Ascendant: Progressing the Bullet

As Mike Carver's comments demonstrated, it had become evident early in the life of British Leyland that there was a surfeit of both marques and models – and the sports cars were an obvious example. 'Of course there were rumours and speculations about MG and Triumph,' says Bob Burden, 'I am sure there was some debate at higher levels, but I thought the decision to badge the new car as a Triumph was a foregone conclusion. Hope for the mid-engined MG was just about abandoned – so the signs were all there.' Although, as we shall see, the MG badge would be considered again in the context of the corporate sports car, it appears that there may also have been thoughts of attaching it to the original Triumph Bullet concept since, as Triumph engineer David Eley told Graham Robson for an interview published in *Triumph World* magazine, 'there was talk of an MG version, so Harry Webster (he was running Austin-Morris by then) came over to Turin to see the prototype'. Soon after came the process that finally determined the definitive form of 'Bullet'.

Triumph Styling experimented with a number of options for their original Michelotti/Les Moore 'Lynx'; this is one sketch by John Ashford. (John Ashford)

Dead End: ADO21 – MG's Mid-Engined Sports Car

After the abandonment of the EX234 project, intended to replace both the MG Midget and MGB, the MG design team at Abingdon was acutely aware that its survival was uncertain under the new order at British Leyland. Encouraged by its masters at Austin Morris, and building on the interest generated by other studies such as the Zanda and Rover P6BS, the MG team was granted the opportunity to develop a new small sports car that could replace both the MG Midget and the Triumph Spitfire and, at a pinch, nibble at the MGB market sector too.

It was swiftly decided that, along with the A-Series engine from the Mini, the still-new E-Series engine/transmission package could be offered, all to be mounted amidships, and offering a theoretical range from 1098cc to 1750cc variants. The rear suspension, the work of MG's Chassis Designer Terry Mitchell, was a De Dion suspension arrangement, a sophisticated semi-independent system well suited to mid- and rear-engined cars (and a favourite of Mitchell's), while the front would adopt simple MacPherson struts. MG's Don Hayter drew up much of the specification and, in tandem with the engineering effort at Abingdon, Austin Morris Styling at Longbridge was engaged to come up with suitable exterior shapes capable of containing the bulky engine and transmission package. A number of attractive Italianate shapes were drawn up by Harris Mann and his colleague Paul Hughes, and while MG experimented with a severely chopped-about MGB GT as engineering test mule, the Longbridge model shop eventually created a strikingly styled full-size wooden mock-up of the preferred ADO21 style. The solution arrived at chiefly by Paul Hughes – Don Hayter credits him with most of the styling work on the ADO21 – was to use 'flying buttresses' between the roof and rear end to disguise the height of the engine cover. Carefully contrived styling creases in the wings gave the illusion, from the side, that the whole car was low and sleek; it was only from the rear that the height of the rear deck became apparent, and even then Hughes had introduced a slope to hide the effect, while the narrow letterbox-shaped rear window was similar to that of the Lotus Europa.

In the meantime MG had realized that, as well as the E4 1.5 and 1.7 units, it could quite easily shoehorn the 6-cylinder E6 in 2227cc guise, making a smooth modern and exotic successor to the MGB possible as part of the project. This risked moving the 'new Midget' dangerously across the line into 'Bullet' territory, but there was no sign initially that British Leyland management would fail to be receptive to a wider ADO21 model range that extended usage of the range of E-Series engines and transmissions beyond their existing applications in the Austin Maxi. The new £16 million Cofton Hackett engine plant was certainly capable of building 8,500 units per week and the ADO21 could have taken a useful part of that output, although one factor that would have militated against the E-Series would be the lack of any work to certify it for US emissions legislation.

In the early stages of the ADO21 study, activity on the programme was quite intense, but those involved say that in due course the impetus simply evaporated. MG engineer Rod Lyne says: 'I never got told it had definitely been canned: I was simply told to leave it on the side in order to get on with other urgent work.' Some evidence that explains this change of pace survives in the minutes of Austin Morris's Product Policy Group (PPG), which was set up in 1969 with a view to coordinating the division's forward programme in tandem with the work of other British Leyland divisions. At the PPG meeting of 21 August 1969 it was reported that '[Austin Morris] Engineering report that the exercise is well-advanced on a Midget/Spitfire replacement which will have common [bodyshell] hard points but different skins'. Two months later, it was reported by Harry Webster that 'the concept for the replacement Midget would be transverse [mid] engine, rear-wheel-drive, 1100/1300/1500/1750cc. It was being designed in conjunction with Standard-Triumph to replace the Spitfire as well. A brochure would be available in six weeks'.

That 'brochure' was the project's so-called 'Blue Book', which set out to define the parameters of the car and was published in December 1969. It proposed that:

> the ADO 21 project is a new rear transverse engine, rear wheel drive, two door sports car model intended as a MG Midget/Triumph Spitfire replacement. The basic body and chassis structure together with the majority of the mechanical components will be common to both MG Midget and Triumph Spitfire models. Body style has yet to be finalized, however a model announcement is tentatively planned for spring 1973.

The idea therefore was that only the outer skin panels would differentiate between MG and Triumph models; this naturally presupposed that Triumph Engineering and Product Planning would be happy to accept the imposition of Austin Morris engines and – presumably – factories for production of Triumph models. It was recognized that, for this programme to proceed, time was of the essence since 'to achieve correct model timing, body styling would have to be agreed early in 1970 to achieve a model introduction in 1973'. By this stage any thoughts of an 1100 version had been dropped: the blue book suggested a choice of 1275, 1485 and 1748cc versions giving a range that, in engine capacity terms, certainly still overlapped the Midget and MGB segments.

At a meeting on New Year's Eve, 31 December 1969, British Leyland Inc Chairman Graham Whitehead commented on the ideas being put forward, stating that 'of all the Austin and MG models in the USA, the Midget is top priority. It competes in the $2,000 Fun Car market, and is under threat from Fiat and Japanese competition. The Spitfire

The mid-engined ADO21 would have been a striking sports car, had it been given the green light. These sketches are of the final concept by Paul Hughes of the Longbridge design studio. (Paul Hughes)

is priced at $2,400 and it is important for the Midget to remain around $2,000.' Whitehead suggested 'either a major exterior and interior facelift, or a complete replacement'. He liked the ADO21 mid-engined concept, but emphasized that 'the base model must retail at about $2,000'. The inability of the engineering team to keep the unit costs of the ADO21 down to this level would ultimately help to seal its fate; by the following spring, PPG meetings record that ADO21 had clearly shifted above the Midget sector, and some consideration was given to an alternative Mini-derived ADO70 'Calypso' project. On 27 January 1970 the Austin Morris finance people reported that projected costs of ADO21 exceeded those of the existing MGB GT. Sales Director Filmer Paradise pointed out that, as the MGB GT then sold for $2,800, it was clear that ADO21 had moved way out of the target $2000 category, and so it was agreed at this meeting that other ideas for a 'new Midget' would be investigated, while ADO21 might still be viable as an MGB replacement. On 16 March Austin Morris Chairman George Turnbull suggested that 'the replacement Midget could be designed and assembled at Innocenti with mechanicals supplied by us. Engineering was working on a design proposal for review on 1 May. ADO21 would also be reviewed on 1 May, but as a replacement for the MGB'.

By the time of the meeting on 8 September the ADO21 was being looked at in a similar sector to the Triumph Bullet and the doubts were becoming obvious: 'It was considered that this programme is dependent on Corporate Sports Car Policy … Mr D. Andrews was asked to arrange a profitability comparison of Lynx, Bullet, ADO21, Triumph TR6 and MGB. A special sub-committee meeting was to be arranged for November, to which Berkeley Square and Triumph representatives would be invited.' By October it was clear that enthusiasm for ADO21 was waning: 'a mid-engined model (ADO21) has been investigated but it hardly justifies development independent of Triumph's plans. As yet there is little, if any, joint model planning but the establishment of Product Planning Co-ordination Department at Berkeley Square should at least ensure that overlapping programmes don't get approved'. On 3 November 1970, the ADO21 and ADO70 models were reviewed by management: 'the wooden model of ADO21 was viewed in the studio. The front end was unanimously admired, but there were some reservations about the rear end. However, in view of the Corporate sports car policy, it was decided that no more work is to be done on this programme.'

The ADO21 was dead in the water, and the outcome of Spen King and Mike Carver's fact-finding mission to the United States only served to drive the nails further into the coffin. A similar fate befell the ADO70 Calypso: costed at £8 million, it was also rejected as an investment opportunity. However even though the ADO21 programme was no more, it was seen as a much more stylish offering than the contemporary (pre-TR7) Bullet, and it was clear that the first thoughts were germinating of marrying some of ADO21's style with the conventional mechanical layout of the Bullet.

An alternative concept for ADO21 by Paul Hughes. (Paul Hughes)

Triumph Engineering was at a crossroads by the time of the British Leyland merger. In 1964 Donald Stokes and George Turnbull had successfully secured a highly lucrative contract from Saab to develop a bespoke 'slant-four' engine to replace their existing units. On the back of this contract, Triumph would later be able to employ a version of this engine for its own use, and at the same time the company was giving first thoughts to a front-engine, rear-wheel drive saloon that would appear in 1971 as the Triumph Dolomite, reviving a pre-war Triumph model name. Strategic ideas about model families and common engineering were hardly novel concepts to the lean Triumph organization, and so the inclusion of what would become the 'Bullet' within the overall programme was entirely logical. The British Leyland merger seemed at first to offer merely the benefits of deeper pockets to support such a programme.

In 1970 the Lynx/Bullet project was already a couple of years old when Triumph Engineering, confident that they would be assuming the mantle of the corporation's sports car supremos,

produced a draft specification for the new range. With this engineering formula agreed, British Leyland's Specialist Car Division Advisory Board approved an order for the necessary production tooling, with a target date for delivery to Speke of spring 1973. The thinking then appears to have been that the Bullet would be launched later that year, probably in time to meet the 1974 US model year.

At this stage, the Bullet/Lynx featured Triumph's own design for the body styling, aided (mostly in terms of prototype construction) by Michelotti but overseen by Les Moore, previously Mulliner's Chief Body Designer and, by 1970, close to retirement. Lynx came first, and Bullet was derived from it. The neat but unadventurous Bullet style, which featured a removable targa-style roof panel, was thought likely to be the preferred option for the new sports car range. Triumph proposed offering the Bullet with a range of engines, starting with the 1.5-litre Triumph four, the forthcoming 2.0-litre slant four (proposed as a development on the basis of the 1.7-litre version designed for Saab) or the 2.5-litre Triumph straight six.

Creating the original clay model for Triumph's own 'Lynx' concept. (John Lloyd)

(Left top and bottom) A remarkably detailed quarter-scale model of Triumph's proposal for their new 'Bullet' sports car, intended to replace the TR line. (Right top) The model of the 'Lynx' proposal was extremely well finished and belies its small size. (Right bottom) The pair of models, photographed on the large playing field behind the Triumph factory. (Norman Rose)

Tony Lee, who reported to John Lloyd and whose photographs are included here, recalls going out to Turin in a convoy of cars along with Spen King, John Lloyd and Alan Edis (then Triumph's new Product Planner) to see Michelotti's Bullet prototype:

> We liked it. It was a sort of 'Bulldog British' version of the TR7, which we certainly thought that the Americans would have liked. Mind you, the Triumph Italia had been another Italian body on a traditional TR chassis, which we had thought was a beautiful car – but the Americans hadn't wanted that as they thought it was too Italian.

Alan Edis remembers that the convoy to Turin included not only the early white pre-launch Dolomite seen in some of the photos (overleaf), but a Triumph 2500 intended to convey Spen King onward to a post-viewing skiing trip, its generous size making it unnecessary to leave the Canley car park with skis ostentatiously strapped on a roof rack.

According to John Lloyd's records, the fastback Lynx, which was intended to donate much of the Bullet structure, would, as initially conceived, have featured a choice of up to four versions; a brace of carburettor and fuel-injected 2.5-litre sixes (115 and 130bhp respectively) as well as two tunes of the 3-litre Triumph Stag V8 – offering a projected 142bhp in standard carburettor two-valve per cylinder guise and a gloriously exotic fuel-injected four-valve per cylinder version expected to produce 233bhp (forecast to

Triumph turned to Michelotti as usual for construction of the first
Bullet and Lynx prototypes; Tony Lee photographed the former
outside Michelotti's premises at Orbassano in February 1971.
(Tony Lee)

The construction of the full-size Lynx prototype actually predated
the corresponding Bullet; here the Lynx is seen shortly after
completion. (John Lloyd)

The nose of the full-size Bullet dispensed with the small
rectangular lights suggested on the quarter-scale model, in favour
of the fashionable quadruple headlamps. (Tony Lee)

One of John Lloyd's own photos of the Lynx prototype at
Michelotti's design premises in 1968. (John Lloyd)

The Michelotti-built Bullet prototype, resplendent in 'Bahama
Yellow', seen alongside a pre-production Triumph Dolomite.
(Tony Lee)

deliver a top speed of 137.5mph/221.3km/h and
a 0–60mph time of 6.5 seconds). Undoubtedly
the Rover V8 might later have come into play,
both for the original style 'Bullet' and 'Lynx', but
this never came to pass and so is academic.

Along with highly detailed quarter-scale
(rather than traditional 0.3-scale) models of
both Bullet and Lynx (John Ashford believes
these were built in the Canley Experimental
Department, next door to styling), full-size versions were built. Work was initially focused on
the Lynx, possibly as a replacement for the GT6,
with Bullet following afterwards; the '1972' and
'1973' licence plates on the finished models seem
to support this.

Triumph Bullet and Lynx Prototypes in the 'X' Register

Project Number	Model	Date	Details recorded in Register
X780	Lynx	1969	1st prototype body, Bahama Yellow

This is the original Triumph Lynx predating the TR7 style. 'Bahama' could have a number of meanings, such as a reference to the 'Bahamas' licence plate seen in some of the photos, or an internal Triumph code predating adoption of the 'Lynx' name (contemporary with 'Bullet', 'Barb', and 'Bomb'). However, 'Bahama Yellow' was also an amber shade used on contemporary Lotus, Porsche and other manufacturers' cars.

Running Prototypes

Project Number	Model	Date	Details recorded in Register
X792	Lynx	13/11/1969	1st running prototype (yellow)
			Probably X780 made into a running prototype.
X794	Lynx	—	2nd prototype (white)
X795	Lynx	—	3rd prototype (colour not stated)
X796	Lynx	—	4th prototype (blue)
X801	Lynx	03/06/70	5th prototype (green; left-hand drive)
X814	Lynx	—	Prototype (blue)
X817	Bullet	04/05/1971	1st prototype, original Michelotti prototype
			A hand-annotated note in the register says 'to be scrapped'. Note that Tony Lee's colour photos of the yellow car taken at Michelotti's premises in Turin date from February 1971.

John Ashford, one of Les Moore's in-house designers, recalls producing renderings showing different options for the rear end of Lynx:

It was a bit ordinary compared to the futuristic look that the Longbridge TR7 style eventually had – at least as far as the nose is concerned, for it had a very conventional front end like a VW Scirocco – a squarish grille with the lamps at the ends – there was nothing radical about that!

John Lloyd's files show that there was some investigation of slightly more substantial wrap-round front bumpers for Lynx, but this was nothing like the much more substantial units that would later become a requirement of US legislation.

In the following months, top company management began to get cold feet over the Triumph styling, and so it was decided to arrange a senior management review, with Lord Stokes presiding. On 23 April 1971 Bruce McWilliams attended a sports car policy meeting convened in the exhibition hall at Brown's Lane, home of the Jaguar:

The meeting was organized by Mike Carver, and chaired by Donald Stokes. A number of competitive cars were on view there, along with the then-proposed replacement for the traditional Triumph TR line. This car [the Les Moore design] had been developed at Triumph prior to Spen King's arrival; it had many awkwardnesses and was really quite out of date and unsatisfactory for a new generation model. Spen King worked on this problem, and I helped to a limited degree because there was no time to do more. The exercise needed to be started all over again.

Brian Anderson of Triumph Engineering often helped organize such events: 'I used to arrange the Product Policy Viewing meetings for the PP Committee. Lyons was a bit of a terror – he was in fact a bit of an old fashioned "bully". He used to stick bits of tape on the models to try to make

A rare photo showing Arthur Ballard, then Triumph's chief body engineer, leaning on the Lynx prototype in Michelotti's yard in Orbassano. (John Lloyd)

Back at Canley, the Michelotti-built Lynx is seen in a studio alongside the contemporary GT6 and forthcoming Dolomite. (John Lloyd)

them look different ...' At this particular meeting, the plan was to review all the sports car ideas still in consideration, from the ADO70 Calypso (the Austin Morris 'Midget/Spitfire' proposal – ADO21 was already dead) up to the Jaguar XJ27, which would become the XJS.

Stokes sought feedback on the Triumph Bullet and Lynx. McWilliams said he believed that the car needed more work and, as a consequence, Jaguar's Sir William Lyons was asked by Stokes to 'see what more could be done'. McWilliams recalls another curious happening at this meeting:

George Turnbull and Harry Webster arrived carrying a huge case, obviously carrying drawings or sketches. I was immediately curious to know what they had up their sleeves. Nonetheless, the case remained firmly planted between their two chairs, its contents never revealed. At dinner that night with Spen King, I speculated that another sports car scenario was evolving at Longbridge and, of course, it soon emerged in the form of Harris Mann's design.

The ADO70 Calypso seems to have been hardly mentioned at the meeting and it soon followed ADO21 into oblivion.

The quarter-scale model of 'Lynx' was tried with slightly more substantial bumpers, which wrapped more extensively round the sides of the car. (John Lloyd)

Before long, Triumph had built a running prototype of the Lynx.
The compact simple nose is redolent of contemporary Italian
designs emanating from Fiat and, before long, VW – though the
Scirocco was still a few years from launch when this photo was
taken in 1969/70. (Norman Rose)

From the rear three-quarters, perhaps the Lynx was a little less
successful as a modern sports coupé, even if it could seat four in
reasonable comfort. Note the style of the wheeltrim, a precursor of
the 1975–77 TR7 style (see page 71). (Norman Rose)

At this time, endurance testing as part of the development of the slant-four engine for Saab was also going on within the dynamometers at Triumph Engineering. Kastner became involved at the periphery of this process:

> Just to cover all bases I guess, Mr Webster sent a complete engine to me at the USA Competition Department in California and gave me certain parameters and limits to follow in doing what I thought for a possible power increase. It was easy. We picked up 25bhp at the flywheel with just a limited compression and a little cam and exhaust headers and few other little tricks. I sent the engine back to Coventry and that was the end of my involvement as I soon after resigned from the company to start my own racing team venture, Kastner/Brophy Racing.

Wedge and Creases

The next stage, in July 1971, was the presentation at Longbridge of the final variants of the Bullet design studies: the rivals were the Triumph proposal and an offering from Harris Mann of Austin Morris Exterior Styling. Alan Edis, then in Product Planning, recalls that, with no axe to grind and less engineering baggage to limit

their imagination, Harris Mann and his team – with the strikingly styled ADO21 and ADO71 projects to their credit – were arguably inspired to be more imaginative than the Triumph team: 'From the outset, the Longbridge proposal was a closed car, and so Harris wanted to do something with an exciting sporty character to compensate for the lack of an open top.' Edis also confirms that the Triumph 'Bullet' on show at this viewing was effectively the same orange car seen in the photographs taken a few months earlier outside Michelotti's premises in Orbassano, Turin.

Mike Dale saw the potential in the Harris Mann styling model too:

> There was a meeting in the UK which Graham, Bruce and I attended where a decision had to be made between Bullet and what was effectively an uprated TR6. The TR6 upgrade was a good piece of work but it was still a convertible and Bullet promised Lynx, a competitor for the all-conquering Datsun 240Z. I went for the Bullet although I remember Bruce cautioning me that the TR6 upgrade was a strong competitor and he was right. The total outcome would have been the same because the company, ultimately, couldn't have produced either of them in a cost efficient, high quality manner.

An early rendering by Harris Mann of what would eventually become the familiar TR7. Note the simpler bumpers and the targa roof. (Harris Mann)

Paul Hughes, one of Harris Mann's colleagues at Longbridge, and the man who drew the definitive ADO21, produced these alternative ideas for Bullet. (Paul Hughes)

Alan Edis describes the following set of parameters that were defined for the corporate sports car:

- There was a need to deal with the endemic reliability problems, and so the car had to be relatively simple and therefore reliable;
- The car should have a high technology appearance belying its simple mechanical componentry (hence the 'pseudo mid-engine style' that emerged);
- There should be a large cabin to compensate for the lack of an open top;
- The comfort aspects should be very good, hence an efficient heater, air-conditioning etc.;
- Safety aspects were paramount, and so the car had to be structurally very sound.

According to Edis, 'the TR7 was a real attempt to build a new sports car which could live in the US market. The original Triumph proposals for Bullet and Lynx had some of these elements, but not all: the work at Longbridge was more free-standing – an overview of what was needed.' Mike Dale was relaxed about the lack of an open top; he felt that a coupé was what was needed in any case:

> Basically I was convinced we needed to break out of the mould of convertibles and compete with a coupé

as well as a convertible. The MGB, backed by excellent advertising and a successful race programme, continued to set sales records so we felt reasonably secure in that area. Nobody with any sense in those days was investing in new convertibles. The TR7 beginnings, from my point of view, were promising: ohc engines, 2- and 4-valve, a coupé which we obviously needed and the styling buck was exciting. Unfortunately this buck was the only TR7 where the panels fitted and the wheels filled the wheel arches!

Meanwhile, Triumph had also been working with the celebrated automotive designer William Towns, stylist of the Aston Martin DBS, who worked on a brace of projects, 'Bobcat' and 'Puma', intended to replace the Triumph 1300 and 2000, respectively. Bobcat appears to have developed as far as a prototype (X824), which was subsequently broken up, but Puma – supposedly related to Lynx – had not progressed beyond model stage. According to Towns, Triumph had tried to recruit him as their Chief Stylist, but the idea of being a corporate man did not appeal to him, and so he worked for them in a freelance capacity alongside Triumph's Les Moore and Ray Innes in a Portakabin at Canley. Towns told Mike Taylor, in an interview for *Classic Cars* in July 1986, that while working at Canley

The original 'Longbridge Bullet' clay begins to take shape under Harris Mann's direction. Note how there is some uncertainty as to how the side feature line should be treated. (Harris Mann)

This second shot of the full-size clay shows that some thought was being given to a bumper with horizontal slots or grooves, which might have made it less massive in appearance and closer to the original sketch in concept. (Harris Mann)

This is the clay finished and surfaced ready for management viewing. Notice some of the features that will not survive through to production: the extension of the side slope down into the sill (just behind the front wheel arch), the recessed door handle, the treatment of the rear edge of the door shut line and, of course, the 'MG Magna' badging. (Norman Rose)

Two alternative front end treatments – both with 'MG' badges and headlamps concealed under 'flaps' rather than fitted in 'pods'. Harris Mann later bemoaned the change from his original design intent. (Harris Mann)

he and clay modeller Eric Ingram had created an alternative 'Bullet' model, since he had felt (like McWilliams) that the Les Moore proposal 'wasn't that appropriate … When the time came for Stokes to view the two proposals [Mann and Moore/Michelotti], Triumph were certain that he would choose Moore's Bullet since around £2M had already been expended on it.'

However, the Triumph team would be disappointed: Stokes was clearly taken with the Longbridge design, which featured the distinctive wedge shape that would eventually become familiar as the TR7, albeit wearing 'MG Magna' badging in the display studio. Mann and his team also prepared an alternative full-size clay, wearing Triumph badging, but representing the concept of different exterior panels on a common base. This alternative clay wore Triumph badges; Mann now maintains it emerged some time after the MG-badged 'Magna' clay. The 'Triumph' badged clay arguably looked more restrained than the now familiar style, but it was the bolder, brasher wedge – complete with diagonal side creases – that Lord Stokes saw and decreed would be the new Triumph TR7. Harris Mann maintains that the badges were in any case merely 'jewellery' added for effect, but the principle of two different versions (one Triumph, one MG) was nevertheless a serious proposal.

In a last-ditch act of desperation, Towns was asked to help save the day for the Triumph team when 'the Triumph executives rushed into my

Harris Mann and his team worked on an alternative design for 'Bullet', seen here in sketch form; Mann maintains that this followed the original, although it is clear that it could have allowed a pair of, say, MG and Triumph badged sports cars to have shared common interior body pressings. (Harris Mann)

The alternative Bullet clay takes shape at Longbridge. (Harris Mann)

The finished 'alternative' Bullet clay, which, interestingly, wore Triumph badges rather than MG ones! (Harris Mann)

studio, took out my clay proposal for Bullet and dusted it off. But, by this time, Stokes had left and the Longbridge TR7 came into being.' Towns told more or less the same story to Jon Pressnell for *Classic and Sportscar*: '[We] were just about to put [the model] on a trolley to wheel it round when someone else came in and said, "it's no good – he's gone." And Stokes had got into his helicopter and flown off to Longbridge. That's how history happens.'

Mike Carver admits that the decision to go for Mann's style was controversial, but:

> there was a consensus that the Triumph style was too conventional; we needed something less dull and traditional. But in retrospect, maybe that wouldn't have been such a bad thing – and some others did feel that the 'TR7' was too extreme. But in the event it was preferred because it was 'different'. These sorts of decisions are rarely as strongly reasoned as you might like them to be – there is always a compromise consensus.

Triumph Engineering's Norman Rose recalls Spen King's report back on the styling competition: 'He told us that our style hadn't won the day – Longbridge had won that battle – and in fact he remarked that only Bill Lyons and one other supported the Triumph styling proposal. However, Triumph retained the engineering of the car.' Spen King confirmed this, adding: 'Bill Lyons, myself and Lyndon Mills – Triumph's sales director at the time – were the only ones to support the Triumph proposal'.

As an effort to recapture the initiative, a modified version of Canley's Bullet 'Mark I', with the Moore/Michelotti style but a Porsche 914-style front end, was cobbled up on the basis of the Michelotti-built car. This was seen by Triumph's US Competitions man, Kas Kastner:

> I first viewed versions of the car in the design studio in Coventry at the request of Harry Webster, the Chief Engineer. That particular day he was mostly interested in my views on the disappearing headlamps. There were several versions to see that had

A Harris Mann rendering of the TR7 Bullet 'after the fact'. (Harris Mann)

Harris Mann

Harris Mann typified the 'new generation' of people intended to be standard-bearers for the glorious revolution planned for British Leyland. In his mid-thirties when he penned the TR7, Mann was already 'Chief Exterior Stylist, Austin Morris Division' and had a number of exterior designs under his belt. He was born in London in April 1938 and came from an engineering background. He started as a draughtsman apprentice at Duple, the bus coachbuilding company, but from an early stage he harboured styling ambitions. At the end of the 1950s, Mann took the bold step of emigrating to the United States, where he managed to work briefly at Raymond Loewy's studio in New York, but caught by a recession in the USA in 1960, he found himself out of work after six months. After returning to England, and a period doing National Service, he briefly rejoined Duple. Before long, however, he moved to join Rootes as a body engineer at the Commer commercial vehicle division. He stayed there for nine months before moving to Ford in 1962. Mann showed his portfolio of drawing work to the head of styling at Ford, with whose support he moved over to the world of styling. At the October 1967 Motor Show it was announced that Roy Haynes, Mann's boss at Ford, would be moving to join the British Motor Corporation as head of the styling department. Within a few months many of the key members of Haynes's team, including Mann, made the move to BMC's new styling section, which Haynes had established at the Pressed Steel facility at Cowley.

By May 1968 BMC had merged with Leyland to form the British Leyland Motor Corporation and Harris Mann was busily involved in a new programme of work for the Austin Morris division of the new organization. By the following year, Roy Haynes had left and Mann found himself heading up the forty-strong Exterior Design team, reporting to Tom Penny, BLMC's Chief Body Engineer. Here, Mann and his team were engaged in various Austin Morris programmes destined for production such as the ADO28 Morris Marina (launched in 1971), ADO67 Austin Allegro (launched in 1973) and ADO71 Princess (also known by the codename 'Diablo', this was initially launched in March 1975 as the '18/22 Series' but re-launched the following September as the Princess range).

As well as these production cars, there were numerous other projects that never saw the light of day and some design studies intended to show off the talent of the newly invigorated design studio. One such design was the Austin Zanda, a wedge-shaped concept for a mid-engined sports car with an Austin Maxi engine in a similar mould to the ADO21 MG proposal. The Zanda concept, drawn up at Longbridge despite being a Pressed Steel-sponsored project, was boldly styled and drew much interest when it was shown to the public as a full-sized plastic model. There is little doubt that this successfully raised the profile of Mann and his colleagues at a time when the company was seeking new ideas for the proposed corporate sports car. As Mann recalls,

> the idea with Zanda was to demonstrate the new Italian digital measuring machine which could record three-dimensional data directly off a clay model – that was something very new at the time. Of course being BLMC, we had to have inspectors to check every measurement rather than letting the machine do it all automatically, which was in reality quite feasible.

He also points out that several features in Zanda were used when shaping what became the TR7: 'Look at the shape of the headlamps (those on the original Bullet clay were the same as Zanda, rather than the 'pods' which the engineers imposed) as well as the sculpting of the wheel arches.' Following the various upheavals at British Leyland during the 1970s, Mann stayed at Longbridge for a time, contributing to the Austin Metro and submitting an unsuccessful but arguably superior style for the Austin Maestro. From 1983, however, he mainly worked as a freelance on a wide range of transport-related design projects: in 2003, for example, he worked under MG Rover Design Director Peter Stevens on the MG XPower SV project.

Harris Mann alongside Chris Turner's immaculate early TR7 at Gaydon in 2006. (Alisdair Cusick)

Paul Hughes produced this idea for an interior for the TR7, which never made it beyond sketch form; Triumph designed its own interior instead. (Paul Hughes)

some Triumph people as the 'Lord Stokes crease', but to no avail; the style of what would become the TR7 had been set.

Harris Mann confirms that there was some debate about the side crease, but only in terms of how it ran down the side of the car: 'As originally conceived on the clay, the swage line ran down behind the front wheel arch, but that was one of the few things that Stokes wanted changed to more or less how it appeared on the final car.'

Mann believes that it was Stokes's unique perspective that allowed Longbridge to style a Triumph:

been mocked up on full-size cars or models as I remember. The resultant design was not present and I was certainly not impressed with the designs I saw, which went from weird to really ugly …

This proved futile, however, for Lord Stokes had decided to go with the Longbridge offering. Spen King tried, as a compromise, to persuade Stokes to abandon the sloping side feature, known to

Of course at the time we did the TR7 clay, Longbridge and Canley were still entirely separate, but Lord Stokes was over us all and so he knew what everybody was doing. Triumph had been having problems modifying their own 'Bullet' to get it into the USA. The Michelotti-built car had been sitting around for some years and it was okay but aged. So we at Longbridge were asked to help come up with a new proposal. We'd recently done the Diablo

At a late stage in the process, the Triumph design people hastily concocted this 'halfway house' facelift of the Michelotti-built Bullet, marrying pop-up headlamps and beefier bumpers along with raised sidelights that looked rather like those on the VW-Porsche 914. It failed to get the management support it would have needed, however. (Graham Robson)

In 1969 Harris Mann and his team were responsible for 'Project Zanda', an idea for a mid-engined sports car that could have used Austin Maxi components.

Although Zanda would first inspire ADO21, many of its defining features, such as the bold wedge shape, pop-up lights and sculptured wheel arches, would later surface in the definitive TR7.

(ADO71) in 1970 and we'd worked on other projects such as Zanda and the ADO21, not to mention the Allegro – so Stokes knew what we were capable of.

Mann's original sketches were certainly inspirational and different from the traditional 'norm', and he freely admits they were intended to reflect American tastes. Even so, like many designers he saw a number of changes imposed on his concept in the transition from feasibility to production. Apart from the headlamp 'pods', which were originally simple trapezoidal shapes set into the front panel facings, various exterior trim details were altered along the way, including recessed door handles and a further lip to the top rear of the doors: 'The original intention was that the whole of the door window frames and cappings would have been satin black, as would the windscreen surround; not a mixture of body colour and stainless steel as was the actual result'. Mann also told Steve Redway, for an article in *TR Action*, that the windscreen rake was designed such that a seated driver could see the overhead traffic

lights in the US – this being a car designed 100 per cent for the US market.

Norman Rose also points out that the side crease was slightly reprofiled, making it dive less steeply at the forward edge, and a small upward kick at the tail end of the door was also deleted, as it would have proved a production nightmare and wasteful of steel at the pressing stage.

Bruce McWilliams, an Anglophile traditionalist with a British wife, readily admits he was never a fan of the new wedge:

> The first time ever I saw a model of the TR7 at the Elephant House at Longbridge, I believed it was a disaster – totally. It totally failed to exploit British sports car tradition, was incredibly ill-proportioned and ungainly. But all those most important to its being sanctioned had wrapped it in praise. It had character all right – the wrong one, and the rest of its life was just trying to make up for a terrible shortcoming.

So the style of the new corporate sports car had been decided: all that now had to be done was to engineer it and build it.

A sketch by Harris Mann of a possible TR7 '2+2'. Mann had no input to the Triumph Lynx that followed the TR7. (Harris Mann)

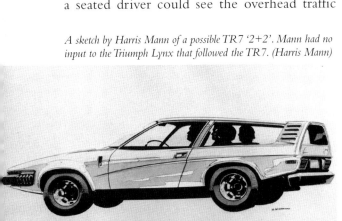

An alternative style that could have formed the basis of an MG version of Bullet, perhaps? (Harris Mann)

3 The Corporate Sports Car

Canley's Challenge

Triumph at Canley may have lost the battle to style the new British Leyland sports car, but as compensation they had won the task of engineering it and making it a production reality. Of course this was undoubtedly the harder part of the bargain, for the task of making a car possible to build and sell had changed dramatically in the previous decade and was certainly not getting any easier. The TR7 was subjected to hitherto unprecedented levels of testing, with impact rigs, seat-belt destruction tests and a panoply of safety assurance virtually unheard of when the TR6 had been designed.

Norman Rose and his team became intimately involved in the engineering of the new Bullet. They were faced with several constraints, not least the limited resources of the company and the shrinking finances available. One of the predictable project parameters was that the new car should dispense with the traditional separate chassis, providing benefits in terms of lower weight and greater strength, as well as torsional stiffness. With the need to engineer the car to meet the new legislation, these were benefits worth having, but they certainly did not make the tasks any simpler. Rose stresses that 'at the original conception, no thought or provision was made for an open body', which of course would lead to considerable challenges later on.

Safety Engineering

Meanwhile, the onslaught of new legislation in both the EEC and the USA was posing many more immediate challenges for Rose's team. 'In some cases, such as frontal impacts, we already had some experience,' he explains, 'whilst in other areas – such as rear impacts – we were breaking new ground.'

The frontal barrier test involved impacting the vehicle with a concrete block at 30mph, initially head-on but also at an angle. 'Requirements were that the steering column should not penetrate more than four to five inches during the impact, that the rear edge of the bonnet should not be driven back through the windscreen and that the windscreen should remain substantially in place'.

The issue of rear impacts had become literally a hot topic in the USA following a series of tragic fuel fires involving Ford's Pinto small cars as a consequence of the rupture of vulnerable petrol tanks in rear-end shunts. Triumph engineers placed the TR7 fuel tank in just about the safest place possible, between the two rear wheels, with a fuel filler just behind the upright rear window. 'Rear impact requirements at 30mph and the 5mph "no damage" bumper proposals were responsible for us designing rear side members into the understructure. Vision angles dictated some aspects of the body style and the no-damage bumpers dictated the bumper shape and position', Rose explains.

For the rear barrier tests, 'the rear of the untethered vehicle is impacted by the moving concrete block. The vehicle is allowed to roll until it stops and at this stage petrol loss is measured with only a certain figure allowed.'

Open Sports Cars Under Attack

From a low point in the late 1950s, US interest in road safety had advanced so far by the end of the following decade that some doomsayers were even predicting the demise of the private car in any readily recognizable form. In addition to the issue of 'conventional' vehicle impacts, well demonstrated in the development of the TR7's substantial bumpers, a factor that had particular significance for the traditional open sports car was the increasing concern with vehicle roll-overs, many resulting in serious or fatal injuries. By the late 1960s, the US government had decided upon legislation rather than moral coercion; having set standards for the interiors of cars, it was evident that the next move would be to consider issues such as roof strength. Some more conventional cars with fixed but relatively unstressed roof structures were part of the problem: it was obvious that a car with no roof would be even more vulnerable to any new legislative moves.

While few would go as far as to suggest the basic objectives behind such legislation were unjustified, the fact was that a new consumer drive, championed by arch-automotive critic Ralph Nader, provided an expedient political momentum for changes to be forced through without much thought about their practicality. America had just managed to get a man on the Moon; the automotive industry's bleatings that these new technical vehicle safety and emissions challenges were unachievable just didn't wash. In this context, the future of the open sports car seemed to be sliding towards oblivion. In January 1972 the US National Highway Traffic Safety Administration (NHTSA) published its latest draft Federal Motor Vehicle Safety Standard (number 208), which called for the safety of vehicle occupants to be ensured with as little conscious effort on their part as possible. The car makers had already begun dabbling with such things as passive safety belts and primitive air bags to complement the passenger-friendly soft and squishy facias with rounded edges that had already been legislated into existence; it was an obvious next step to ensure that the safety of passengers inside the vehicle should be maintained as far as possible in the event of a catastrophic loss of control such as a roll-over. The roll-over criteria decreed that occupants should remain wholly within their vehicle while it was propelled sideways from a platform moving at 30 mph. For many US domestic manufacturers, this effectively saw the end of low-volume convertible offshoots of their two-door sedans and coupés, while a few others explored targa-roof arrangements in the style of the Triumph Stag or lift-out roof panels (Datsun 280ZX).

However, the part of the legislation that seemed destined to force the introduction of air bags led to the domestic manufacturers mounting a challenge to FMVSS208. Chrysler took the US government to court and joined forces with the Automobile Importers of America (AIA), which took up the cause of the open car as part of the battle. In December 1972 the alliance won a victory that resulted in a pause in the legislation. As a key part of the final judgment, the compulsory fitment of air bags (something of an unknown quantity for open cars) was delayed indefinitely. The court further found that the Highway Safety Act of 1970 did not empower the NHTSA to outlaw any existing categories of vehicle, particularly open cars. The legal opinion was that 'people knowingly accept certain risks when they choose this type of machinery over what may be a safer automobile'.

By now, however, the open car market had been decimated and, with plans for the TR7 and Jaguar XJS already far advanced, both would appear on the market little more than two years later without the traditional open roofs that the market expected. Mike Dale of British Leyland's North American office at Leonia claims that in addition to worries about legislation, there was a belief that the love affair with the convertible was on the wane in any case:

> Our competition, far more able than BL, had adjusted quickly and left the convertible market because it was too insecure. The Datsun 240Z was the prime example. The BL dealers and distributors were panic-stricken because we didn't have a coupé so we invented the 'disappearing convertible market' as a ploy to show them the glass was half full, not half empty, and we now faced a great marketing opportunity. Bob Burden will tell you it was one of our better pieces of bullshit which we manufactured to keep ourselves alive! At the time we had our tongues in our cheeks but, to some astonishment, it turned out to be true and, while we lived in trepidation that the ruling would be reversed, we started setting sales records partly because we owned most of the market.

Fulfilling this role, the MGB, which the TR7 had been expected to usurp, was able to live on to satisfy the demand for the time being.

Bayer was proud of its part in the creation of the TR7 bumpers, as witnessed by this advert from Autocar *in September 1975.*

Although the car in the photo is a Spitfire, TR7 prototypes were similarly subjected to pendulum rig tests at Canley. (Norman Rose)

Initially, as elsewhere in British Leyland (notably Jaguar, with their XJS, and MG, with the 'rubber bumper' MGB), Triumph Engineering struggled to determine the optimum bumper solution. The original proposal, seen on photos of an early plastic full-size model, would have involved concertina style ends to the front bumper on the assumption that moving armatures would be necessary. In the end, polyurethane mouldings (the Bayer 'Bayflex' material) were fitted over high-strength steel fixed armatures, although there would be something special much later for the open cars (*see* Chapter 7).

The decision to incorporate the sidelamps and front indicators into the front bumpers was taken with some hesitation, given the requirement of the US legislators that no damage be incurred in impacts of up to 5mph, including to the lamps themselves. However, as Mick Bunker related in a paper he presented to the

Institution of Mechanical Engineers, tests were undertaken whereby lamps were mounted on a length of rolled steel joist (RSJ), mounted on coil springs and fixed on the front of a Triumph Stag. Repeated hand-propelled runs into the test barrier with lamps both illuminated and switched off failed to damage them.

Norman Rose explains the method in more detail:

Bumper legislation had been developing in the early 1970s and had now reached the 'no damage' situation as distinct from the earlier situation that allowed damage provided essentials such as lights still worked. The route chosen was using a polyurethane ribbed moulding mounted on a steel armature and using test sections a load/deflection curve for a basic section was established. One of the problems with the front bumper on TR7 was always the excessive 'vee' plan shape, which gave a heavy load concentration at the centre. To assist

A substantial rig was necessary to test roof crush strength, in this case with a TR7 prototype about to undergo testing. (Norman Rose)

this the armature did not follow the vee shape, allowing more urethane depth in the centre. The armature was constructed from high press steel as a box section with additional reinforcement at the centre.

The other end of the TR7 did not suffer from the problems of a non-square profile and so the challenge was subtly different: 'The rear bumper was of similar construction except that the horizontal ribbing of the front bumper was replaced by vertical ribbing. Even so, it was still necessary to add two over-riders to the main moulding to achieve the required compliance at all service temperatures.'

Outside the US market, impact-absorbing bumpers were generally less of an issue: 'Bumpers for cars destined for the rest of the world were manufactured from polycarbonate or nylon as the impact requirements were at that time much less than those for the USA.'

Other tests looked at the effect of the vehicle rolling over (for this test, the side of the vehicle was impacted and the vehicle allowed to roll until it stopped) and a series of 'static' tests, which Norman Rose describes:

Roof Intrusion: this required the application of a load equivalent to one and a half times the vehicle weight to the top of the windscreen pillar at a prescribed angle. Penetration was required to be limited to six inches and needed a substantial rig structure to enable the test to be carried out.

Side Door Intrusion: the requirements of this test meant loading a ram simulating a telegraph pole against the door in three phases, the ultimate one being a load equivalent to twice the vehicle weight with a specified maximum penetration. To achieve this, a multi box section beam has to be incorporated into the door structure between the outer skin and the door glass in its lowered position.

Seat Belt Anchorage: A feature incorporated on TR7 was to mount the lower anchorage onto the seat frame so that the position of the belt relative to its occupant remained the same irrespective of seat position. Thus the loads were imposed on the seat slides, which had to be designed to take these loads. The upper anchorage was concealed behind the parcel tray. The anchorage test involves a static rig with the designated loads applied through a body simulation block. Some structural deformation but no tearing of metal or breaking of spot welds is allowed – this test is carried out before the 30mph barrier test which proves the dynamic ability of both belts and anchorages.

Meanwhile, careful study and assessment of the packaging and regulatory requirements led to other unforeseen departures from the original Harris Mann clay. It was found necessary to widen the body, lift the roof line and to lower the headlamp shrouds in the 'up' position. 'The raising of the roof could be done on the clay,' Rose remembers, 'but the widening of the body was not modelled and was achieved subsequently during the "line take-off". A further viewing was held in the drive outside the styling block at Longbridge in August 1971, with such competitors as the Toyota Celica parked alongside.' By this stage, the plan was for production to commence in January 1974 for a June 1974 launch, so a very tight programme was already envisaged.

The next stage was to take the clay to Cowley, where it could be measured by the state-of-the-art Alpha 3-D measuring machine during September 1971. 'This machine comprised a three-dimensional probe which allowed recording of all the body surface contours', Rose explains. To achieve the required widening of the body, the machine was programmed to read off widths plus half an inch, so in effect a whole inch was added to the width of the body at the centre line. 'From the recordings taken on the Alpha machine, the skin lines were mechanically drawn by a Gerber draughting machine onto "permatrace" film, and we were also given a complete read-out of the ordinates of every line.'

Whereas nowadays this raw data is 'smoothed' by sophisticated computer programmes, such techniques were not available in 1971, so the line information was delivered 'unsmoothed' to the Triumph body drawing office at Canley. 'The clay model was then used to take off a fibre-glass mould from which several fibre-glass shells were moulded. These were then used for interior bucks, wind tunnel assessments and on-road vision checks.'

The body engineering programme called for completion of release of skin panels by 1 January 1972 and for major structural panels by 1 April. According to Norman Rose,

> the first panels to be completed were in fact the bonnet and trunk [boot] lid by November 1st 1971, followed by the doors, rear deck and front upper exactly a month later. The fenders [wings] front and rear and sills were completed by January 1st 1972 and only the roof and screen panels ran late, to February 1st 1972. Most of these drawings were 'line' drawings – undimensioned apart from aperture lines, hole centres and sizes. The major part of the 'body in white' design programme was complete by the end of June 1972, and by this time the interior bucks had been progressed to a habitable degree.

The First Prototype Programme

With the form of the key body panels determined, the next stage was to initiate a prototype build programme. The decision was taken to

A full-size plastic model of the TR7. Note the proposal for 'concertina' ends to the bumpers. (Harris Mann)

build fifteen bodyshells and two front end units for separate testing. According to Norman Rose, 'the first front end unit was completed in June 1972 and the first shell at the end of July. Shells were built at the Castle Bromwich plant and also at the Triumph plant.' This was the highest number of prototypes ever ordered by Triumph up to then and was a necessity because of the high number of 'write-off' tests involved and the need to install various engine options. Some of these prototypes became fully built cars, such as X827 and the other cars listed in the Appendix. The five key cars were as follows:

No. 1: pavé car TR7, 2-valve, right-hand drive (probably X827)
No. 2: general development TR7, 2-valve, left-hand drive (probably X828)
No. 3: body development TR7, 4-valve (Sprint), right-hand drive
No. 4: general development TR7, 2-valve, left-hand drive
No. 5: general development TR7, V8, right-hand drive

In addition, test programmes had to cover all the dynamic and static tests described earlier. These were collectively guaranteed to result in a high rate of attrition for these expensive hand-built prototypes, but they were vital if the Federal safety standards were to be met and demonstrated.

Testing of early prototypes followed standard British Leyland practice of 1,000 miles of evaluation over a simulated Belgian pavé road, a rough cobbled surface (built at the Motor Industry Research Association facilities near Nuneaton) guaranteed to show up and accelerate any inherent vehicle weaknesses, effectively providing wear harder than a vehicle might experience in a lifetime of normal use – and loosening the fillings of the unfortunate test drivers. The triangular track has three different levels of cobblestones, ranging from minor undulations to virtual potholes. Norman Rose describes the experience:

Driving the third track was how I imagine using a pneumatic drill would be. This test was estimated to

equate to 100,000 miles of normal running and could now only be undertaken after all the safety tests. Door, boot and bonnet latching and window winding were also endurance rig tested.

This harsh test regime inevitably showed up a number of minor structural issues and potential weaknesses that, once identified, could be designed out for production. A pre-production TR7 prototype and a TR7 V8 convertible were subsequently subjected to the same test as validation.

A related assessment exercise for the TR7 was the '90 day corrosion test', for which a prototype was built without the usual zinc primer or anti-corrosion treatments and the body painted white, the best colour to show up any rust streaks. As Norman Rose explains, 'this prototype was run around a variety of road surfaces under wet conditions and then the damp areas were checked. The vehicle was then fitted with a series of nozzles which sprayed salt solution into these same areas, fed from special built-in tanks mounted within the vehicle.'

The TR7 saw a number of innovations, not only for Triumph but for British car building as a whole, including pop-up headlamps and a bonded-in windscreen, which contributed to structural stiffness of the body. The 'Solbit' system had already been used by Fiat, and a team of British Leyland engineers visited a plant in Italy to see the process in operation. The system used a pre-formed adhesive with a metal core, using heat to cure it. This required special storage of the adhesive, which led to an interesting sequence of events at Speke (*see* Chapter 4).

The facia was styled at Triumph, very much inspired, according to Norman Rose, by the experience of Spen King, who had been responsible for the Range Rover. 'It took the form of a one-piece 'Noryl' moulding and was subject to all the head impact legislation which was by now mandatory. Because of its large size, the fixings had to take account of expansion and contraction under temperature variations.'

Although the requirements of new legislation provided awkward hoops through which all car

Pop-Up Headlamps

Even if they had been shown previously on one-off Triumph prototypes (TRX and Fury), concealed headlamps, 'popping up' on demand whether for flashing (except in the USA, where this was illegal) or for night-time illumination, were a novelty for British Leyland in 1974. In truth, few other car makers had much experience of them either: General Motors had used them for their Chevrolet Corvette and Oldsmobile Toronado, and a few other cars had seen partially concealed lamps behind movable grilles. The only small British sports car of note that had previously used 'pop-up' lamps was the low-volume Lotus Elan, introduced in 1962. 'For some time, we followed Lotus in the use of a vacuum operated system,' Norman Rose recalls. 'However, our standards had to be higher because US legislation demanded certain performance levels.' The vacuum system soon fell out of favour:

The Triumph Fury prototype had been a one-off exploration of an open monocoque sports car. The pop-up lamps helped keep the nose low and sleek. (Norman Rose)

> After many frustrating months of seeing headlamps creep up on the road and – worse – creep down again – we also had concerns about the viability of the system to sustain weekend garaging and still have some vacuum lift left, we were literally saved by the bell, which in this case was the arrival on site of a Fiat X1/9.

The Fiat had pop-up lamps that used electric motors; these were soon stripped off and within eight hours had been fitted to a Bullet prototype, where Rose says they worked very well. In practice, Rose and his team turned inevitably to their friends at Lucas and adapted a pair of windscreen wiper motors, resulting in a system that allowed the lamps to raise through an angle of 37 degrees in around 0.8 seconds. To cater for the possibility of motor failure, it was possible to manually lift the lamp units. In service, poor weather-sealing would prove to be a bugbear, leading to many motor failures before a modification early in production.

The distinctive headlamp 'pod' of the production TR7. (Alisdair Cusick)

The housing in which the lamps were fitted was originally intended to have been assembled from a number of steel pressings, but the harsh pavé testing regime showed a tendency for these early prototype lamp units to shake themselves apart and so an alloy casting was used for the 'pod' with a front facing of black EPDM rubber. It is possible that this was one of the key reasons why Harris Mann's original proposal for a 'lidded' headlamp was dropped in favour of the familiar 'pods', a change that Mann dislikes to this day. One worry was how these pop-up lamps would cope in certain markets that require headlamp wash-wipe units, such as Sweden. 'We did get a system to work,' Rose remembers. 'It had a flexible drive to the centre of the headlamps with a spindle driving the blades through 180 degrees each.' The prototype worked well but was not needed in practice, as the TR7 was not marketed in Sweden. In production there were various problems with paint adhering to the alloy lamp housings and these were only adequately addressed after some time (*see* Chapter 4).

This rather ungainly effort was clearly an attempt to do away with the complications of pop-up lamps. The idea never progressed very far, although late in the TR7 rally programme, Vauxhall Chevette lamps were tried! (Norman Rose)

The TR7 dashboard with its clear layout was one of the more highly regarded aspects of the car, even if it was very much more 'plastic' (actually Noryl) than the traditional Triumph timber facias. Much of the work on the dash was carried out at Triumph by Dave Jeanes. (Alisdair Cusick)

makers had to jump, British Leyland's American representatives saw another side to this. Bob Burden quotes a BMC distributor who said to him, 'Thank God for the safety regulations – at least they force the factory to make changes to the cars every now and then!' As Burden notes, safety and emissions legislation were blamed for many problems, and sometimes with good reason. 'But industry intransigence often made companies impossible. How do you respond to a company president who tells you, as I was told, that seatbelts made people drive unsafely?'

In Burden's opinion, many engineers (in company with doctors and lawyers) 'rank second only to God, and I know at least one engineer who would dispute that ranking. It was futile for us mere marketing mortals to challenge designs; they could always marshal up a myriad of reasons – or excuses – and legions of cohorts to support their positions.' Burden noted, however, that there were some voices to which the engineers and their managers remained sensitive: 'They acknowledged the power of the press

– particularly the more opinionated writers like David E Davis and the more knowledgeable like Pat Bedard.'

The attitude of the press to the future corporate sports car would undoubtedly be critical, and this was one area where the Leonia team was at one with the British Leyland engineers. 'Mike Dale and Bruce McWilliams were not unaware of this,' Burden explains. (For the way that the press were tackled, *see* Chapter 4.)

Thin End of the Wedge: Building the Bullet

By the late summer of 1971, when the hardtop wedge-shaped styling of the TR7 was frozen, and as Norman Rose and his colleagues were just beginning their work to translate the design from a clay styling model into a real car, the original quotation from Karmann (suppliers of the TR6 tooling) for 'Bullet' body tooling had meanwhile become time-expired, and it would no longer be possible for the Osnabrück company to deliver

This amusing series of cartoons poked fun at some of the TR7's contemporary rivals and was intended for use as part of a presentation on the new Triumph's virtues. The titles were 'detachable roof panel' (Fiat X1/9), 'gas guzzler' (Opel Manta) and 'headroom' (Matra-Simca Bhagheera). (Norman Rose)

tools in time for the projected launch date, which by now had slipped well into 1974.

In an effort to promote interdivisional working and to safeguard the programme, Austin Morris's body engineering division, effectively the former Pressed Steel Fisher unit, was strong-armed by senior management into agreeing to make and deliver the necessary tools by late 1973, which would have been a very tight timetable even for a company with the right resources and free of other problems. As will be apparent from the timetable given by Norman Rose above, with the best will in the world this would be a tough challenge for the body tooling people as they were always going to be very much dependent upon the release of body panel designs and the outcome of testing. These problems would soon haunt the pre-production phase of the new car.

At the same time, some debate continued about where exactly the new corporate sports car would be built. Austin Morris, with MG in its camp, lobbied on behalf of the MG factory at Abingdon, coupled with the concept of the 'body in white' and painting work being carried out at Cowley instead of, or perhaps in addition to, Speke. As late as the end of November 1971, the Specialist Products Division Advisory Board (SPDAB) was reporting that:

> No decision has been taken on the location of trim and final assembly of Bullet, both Canley and Abingdon having been considered, but further detailed study by the Division and Central Staff of the labour implications of the two alternatives was needed before a decision could be reached. Central Staff was co-ordinating the work and a further presentation was to be made to a later meeting of the Board.

However, this appears to have been something of a forlorn hope championed by Austin Morris, in particular by its Managing Director, George Turnbull, since a decision had already been taken in principle the previous month to sanction Speke as the one and only home for 'Bullet'. The subject came up again in April 1972 at a meeting of the SPDAB attended by both Lord Stokes and Geoffrey Robinson, then Cost Controller for British Leyland. During the meeting, it was reported that:

> Mr Robinson reported on meetings and discussions that had been held with 'Austin Morris & Manufacturing' on the manufacturing location of sports cars in the future. Whilst it had been previously agreed (and minuted at a meeting held on 4th October 1971) that Bullet would be manufactured at Liverpool, Mr Turnbull had expressed doubt as to whether the replacement MG should also be assembled there.

The notes of the meeting record Lord Stokes's reaction in the usual understated style of a minute-taker, but reading between the lines one can imagine the tone in which the Chairman's response was delivered from the careful choice of wording:

> The basis on which the previous directive had been made was pointed out and, additionally, if the MG version was not manufactured at Liverpool it would be less viable and would result in unused capacity. It was agreed that the policy of manufacture of Bullet and all its derivatives at Liverpool is confirmed and planning should proceed on this basis. The Chairman [Lord Stokes] instructed Mr Robinson to draft a letter to this effect to Mr Turnbull for his signature and discussion with Mr Turnbull.

At this stage, of course, the threat of US legislation against open cars was still unresolved, and so the decision was taken to keep the MGB in production as an insurance policy – with the new 'O' Series engine under development – but a question mark remained over the long-term future of Abingdon. Central planning vacillated over the question of the MGB in forecasting the timetable for the new 'O' Series engine as a replacement for the venerable 'B' Series engine; the proposal was that the TR7 would replace the MGB altogether in the winter of 1972/73, but by May 1973, and with the threat to open cars past, the MGB received a stay of execution – at least until an open version of Bullet could be made ready. However, for the time being no further thought seems to have been given to an

MG version of Bullet. Certainly, in an article about the TR7 in the 1 February 1975 issue of *Autocar*, it was suggested that there were no plans for an MG version of the new Triumph.

Production Engineering: A Battle Against the Odds

Perhaps unsurprisingly, the promises that had been wrung from Austin Morris for early delivery of tooling proved impossible to keep, and early indications of this appear in the minutes of what had become the Jaguar and Rover Triumph Advisory Board from 2 March 1973, when it was reported that:

> the latest Bullet programme analysis showed it would not be possible to obtain adequate supplies of components off production tooling in time for Method Build in October 1973. There is an indication there may be a conflict of interest at Cowley producing tooling for Triumph and Austin Morris. The Chairman asked for it to be looked into to ensure this was not a problem for SD1.

Needless to say, although there were various positive noises and fair intentions, the 'conflict of interest' at Cowley – busy on other projects, such as the ADO71 saloon – did not go away. When none of the tooling had appeared by early 1974, some months after the original date, an argument erupted between Rover Triumph and Austin Morris. John Barber, Stokes's deputy, intervened when a new date of October 1974 was stated as unworkable by Spen King of Triumph, but while Barber was sympathetic, and offered to investigate a possible delay in the launch, his colleagues at senior board level were evidently less accommodating, for the US introduction date of January 1975 (and a planned UK/ Europe launch in May 1975) held firm. By early April 1974 the Rover Triumph Advisory Board resolved that the timing was so sacrosanct that 'only a major catastrophe would be permitted to interfere with these dates'.

There continued to be a struggle between the competing forces of engineering, production and sales over the timetable. At the meeting of 4

John Lloyd: Mister Triumph Engineering

John Arthur Edward Lloyd, born on 5 September 1923, began his engineering career with an apprenticeship at Armstrong Whitworth Aircraft at Coventry, where he had lived since his parents moved there from New Tredegar, South Wales, in 1936. During the Second World War Lloyd served in the Royal Navy on HMS *Grenville* as an electrical artificer and was awarded the Burma Star. He was one of the early visitors to Hiroshima shortly after the devastation caused by the atomic bomb in 1945. After hostilities ceased, he joined the Standard Motor Company in September 1946. From 1947 he was a research technician, and by 1955 he had risen to the role of Experimental Shop Manager. By the early part of the following decade he was working on the engineering of what would become the Triumph 2000 and from 1966 he was Triumph's Deputy Chief Engineer, reporting to Harry Webster. By the time that Triumph's own early proposals for the 'Bullet' sports car were being formulated, Lloyd had risen to become Executive Director and Chief Engineer of Triumph. In the wake of the British Leyland merger, however, Spen King took on the role of Triumph Engineering Director, with Lloyd continuing to look after Triumph affairs but reporting to King.

In July 1974, however, just as the final stages of 'TR7' Bullet development were in full swing, Spen King moved over to a more central role in British Leyland engineering, leaving John Lloyd to assume the role of Director of Vehicle Engineering, Leyland Cars, with a seat on the Rover Triumph Advisory Board. This undoubtedly became a poisoned chalice, coming as it did just as the company was going through its tough transition from private to public ownership. Writing in an article about Lloyd for *Motor* magazine (2 August 1975), 'Jonathan Edwards' (now known to be a pseudonym for Graham Robson) recorded how Lloyd found bureaucracy frustrating: 'In the old days, I could have spent a lot of time actually designing things – something I would enjoy – but there is so much involvement with Product Planning Committees, liaison between design offices, liaison with so many people, that I have to delegate almost everything.' He went on to say, rather poignantly, 'I miss my old days in the development shops, my development time, very much. I have to drive experimental cars at night-time, early mornings, Saturdays and Sundays'. Certainly Lloyd's son Martin remembers that his father always had papers to read at home, simply because he had insufficient time to deal with them during the office day, which usually started for the early-riser at 07:30. Between 1978 and 1980 Lloyd was Director of Product Engineering for Rover Triumph, but in 1980 he was promoted to the position of Leyland Quality Director – but this was a far cry from the times he had enjoyed in earlier years at Triumph. He retired from British Leyland in 1980 and returned to South Wales.

John Lloyd in the studio with the TR7. (Martin Lloyd)

As part of the test programme, TR7 prototypes were driven extensively in Timmins, Ontario, in northern Canada …
(Tony Lee)

… At the other extreme, TR7s were taken to Arizona.
(Tony Lee)

April 1974, Manufacturing Director Bill Sanders expressed his concern at the progress of body tooling for Liverpool by Austin Morris Body Plant: 'of 40 sets of tools for Liverpool, only 13 have been delivered to date. There is a serious danger of several sets of tools arriving together at Liverpool and causing a "log jam" on initial press runs.' Sanders, who would be dead within four months, said he was 'in touch with Austin Morris and arranging for a further schedule of promised delivery dates to be prepared'. Spen King cautioned that 'the tools must be properly checked and be acceptable to our Quality Department' and E.G. Bacon of Quality Control 'was asked to persuade Austin Morris to further involve their own Quality Department and Mr Sanders said that he was arranging for all modifications to be listed and analysed so that priorities could be determined'.

During 1973 and 1974, endurance testing of TR7 prototypes was undertaken in various locations, the remote parts of Wales around Bwlch-y-groes being a popular, relatively local venue frequented for many years by both BMC and Standard Triumph engineers, although history does not record if the two groups ever met! Prototypes were also driven at the MIRA test facility and in more extreme 'real world' conditions in the Canadian Arctic (for sub-zero temperatures), the Arizona desert (dry heat) and the Mississippi basin (for humidity). Such locations were regarded as sufficiently remote or secure that it was deemed less likely that industrial spies or the general public would stumble upon the prototypes out in the open. Brian Anderson was part of the well-travelled TR7 road-test team:

We went to Arizona for the hot climate testing, to Mount Evans, at an altitude of around 14,000 feet

above sea level – Pikes Peak – in Colorado for altitude testing and Timmins, Ontario, for the cold-weather testing. The TR7 was the first vehicle which we took to the USA for major testing in that way.

While testing in remote overseas venues posed relatively few security headaches, prototypes (both 4-cylinder and V8 versions) for testing in the hills and valleys of Wales were fitted with riveted-on disguises aimed at concealing the startling new shape. John Lloyd, Tony Lee, Brian Anderson and Mick Bunker drove the brace of prototypes seen in the photographs overleaf, which are dated 1974, even though PVC 212L was first registered in November 1972. Tony Lee points out how the strips along the tops of the front wings broke up the line visually, but caused some concern among the test crew: 'We drove the cars for so long like that, that we began to wonder if they were in fact stabilizing the car, and so we had to do some runs without them!'

Spen King was particularly frustrated that such security restrictions limited his ability to test prototypes on the public highway, and he brought up his concerns at the Rover Triumph Advisory Board meeting of 2 May 1974, where it was recorded:

Mr King raised the question of when security on Bullet could be lifted to enable essential road-testing. But Mr M.W.J. Sanders said the break should be delayed as long as possible. Mr Carver said that it was essential to drive the cars somewhere sensibly and with discretion. Mr Jackman asked Mr Carver to discuss the matter with Mr Bacon and Mr King and present a paper to the next meeting asserting that the tight schedule restricted essential road testing of the prototypes.

One of the early test cars on the road near Bwlch-y-Groes in Wales, in late 1974. John Lloyd is in the (LHD) driver's seat. (Tony Lee)

King's view was that the sales people were prohibiting him from using public roadways (British Leyland had yet to acquire its own test track). Perhaps unsurprisingly, sales insisted that secrecy remained necessary to maximize launch publicity. Meanwhile, Sanders (Director of Manufacturing) sought a temporary halt to the road-testing programme to accommodate the additional time he needed to allow the installation of dies and equipment. Perhaps unsurprisingly, in the slightly crazy 'do-or-die' climate, this request fell on deaf ears; the Rover Triumph Advisory Board responded simplistically that 'each department has adequate time to complete its tasks'. The launch date was reaffirmed and sales agreed to road testing as long as the car was camouflaged.

As the summer of 1974 approached, and as British Leyland teetered on the brink of a financial abyss, the TR7 pre-production programme staggered onwards. Norman Rose records that by June 1974 there were thirty prototype vehicles in existence and the first pilot build of seventy pre-production cars was built in September. Meanwhile, however, the continued lack of critical tooling meant, as Sanders had predicted, that the first cars that should have been 'off tools' were still being largely hand-built. In the meantime, 'Quality Control identified at least 300 technical faults. The most serious was the rear axle's tendency to strike the body shell upon encountering bumps.' Triumph's Chief Engineer, John Lloyd, suggested that the remedy would be to redesign the suspension and the tail, but the Rover Triumph Advisory Board rejected this outright on cost and time grounds; instead, modifications to the springs were authorized as a partial remedy. Mick Bunker does not recall this problem – despite the fact that he was largely responsible for the design of the TR7 rear suspension, under Spen King's direction that there should be plenty of suspension travel.

British Leyland's cost controller, Gerry Wright, who was subsequently rewarded for his efforts by being made Leyland Finance Director in May 1975 under the Ryder plan, but who would fall victim to an early Edwardes purge, brought the mounting problem of a budget over-run on TR7 development to the attention of the old Board in mid-1974 – just as management's focus was preoccupied with keeping the whole vessel afloat.

Another minor calamity followed when the slant-four engine twice failed the US Environmental Protection Agency (EPA) emissions tests. At the Rover Triumph Advisory Board meeting on 31 July 1974 John Lloyd reported that:

> some re-testing of Bullet may be necessary as the cars had failed to meet Federal regulations when tested in Detroit although they had been satisfactory in Coventry. He was hopeful that the 're-set' vehicles would satisfy but if not, re-testing or re-specification may be necessary which could delay matters by five months. The results would be known in about seven days.

This is an interesting photo since the car in the foreground is clearly a V8-engined TR7. Popular speculation in the past has suggested the date is 1972 or 1973, based on the registration numbers. However, the photo is dated 1974, which seems to fit with the date of the first V8 TR7 recorded in the Triumph 'X' Register. Behind the car are (left to right) Brian Anderson, John Lloyd, Mick Bunker and Tony Lee. (Tony Lee)

Fundamental problems with the engine continued to dog the TR7 throughout the remainder of its development period, matching the mechanical woes brought about by the weaknesses inherent in the uninspiring Morris Marina (but admittedly Triumph-developed) gearbox. Less than a week before pilot production of the TR7 was scheduled to start, in October 1974, a further batch of engineering design changes were made to both the engine and the transmission in an effort to stem unwanted vibrations. Lloyd reported that:

Vibration problems exist in production Bullets, particularly air-conditioned vehicles, which is causing some concern. To overcome these problems, it is necessary to introduce a modified constant-velocity type of propshaft, a stiffener for the gearbox tail extension casting and an harmonic damper. Work is currently in progress to release the necessary design instructions relative to the re-work of all vehicles. To effect an improvement in exhaust noise an intermediate insert scheme for the tailpipe has been released, to be followed by a revised tailpipe design.

Lloyd also warned that an unspecified but apparently 'considerable number' of components had still to be finally approved and some remained to be tested – barely three months from launch. Mick Bunker remembers the problem with the optional air-conditioning well: 'this was only an issue on pre-production, but I recall that the vibration from the engine was shaking the compressor to such an extent that the clutch inside it failed.'

Although Triumph made much of the modern, lightweight construction and low height of their slant-four engine, the TR7 drivetrain (in its original guise) was going be a poor relation to the classic Triumph six and, at least in the early days, was rarely better than uninspiring. From his vantage point in British Leyland's US office in

Keeping the TR6 on Sale

British Leyland's North American outpost was nervous about the TR7 from well before its launch – and not without justification. Apart from the fact that the new car was such a dramatic departure from the 'traditional' TR, continual development problems and risks of programme slippage meant they wanted an insurance policy. The only solution that presented itself was to extend the life of the TR6 to overlap generously with the TR7 launch. An early record of this as a serious option appears in the minutes of the Rover Triumph Advisory Board meeting of 11 April 1973, which records that 'although the US had asked for a January launch of Bullet, additional work on the TR6 engine to bring it up to Federal emissions standard was being undertaken as a safeguard'. A month later, the same board was told by M.W.J. Sanders that:

> some TR6 cars must be reserved for Europe to bridge the gap while waiting for Bullet, but we could not produce TR6 after December 1974 without a corresponding reduction in Bullet. He was asked to check this situation and Mr Wright [cost controller] said that this matter should be fully ventilated and definite solutions made.

Later that month the board met again and heard that:

> by adjusting schedules adequate TR6 stocks would be available without building after December providing UK/Europe launch was not delayed. It was decided to examine all the implications of running TR6 beyond December and report to the next meeting for final decisions to be made by end of June if possible or end July for certain. It would be sensible to have a contingency plan to bridge the gap for the first 3 months of 1975. It was agreed that any extension of the TR6 would be for USA only.

In the meeting of 26 July 1974 the question of continuing TR6 production after December 1974 was again discussed:

> Mr M.J.W. Sanders outlined the labour problems that could arise, and it was generally agreed that production should continue for a minimum of 3 months and a maximum of 6 months providing USA sign off the quantities to be shipped and that the labour problems, to be discussed with Mr Jackman, could be resolved. Production would cease entirely when the TR6 labour at Liverpool is finally absorbed by Bullet production. Clearance is to be given to Mr Fernyhough not later than the end of July. Mr [Alex] Park said that the Shipping Department should be advised of volumes as soon as possible so that space may be reserved.

At the end of July the matter was still a key issue of discussion, with input received from an anxious US sales team by now clearly angling for TR6 production to continue as long after the TR7 launch as possible:

> It was reported that USA had agreed in writing to take 1200 units per month for 18 months commencing 1st January 1975. Mr M.W.J. Sanders said that production after September 1975 meant an urgent look at bumper modifications and other engineering features. Also the labour situation would need close examination. Mr

The TR6 was extended beyond its intended lifespan, remaining on sale in the North American market for almost 18 months beyond the launch of the car intended to replace it.

Jackman said that the decision as to how long to continue would depend on whether the cost of the bumper modifications justified continued production. If too much Engineering effort had to be devoted to the bumper modifications it may be advisable to cut off at September 1975. It was decided to discuss the matter further outside the meeting and lay it before the Product Policy Meeting.

The solution to the bumper problems would be the massive TR6 overriders seen only on 1976 model year North American specification TR6s.

On 28 August 1974 the possibility of continuing TR6 production beyond August 1976 was discussed, together with the financial considerations: 'It was resolved that production would cease at the 30th June 1976 and that Mr Carver prepared a statement to that effect for communication to Central Staff, BLI and other interested parties.' This then was the decision taken, although the team at Leonia would have liked more: at the Rover Triumph Advisory Board meeting in January 1975, a few days after the launch (*see* Chapter 4), it was reported that 'they [USA] are asking for TR6 to be produced for another 2 years'. This, of course, necessitated the requisite engineering, testing and certification, and even here the path was not a smooth one for, as John Lloyd told Jonathan Edwards for an article in *Motor* in August 1975:

> Last year we were running a couple of TR6s on 50,000 mile endurance to meet the North American emissions laws. At five o'clock one morning I had a phone call to say that both the cars had crashed! Their mileages that night were 49,500 and 48,000 – that close to the finish of the tests. What's more they had actually managed to hit each other – one crawled up the back of the next when they were running in convoy. I don't want to repeat that sort of thing, thank you very much!

In the end the TR6 was discontinued for the UK and Europe on 7 February 1975, but production for the North American market continued until the last TR6 went down the Canley production line seventeen months later on 15 July 1976.

Leonia, Mike Dale could see the problems building up even before the launch:

> The performance was starting to show deterioration against the plan. The engine was not offering any real power and yet the four-speed gearbox was proving so weak that they had to put a high first gear in order to stop tearing it out on heavy acceleration. The later, stronger five-speed box was really only put in to improve its low-end performance and warranty costs.

Meanwhile, as the TR7 moved closer towards the launch deadline, the problems mounted. The Rover Triumph Advisory Board worried that further development work would serve to delay the actual launch, something they remained determined to avoid. The news in late October 1974 that the first 120 pre-production TR7s built had required an average of twenty hours of manual rectification each did not deflect them from this objective. John Lloyd reported that forty further crucial design modifications were needed and, in a frenzied period of activity, a remarkable 1,300

changes were instigated in a three-week period while the programme was temporarily halted.

By November 1974, just two months from the launch and with full line production starting at the Speke factory, the rectification department was expanded in anticipation of the problems to come. Some of the first line-built cars were even shipped to Canley for further rectification prior to their shipment to the USA in time for the launch; among these were some of the cars in the batch sent to BLMC's US subsidiary for use as part of the press and dealer launch (*see* Chapter 4). As that story will show, the quality of these cars was still appalling.

Perhaps recognizing the minefield that lay ahead, the Rover Triumph Advisory Board authorized the contingency plan of even more rectification capacity at Rover's Solihull plant in case the rectification sections at Speke and Canley could not cope with throughput. The first customer cars were scheduled to reach their new American owners in April 1975, although there was a strike at the Canley plant before that

Tony Lee (left) and John Lloyd stand either side of TR7 prototype X828 in the Welsh hills, in late 1974. (Tony Lee).

could happen. Throughout the British Leyland organization, fingers were collectively crossed.

On 27 November 1974 the Rover Triumph Advisory Board heard from Dick Perry that:

> the first four Bullets destined for the USA were ready but trapped at Canley by the dispute. He was endeavouring to get them released. Build had been stopped for three weeks to allow production problems to be overcome. People were being sent to Liverpool to assist and organize a rectification area. Production was due to re-start today but have to end on Friday due to the dispute at Canley. Mr Bacon said that emissions testing could be done at Solihull if necessary. Mr Jackman said that although it appeared the US launch vehicles would be ready on time, the back-up programme may need revision if the strike continued.

A fortnight later, on 10 December, the next Board meeting heard an update on the matter of 'Bullets' that had been prepared for the American technical press. 'These cars are confined to the Canley factory due to the strike', Rover Triumph Chairman Bernard Jackman reported, adding that the Leonia team should 'be approached to ascertain the deadline by which the cars could be flown out. It may be possible to bring one or two others up to the required standard using Solihull labour.' Two days before Christmas 1974, however, the Rover Triumph Advisory Board met again for the last time before the planned US launch and heard that '34 cars will be provided for Press launch thanks

to a splendid performance on the part of Quality Control'. How splendid the quality of those cars really was will be considered in the next chapter.

The Ryder Plan

Just before Christmas 1974 Sir Don Ryder, the government's Industrial Advisor, was appointed to investigate the problems of BLMC. His report, *British Leyland: The Next Decade*, was completed at breakneck speed and handed over on 26 March 1975. It was rapidly endorsed by Prime Minister Harold Wilson's cabinet and was made public on 23 April. Chronologically, the story of the Ryder Plan, which took effect just as the TR7 went on sale in the United States, belongs in the next chapter, but its background and its effect on the TR7 deserves separate comment.

The TR7 was the first TR to use the company's slant-four engine. (Alisdair Cusick)

Teetering on the Brink: The Financial Crisis of 1974

When British Leyland was formed, Sir Donald Stokes knew his board of management faced a Herculean task, but with salesmanship as his principal strength and the sheer unwieldiness of the new corporation, there was perhaps a stronger focus on keeping production volumes up and product in the showroom than the slash and burn necessary if the corporation was to reduce capacity and rationalize the product range. In fairness, some major investments were made, and within a few years their benefits were being felt, but British Leyland's profitability in the early 1970s was fragile. The year of the Austin Allegro, 1973, proved to be an unfortunate turning point. The company was still wrestling with the inevitable indigestion caused by a change in the way that production line workers were paid (from 'piecework' to 'Measured Dayworks'), which brought with it increased industrial unrest. The main problems, however, were not directly of British Leyland's making. The Arab-Israeli conflict of October 1973 brought with it a rapid escalation in fuel prices, inflation (which peaked at 27 per cent in August 1975) and related factors had a negative impact on sales and productivity. The fuel crisis not only made it unfashionable to run the more powerful cars in which Rover Triumph specialized, it also contributed to political turmoil, the miners' strike and the infamous three-day week that precipitated the downfall of Prime Minister Ted Heath's Conservative government in February 1974. In its fragile financial position British Leyland could not cope, and a forecast multi-million pound profit swung round to a mammoth loss.

In April 1974, Lord Stokes referred to the problem of union militancy during an after-dinner speech: 'Too many industries are being deliberately ruined by the divisive and destructive attitudes of a very small minority who appear to hypnotize so many of their complacent colleagues.' A month later, Derek Whittaker, Managing Director of British Leyland's Body & Assembly Division (and later to become head of Leyland Cars under Ryder), wrote to employees warning that the company was facing its worst crisis yet:

> During the first half of the Financial Year, the Corporation lost £16 million. We started the year with £50 million cash reserves. This has now gone; and we are now having to borrow money on an extensive scale to finance our current operations and the development and introduction of new models.

There was worse to come. From a peak of 18s 3d (91.5 pence) in 1969, British Leyland's shares slumped to 10.5 pence each in June 1974, below half the nominal issue price of 25 pence. According to the *Financial Times*,

> The cash crisis is so severe that Leyland are borrowing money merely to pay wages. The company is perched precariously on an ever-growing mountain of debt. Total borrowing is estimated at over £100 million – that is almost double the total worth of the company's 592 million shares valued at their current price of 10.5 pence each.

By July, British Leyland's deepening cash crisis forced a meeting with four banks (Barclays, Lloyds, Midland and National Westminster) to support a reduced investment programme and a £150 million loan. The oil crisis and rampaging inflation had contributed to a reversal of a £50 million profit in 1973 to a £35 million deficit.

The situation was no better by November, and on 6 December Tony Benn, the Industry Minister, informed the House of Commons that the Labour government would step in and guarantee BLMC's capital. This was tantamount to saying that the government would bail BLMC out if private finance efforts failed. This naturally put a different complexion on the corporation's chances, but also placed a question mark over the heads of its board of management. The front page headline of the next day's *Daily Mail* read 'Leylands ask for state aid – Motor giant may need £50 million to beat cash crisis'. Just before Christmas, Sir Don Ryder, the government's Industrial Advisor, was appointed to investigate BLMC. And all this was happening just as the TR7 was being unveiled on the world stage.

A trait prevalent in much of the indigenous British car industry of the 1960s and 1970s was vastly exaggerated forecasting of projected sales of new models. This was a practice that had seen sterling service within the old BMC group, but within the new company the trend reached dizzy heights, with the added feature of forecasts zigzagging up and down. The TR7 was sadly swept up in this process for, like its near contemporary the Rover SD1, projected sales figures were massaged to justify the investment needed for the new production plant and equipment. The eventual price that would be paid for this would include under-utilization of plant, feeble productivity from an unmotivated workforce, woeful industrial relations, often appalling product quality

The Speke Factory

Even before the intervention of Leyland in Triumph affairs, plans had been put in place to create a new production facility to support the 'home' plant at Canley and to help reduce Triumph's critical dependence on certain outside suppliers, most notably Pressed Steel. Common sense would surely have dictated that an ideal place to build the new factory would be in the Coventry area, or at the very least not too far away, in order to draw upon a pool of labour already well versed in the art of car building and spread generously throughout the Midlands. However, commercial common sense and politics do not always go hand in hand, and successive British governments had used various blunt-edged tools to leverage investments by high-earning car makers into regions identified as areas of high unemployment. Car makers were forced to apply for special Industrial Development Certificates in order to be able to build new factories, and the government ensured that these IDCs were rationed to cover deprived areas, irrespective of any paucity of car-building traditions or the availability of a relevantly skilled workforce. In Triumph's case, the company eventually settled upon Speke, situated on the edge of Liverpool.

Triumph Speke, established in a factory formerly owned by Hall Engineering, first opened in 1959 with a workforce of 900 making Triumph parts. The following year a £3.4 million extension created the press shop and assembly plant that made up the 'Speke Number One' plant. At the same time Standard Triumph International set aside an adjacent undeveloped 104-acre site for expansion. When Leyland took control in 1961, however, this plan was temporarily shelved. It was reawakened seven years later, in the aftermath of the formation of British Leyland, and by 1969 work was in hand on 'Speke Number Two', with plans for substantial body-pressing facilities on site. A cynic might question the need for this when Pressed Steel was by now part of the wider British Leyland family, but in mitigation the plans for Speke 2 were already far advanced by this stage, and the greater challenges of the British Leyland merger were yet to be addressed. 'Speke No. 2' included a body plant that welded together the sections of the bodyshell (pressed at 'Speke No. 1'), a paintshop where the body was painted, a sewing room that produced the cushions for the seats and the rest of the interior trim, and a trim and final assembly plant that completed the car. Plants in the Midlands delivered axles, engines and transmission units. However, as Huw Beynon recorded in his study of Speke:

> production at Speke was always part-production: the TR6, the Stag and the Dolomite range were all part-produced at Speke and shipped (in various stages of completion) to the Midlands to be finished. It was not until the early 1970s, with the production of the Toledo, that the Speke plant produced a motorcar on wheels.

There is a popular misconception that the transfer was by rail, although this was not the case. Ken Hazelhurst explains:

> the factory did not have a rail link, despite being adjacent to a railway marshalling yard. All cars being shipped out of the Factory were transported by road on purpose-built LGV trailers, known as 'rigs', which had a system of what is known as roller beds built into them, in two tiers, which where electrically wired to take power from the factory mains. These vehicles were very distinctive due to their shape. Basically a flat bed trailer with canvas sides and a roof which tapered at the top. At the rear a light metal door ran from bottom to near the top, then a large gap up to the very top, similar to a horsebox. They were known to the workforce as giraffe boxes because of their height, which was a lot higher than most LGVs at that time. The Transport Contractors responsible for this operation was a company by the name of William Harper from central Liverpool. Movements took place over a 24-hour timetable.

With plans for a corporate sports car advancing, the idea of a corporate sports car factory must also have seemed particularly appealing by doing away with the need for a 'road train', and in theory the Speke complex could almost take an iron ingot in at one end and spit a car out of the other. This view was further reinforced by British Leyland's own Sports Car Advisory Committee, who decreed that ideally all of the company's small and medium sports cars should be built at a single purpose-designed facility and be based upon a common set of components in order to maximize economies of scale – a microcosm of the ethos behind the entire BMH/Leyland merger. This idea of a dedicated sports car factory would also be championed by Sir George Farmer, the ex-Rover director who was appointed to run the merged Rover Triumph division from March 1972.

By 1970, meanwhile, Speke had begun producing bodies for the Triumph Stag (launched that year but with final assembly still at Canley) and was later responsible for building the Triumph Toledo saloon (the rear-wheel-drive

The Speke factory was the place where the TR7 was assembled – from welding up of the bodyshell, as here – through to final assembly. (Graham Robson)

successor to the Triumph 1300) until that car was transferred to Canley in 1974 in order to make way for the TR7. By the following year, TR7 production was in full swing and plans for the rest of the TR7 'family' were in hand; it was already painfully apparent that these derivatives were going to be urgently needed if the plant were to operate anywhere remotely approaching its capacity. In 1977 the Triumph Stag was discontinued, and the redundant equipment was cleared away to make room for the 'Lynx', planned for introduction in 1978. However, Speke's future would soon be rewritten.

and the eventual fall in sales and transfer of the manufacturing of the TR7 to another factory.

British Leyland management saw in the TR7 salvation for their sports cars – significant dollar-earners for both the company and the nation – and, thus enthused, they viewed it as a route to ease some of their cash-flow problems. However, as we have already seen, not all the troubles with the TR7 lay simply at Speke's door.

When Sir Don Ryder (Lord Ryder from July 1975) scrutinized British Leyland in the spring of 1975, attention rested on four key new car programmes. The TR7 was the most recent launch, to be followed in fairly short order by the Austin Morris 18-22 series (another design from the pen of Harris Mann, initially launched in March 1975, but relaunched the following September as the

Leyland Princess range), the Jaguar XJS (September 1975) and the Rover SD1 (June 1976). With these programmes so advanced, and investments largely committed, there was little option for Ryder other than to keep the 'Specialist Cars' supertanker on course or swallow huge write-offs of investment.

Before the new management structure could begin to operate, however, there would be many changes in both organization and personnel – and the resulting shuffling of responsibilities hardly helped the ongoing process of development and manufacture. The evening following the government's acceptance and publication of the abridged version of the Ryder Report, the British Leyland board met at Leyland House in Marylebone, London. Lord Stokes reported what had been announced, and minutes of the

The New Dolomite That Never Was: Triumph's SD2

One of the many tragedies of the British Leyland collapse was the fact that a number of programmes that had a good deal of merit, on the surface, never saw the light of day. The Triumph TR7 'Bullet' was intended to be the kernel of a whole family of Rover Triumph products that might, if events had panned out differently, have formed the basis of a successful Specialist Cars division in the 1980s and beyond. The Triumph Dolomite, in particular the race-winning Sprint, had shown that there was a place for a compact rear-wheel-drive saloon that offered a British alternative to the BMW. (There is no little irony in the fact that, nineteen years after the launch of the TR7, the Triumph name would be part of the war chest of brands acquired by BMW.)

The new large Rover, known by its codename of 'SD1' for 'Specialist Division – Project Number One', had grown out of the need to replace the Rover 2000 and Triumph 'Innsbruck' 2000 ranges, both still deservedly popular and respected, but unquestionably long in the tooth. Rover had won the battle of marque identity, but Triumph Engineering at least had the consolation of developing the new 6-cylinder engines for the 2.3- and 2.6-litre SD1 variants. After SD1, however, came plans for SD2 to replace the Triumph Dolomite, still a relative newcomer in the range but nevertheless based on an ageing Triumph small car platform. SD2 swept away previous tentative Triumph desktop projects such as 'Bobcat' and 'Puma'. With Spen King in charge of Rover Triumph, a commonized family of components was planned that would encompass not only Bullet and SD1 but also a number of other models – with a 'new Dolomite' seen as the key to maximizing volume and profitability.

SD2 was initiated in May 1972, just two months after Rover and Triumph management had been merged. The basic specification was laid out, adopting MacPherson Strut front suspension, a live rear axle suspended by coils and trailing arms and a Watts Linkage. With the undoubted beauty and appeal of the Rover SD1, it was obvious that David Bache and his team would be expected to contribute a style for the new car, but British Leyland management was determined that what should be a 'style setter' should have the best design, and so an alternative proposal was commissioned from Pininfarina. Malcolm Harbour of Product Planning told enthusiast Keith Adams:

> There were many people including myself who rather liked the Pininfarina style: it was slightly less controversial than the final SD2 style, with the very pronounced swage, and the cowled wheel arches, and there was quite a lot of discussion with management about which was the way to go, but in the end they chose the in-house style.

Triumph designer John Ashford puts an even more interesting slant on the story: 'Farina's proposal was tucked behind the curtains when the senior management viewing came along. Too much of a competitor, you see! Dave Bache wanted to do his thing and what he came up with was very controversial – very heavy over the rear wheelarches.'

The management decision was recorded at the Rover Triumph board meeting of 28 September 1973, where it was reported that 'the more dramatic Rover-Triumph style has been selected although the final choice between this and the Farina style had been very marginal'. The meeting was told Pininfarina had been advised of the outcome but that he still wished to come and see the Rover Triumph people. British Leyland Vice Chairman John Barber was at the meeting and said that 'we should seek to maintain a relationship which would keep Farina available', adding that he would also like Giugiaro to be invited to bid for future work. Barber also suggested that the Pininfarina design 'might be a contender for ADO77 as the dimensions [are] the same'. In that sentence lies a clue to part of the problem for SD2: Austin Morris was also working independently on a medium-sized saloon car (to replace the Morris Marina) and the parallels between these two independent programmes would be ever harder to justify in the coming period of turmoil.

Work on SD2 was continually sidelined because of the more pressing issues with the Bullet and SD1 programme, but even so costs were seen to be escalating alarmingly. Engine and equipment choice oscillated as the studies continued – in the beginning there was talk of a 1500cc version and even an idea to develop an all-new 4-cylinder from the basis of the new SD1 PE146/166 straight six – although for most of the SD2's life it seemed most likely that there would (at various times) have been either or both the Austin Morris 'O' Series and Triumph's own Slant-4 engine, the latter probably in 16-valve 'Sprint' guise. There was a great deal of determination within Rover Triumph to retain the Triumph unit in the face of logical demands for it to be supplanted by the 'O' Series; at the meeting of the Rover Triumph board in May 1974, it was reported that only the Slant-4 engine would be used, but two months later the same group was told that the Slant-4 had been dropped (and that launch of SD2 had been pencilled in for October 1977). Doubtless to their approval, however, the engine was once more back in the frame by October 1974, at which point Rover Triumph Chairman Bernard Jackman determinedly stated, 'Slant-4 is a very economical engine and we need as many as possible in our products in the future'.

Even before that telling statement, the omens for SD2 were not looking good; at the meeting of the same board in September, Staff Finance Director C.J. Peyton reported that 'SD2 was meeting some opposition in finance areas as the return was not considered adequate. A re-appraisal was being carried out.' This scheme was expected to 'probably cost in the order of £20 million', a significant sum when other programmes were competing for limited funds. Of that figure, £1.5 million was to be set aside for development of the 'O' Series engine. At a Rover Triumph Advisory Board meeting on 26 March 1975, the same day that the Ryder report was presented, Bernard Jackman stated: 'neither the Bullet nor SD1 should be sacrificed for SD2 … we should try to clear all matters affecting Bullet before we become too much involved in SD1.' With the upheaval post-Ryder, SD2 was an early candidate for cancellation, although in September 1975 it was briefly resuscitated as part of a joint project called 'TM1' ('Triumph-Morris One') in an attempt to bring together the basis of SD2 with the faltering and even less advanced Austin Morris ADO77 project. Bryan Reynolds remembers that most of the SD2 prototypes (apart from the one survivor now part of the Heritage collection at Gaydon) were scrapped, some without any development mileage on them, adding that 'this was a very disappointing time for those of us that had worked hard to build them'. The only positive aspect of the final cancellation of SD2 in February 1976 was that it allowed scarce resources to be freed up to work on the open-topped TR7. Meanwhile, TM1 came and went with barely a whimper, and with its demise ended the prospect of a new Dolomite. The 'Bullet' would have to follow its own trajectory.

subsequent Rover Triumph Advisory Board referring to that meeting record that 'Lord Stokes had recommended acceptance of the Ryder report and that an Extraordinary General Meeting would be held on May 9th 1975.'

Along with a recommendation that Lord Stokes should resign (later ameliorated at Harold Wilson's insistence to a move for Stokes to a largely figurehead role), the Ryder Report proposed that capital expenditure of £1,264 million would be required from the government, along with £260 million of working capital, with the pressing task of wholesale plant, equipment and model overhaul and renewal. To some ears it sounded like manna from heaven: to others it was folly and madness. By the summer Stokes had duly assumed the largely powerless title of President, ironically slipping into the sort of role that BMC's Sir George Harriman had been pushed into when Leyland merged with BMC.

Ryder set out to plan substantial consolidations, most controversially of the different brand identities that made up British Leyland, but the basic structure of Austin Morris and Rover Triumph proved hard to unravel. However, it became even more apparent that the structure in place was unlikely to generate sufficient sales revenue to support further development of all these different model strands. Ryder's answer was chiefly to throw money at the problem; it would be some years before a different management would take the harder but more commercial choice to terminate model lines. Although the new British Leyland management remained committed to these four new models, however, they did start to prune back some of the other programmes lining up behind.

One early casualty would be the SD2 and its short-lived successor, the 'Triumph-Morris' TM1 programme of rear-wheel drive cars, which were intended to replace the Triumph Dolomite and Morris Marina and share engineering with the TR7 and SD1; both would have utilized a combination of the new Austin Morris-designed 'O' series and the Triumph Dolomite Sprint four valve per cylinder slant-four engines. Instead, Ryder decided to focus on a project to replace the Mini with a newer, more competitive small hatchback (ADO88).

Meanwhile at Speke Number Two, preparations for the new TR7 had already involved clearing out the Triumph Toledo saloon lines and recruitment of engineering staff. British Leyland did not make the latter task any easier by refusing to pay enhanced rates in the Liverpool area for fear of fomenting disquiet at Triumph's home plant in Coventry; the fear was that Canley staff

The David Bache style for SD2 was distinctive, if likely to have proved something of an acquired taste. (Norman Rose)

would seek similar increases in order to maintain a differential with their north-western colleagues. This shortage of adequate resources had already contributed to substantial cost over-runs for the TR7 programme of £1 million by the middle of 1974, just months from launch. Much of this over-running was undoubtedly due to the continuous round of engineering problems and the attempts to remedy them by late re-engineering solutions, often after significant abortive expense.

However, these problems persisted, to the extent that work on the SD2 programme was suspended while efforts were focused on the TR7 (by now in production) and the SD1 (months from launch). The consequence was that British Leyland launched the TR7 while the car was effectively still in development, therefore exposing the cars to their harshest critics – the customers – before all the faults had been identified and designed out. Ryder's bold ambition for British Leyland would be too late to have any real effect on these problems – and, as we shall see, the Ryder Plan was in any case a fairly short-lived experiment.

The interior proposed for SD2 would have been a model of simplicity, like that of the Rover SD1. But it was not to be. (Norman Rose)

4 The TR7 in Production

The Shape of Things to Come

British Leyland management was absolutely determined that the TR7 would go on sale on schedule, and consequently pulled out every stop in an effort to ensure that North American customers could take delivery as soon as possible. The very first pre-production TR7s using production-specification tools had been built in the summer of 1974, but problems with delivery of some of the tooling, being made by Austin Morris, meant that the first batch of cars tested by motoring journalists used a mixture of mass-production and hand-made parts.

The launch had been set for January 1975, with a major press event at Boca Raton, Florida. The initial effort was to satisfy US sales, with a promise that home market sales would follow later the same year; in the event the European launch would slip twice – first from Paris in September 1975, then to Geneva in March 1976, and would finally be delayed a further two months to May 1976.

Back in the autumn of 1974, however, and with US sales crucially important to the new Triumph, it was obvious that the sales and marketing people would need to have access to early specimens, and so a pre-production prototype was duly shipped to British Leyland's offices at Leonia, New Jersey, a few months before the planned launch. One of the first to get his hands on the TR7 was Mike Cook, Press & Publicity Manager, whose initial impressions were not that encouraging. As he records in his excellent book *Triumph in America,* his first thoughts were that the car was:

short, high off the ground, and dull-looking, with no bright metal trim except wheel trim rings. I got in and faced an interior that was all black apart from upholstery to dashboard. There was no chrome or bright trim, and only the instrument markings and the lettering on the switches and knobs provided contrast.

Cook's opinion hardly improved when he turned the key in the ignition: 'Starting it up and hearing the flat, dead sound of the highly-touted (but de-tuned for the US market) overhead-cam engine, many of us were glad that the TR6 would be built for a least two more years.' Reserving judgement, Cook took the wheel for his first TR7 ride over some streets near Interstate 80:

There, on pathways usually used by kids on dirt bikes and off-road Honda three-wheelers, we did broadsides through turns and vaulted ditches and did hands-off braking tests. The little car was willing enough and took the punishment without breaking. It was

The neat and simple logo of the Speke-built TR7, the best graphic design of all three variants in the view of many TR7 fans. (Alisdair Cusick)

comfortable despite the short wheelbase and had to be the widest sports car that any of us had ever seen.

Writing more recently for *Vintage Triumph* magazine, Cook admits he and his colleagues could hardly evaluate performance and speed over the short distance of their furtive drive,

so we contented ourselves with thrashing the car around muddy curves and bouncing through potholes. We were actually only a couple of hundred yards away from Interstate 80 but the car and our activities were hidden from view by eight-foot-tall marsh reeds. I had the wheel for perhaps ten minutes and got to drive the car back to the shop.

Cook's colleague Bob Burden acknowledges the positive aspects of the TR7:

The car obviously had features that reflected American 'wants and needs' such as the really good interior room, seating comfort, air conditioning and eventually an automatic transmission. Colour and trim combinations also reflected American tastes at the time, although some seemed to be more on what the English management thought the 'colonies' wanted!

The ex-Marina gearbox and back axle did not inspire confidence, and the fact that the TR7 was only going to be available as a coupé was an obvious handicap, but whatever Cook and his colleagues

Triangles were an obvious concept for the marketing people to latch on to in 1975, as in the cover of this launch brochure.w

thought, the fact remained that they were going to be tasked with selling the new car, and their first mission was to get it in front of the press.

Overall, Bob Burden had very mixed emotions about the TR7:

On the one hand, the organization desperately needed a new car, preferably a sports car. On the other hand, it didn't look any better to me in real life than it did in the photos. The shape was 'different', but notice that Sir William Lyons never included different in his styling criteria. I liked the front half, but the rear simply didn't complete the design – it seemed awkward, a box grafted on to the back end with a crude black bumper and inelegant tail-lights accentuating

It has to be said that not everyone appreciated steel wheels and black polycarbonate trims on a sports car, even in 1975. They are nothing if not distinctive, but the US marketing people hated them. (Alisdair Cusick)

the heavy back end. Some of this could have been relieved with bigger tyres that filled the wheel wells, and/or wheels that had some presence; instead we got go-kart wheels and tyres.

Burden and his colleagues were often exasperated that, to their eyes, 'the English took some time to realize that wheels and tyres are cosmetic.'

However, it was the detailing and quality that really shook Burden: 'the black polycarbonate wheel centre trims and rear quarter grilles, the decals for name badges, the ill-fitting roof/screen pillar mouldings, the skinny little tyres … and the quality of materials and of construction were unforgivable'. Cook adds:

This all happened in the early fall of 1974. We knew that we would be launching the TR7 in January of 1975 with sales beginning in April. Fingers crossed, we said, to ourselves, it was a well-worn test car, which explained the lack of power; a good paint job would improve the appearance, we could get used to the dull interior, etc. And we climbed into our TR6 company cars and went home.

All that Dale, Cook and Burden had to do was convince the dealers and the world's press that the sun shone out the TR7's tail pipe.

A Hot Date in Florida

The all-important US launch of the TR7 was scheduled for January 1975 – and British Leyland was determined that, come what may, this was a deadline that would not slip. Mike Cook and his colleagues cast around for a suitable venue and settled upon the Boca Raton Hotel, Florida, a few miles south of Palm Beach. With a January launch – and a launch with international significance, as this would be the world debut of the TR7 – much midnight oil would be burned over the December holiday. Cook records how 'with scant attention paid to Christmas and the New Year, we got busy'. As well as seventy-five journalists, several hundred British Leyland dealership owners and employees would be given a guided tour of the new model over a period of

A TR7 receives its wheel assemblies, bolted through the distinctive black polycarbonate wheel trims, on the production line in February 1976. (Graham Robson)

several days: the logistics called for military precision and the patience of a saint. Bringing the dealers to the same venue clearly made sense, as Mike Dale explains: 'this made it efficient from both a management and logistical angle because we needed the same people for both purposes and Sales and Marketing obviously had more people, money and so on than the PR department.' Donald Stokes, British Leyland's Chairman and Chief Executive, would be on hand to provide corporate support, while John Lloyd, Triumph's Chief Engineer, had been asked to provide a technical overview of the new car.

The first major headache came when a strike centred at Canley (rather than Speke) put paid to any chance that there would be true production-built cars at the launch: Cook and his team would try to put a positive spin on this story, but it was hard to prevent one or two of the press reports mentioning the strike. Cook's boss, Mike Dale, shared the exasperation:

As the factory was on strike, the press cars were only got out with some extreme ingenuity from the UK. It always seemed that in the middle management of BL there were a load of Brits who were remarkably good at crisis management and, indeed, seemed to enjoy the challenge. I may have to admit some fellow feeling here because I enjoyed the crises too to some extent!

Mike Cook records that the UK strike was only the start of his problems:

David Bate, from British Leyland's service division, was in charge of getting the test cars ready. Arriving two weeks ahead of the meeting, his first job was to oversee getting the cars off the ship at Jacksonville and transported from the port to a big tent in the grounds of the Boca Raton Hotel and Club, where they were to get the final adjustments, wash, polish etcetera. One look at the cars and he was on a pay phone from the port to me, panic in his voice.

The cover of the TR7 press pack issued to journalists at the Boca Raton Hotel.

The factory had shipped over thirty-five cars, supposedly to ensure that the Leonia team could find enough adequate specimens for their purposes, but Bate had found that they were a motley bunch with, as Cook remembers, 'ill-fitting bodies, shipping damage, bad paint, broken windows and missing parts' – and these were supposed to be cars suitable for setting before the critical eyes of the press. Even worse, when they were driven none was found to be suitable for any serious road testing use. David Bate had neither the manpower nor the time to sort these problems out inside two weeks, and potential disaster loomed.

Fortunately, British Leyland had some good friends and allies in North America, including the Group 44 Inc. race team. Bob Tullius recalls getting the call:

> Mike Dale and Mike Cook conspired to have Lanky (Lawton Foushee – Group 44 Inc.'s crew chief) come to Boca and help. When he arrived he took one look at the situation and called me to ask if I could send the entire Group 44 Inc staff to Boca (about 10 men): without them there would be no introduction, or at a minimum it would be a disaster!

Within twenty-four hours they had rallied round and were busily working on the cars inside the marquee at Boca Raton, as Cook remembers: 'the flurry of activity from then on made the walls of the tent bulge. The roads around Boca Raton were sprinkled with undisguised new Triumphs, still wearing their shipboard "Cosmoline" coating, going through their paces with sweating drivers trying to decide if the amount of repair works required disqualified the car from the start.' Mike Dale adds: 'the inside of that tent was littered with the remains of the cars which they had stripped to make the others whole and the tent was tightly secured so no one could look inside. There were, of course no parts for the TR7 in the US.' Meanwhile 'running in' of the cars continued. According to Mike Cook, 'in the Florida heat, the AC worked great but pressing too hard on the control levers would sometimes cause the knobs to break off. As the auto journalists began to arrive, everyone from BBC TV to the *New York Times*, I had a whole migration worth of butterflies in my stomach'.

Eventually, the Group 44 Inc. team managed to salvage seventeen presentable cars. With fingers crossed, on Thursday 16 January 1975 Cook reported to his managers, Mike Dale and Graham Whitehead, that the fleet of road test cars would be ready for their first exposure to the dealers and the press – scheduled to begin at the weekend. Even so, their problems were far from over, as Dale explains:

> by the time John Lloyd, Triumph's chief engineer, arrived we had discovered 15 basic engineering problems with the car to which John could offer no solution. The meeting was testy. The dealers were arriving in the hotel, the presentations were set and there was no practical way of stopping the launch. I remember remarking to someone that I now knew what the Light Brigade felt like at Balaclava …

The Early Federal TR7

Whereas the non-Federal specification cars would benefit from the traditional twin SU HS6 carburettors, providing a reasonably healthy 105bhp at 5,500rpm, the TR7 sold in the USA had to make do with 92bhp at 5,000rpm from twin Zenith-Stromberg 175CD2SEV carburettors and was strangled by the legally obligatory anti-emissions equipment, including an engine-driven air-pump that recycled exhaust gases back through the engine intake. TR7s destined for California had catalytic converters and a single Stromberg carburettor rather than the conventional exhaust system and dual carburettor intake for the other states. Power in the California model dropped to under 80bhp, and fuel economy also suffered by about 10 per cent, according to contemporary United States Environmental Protection Agency (EPA) mileage tests.

All this variety and challenging emissions requirements made for busy times at Rover Triumph. Talking to Jonathan Edwards for *Motor* in August 1975, John Lloyd bemoaned the enormous workload required as a consequence:

> We never have time to tune engines just to see what happens, not any more. There used to be time, once, and we enjoyed the job, but not now. At present we have three emission engine tunes going for 1976, and three more for 1977, more for the year after – that's where all the test bed capacity goes, and that's just for one car – the TR7.

Power in the TR7 was taken to the rear wheels via the rather unpromising means of a four-speed single-rail gearbox based closely on that of the Austin/Morris Marina (this unit in turn having been evolved from the basis of the one in the Triumph Herald). The contemporary Triumph Dolomite, which used essentially the same slant-four engines, could be had with an optional overdrive, but this model was not sold in North America and, doubtless as a combination of drives for cost and weight saving (and with a five-speed option waiting in the wings),

The distinctive 'pop up' headlamps on an early home-market TR7 are adjusted on the assembly line in February 1976, a few weeks before the European launch. (Graham Robson)

the option of an overdrive was ruled out for the TR7, just as the overdrive was dropped from the US-market MGB at around the same time.

Within a year of the launch, a Borg Warner three-speed automatic gearbox became an option: an early US TR7 thus equipped had hardly a 'sporty' performance, but widened the car's potential sales pitch considerably in a market where the manual transmission with its 'stick shift' was still regarded by the average American motorist as something of a novelty.

British Leyland was particularly proud of the structural strength of the TR7 (aided significantly by its fixed roof) and proclaimed that altogether the bodyshell of the new model was about three times as stiff as that of an average sports car (carefully omitting to mention that the company probably also built that 'average' sports car!). As we have seen, the body was planned with safety in mind, with, for example, catches designed to prevent the bonnet from slicing rearward towards the cockpit in the event of a heavy front-end shunt, and the separation of the centrally mounted fuel tank from the cockpit by means of a structural bulkhead.

Inside the car, the well-trimmed cockpit featured a rather imposing but clearly laid-out dashboard with a simple gauge layout. The heating and ventilation was the same basic corporate system that had been developed for the Princess and the forthcoming Rover SD1 (the Allegro, Marina and Sherpa van shared a cheaper one). Much of the early development was carried out by Rob Oldaker, who swiftly moved over to chassis work and much later would rise to the position of Chief Engineer for MG Rover. Exterior trimmings were fairly spartan and the only 'shiny' bits were the stainless-steel windscreen framing and the chrome-plated door-handle pulls. Coupled with the unremittingly black bumpers, this made the TR7 particularly susceptible to choice of paint colour.

The fact that the early TR7 suffered poor quality from the start was compounded by the UK side of British Leyland escalating its demands for higher and higher retail prices in a desperate ploy to mitigate the corporation's financial losses in the wake of the recent collapse and to compensate for rampant inflation. This was another problem for Mike Dale and his team: 'the first signs of trouble were the escalating demands from the UK for higher prices than the program price/volume planning called for. By the launch the price had grown to 30 per cent over plan and the UK still wanted the same volumes!' Eventually Dale and his team indulged in virtual smoke and mirrors:

We constructed an argument for the dealer presentation that showed the price should have been a thousand dollars more than even the actual inflated price forced on us by the factory and then disclosed, to shouts of delight from the dealers, that we were going to sell it at the lower price. It's an old trick but it worked like a charm. The euphoria did not last long.

There were a number of other problems that came to light as production got under way; according to Mike Carver, 'Although the plastic model had been approved, we found that Engineering had essentially raised the rear suspension to give the car greater wheel travel – and this caused a great ugly gap at the rear – this was down to Spen King's love of long suspension travel'. He confirms that 'the US [Leonia] hated it. We tried to tie it down, but even in production it was visible above the tyre. That told against the style.' Bruce McWilliams says that he only saw the TR7 style some time after it had been signed off: 'it was too late by then – and everyone whose voice mattered had declared it a winner'.

In time, McWilliams's involvement in the TR7 became considerable (for the US limited edition models he helped to create, *see* Chapter 4), but his first involvement related to Mike Carver's concerns:

> It actually started with a bit of drama on the first day of [TR7] production. Mike Carver called to say that the cars coming off the production line had their tails in the air, and he didn't think I was going to like it. I left New York for the UK the next day – and he was certainly right! A meeting had been arranged at the Rover showroom with John Barber and others, where I was to view the car. It was awful. Their bodies were so high in the air that you could, indeed, look straight through over the top of the rear wheels and out the other side.

The options to deal with this problem were limited since, as always, time and money were in short supply, and 'after much discussion it was agreed to try to get the height down a bit and to add a shield to get rid of the see-through effect. These actions helped, along with others taken later, but the car was never really right in this respect and, regrettably, many others.'

Press Reactions

The TR7 was designed with Americans in mind and so was decidedly 'American' in concept, a philosophy that did not necessarily strike a logical chord with a sizable body of traditional American fans of British sports cars. Nevertheless, the TR7 was a bold departure from everything that Olde England had thrown at the Colonies in the past and, if only for that reason, many of the US testers who approached the new car were prepared to give it the benefit of the doubt.

Some time ahead of the launch, in the cold wintry days of December 1974, *Motor* journalist Mike McCarthy and his colleague Lawrence Watts, cutaway-artist extraordinaire, were among the very first journalists to see the TR7 up close, their mission to Canley being to examine it so

that Watts could produce the drawing that *Motor* would use in its TR7 launch preview issue in January. Writing some years later for *Classic & Sportscar*, McCarthy recalled being 'ushered into the holy of holies, the engineering development garage. There were a number of [TR7s] around, some of them ready to run, some in varying amounts of déshabillé.'

The first proper exposure that the dealers and the press had to the TR7 was on the morning of Saturday 18 January 1975 in the Boca Raton Hotel's 1927-vintage banqueting hall. Preliminaries over, an early highlight of proceedings was a brief film of early TR7 testing and development, followed by technical and marketing presentations given, respectively, by Triumph Chief Engineer John Lloyd and the local team of Graham Whitehead and Mike Dale, his deputy. Dale had to improvise with the technical presentation:

> I had tried, in vain, to solicit from Triumph engineering some logic for the way the car was designed and so we had to find our own way. Happily, we were used to having to justify remarkable gaps in the rationality of our employers and I wrote a small thesis on the suspension and steering layout based on my skimpily based knowledge of what had succeeded in my Bug Eye Sprite race car. I sent it, in some frustration, to John Lloyd asking him to critique it before we used it as a basis for the sales pitch. I got a short note back saying it looked fine to him. John was a nice man and I think he was somewhat amused to find out how clever Triumph engineering had been without knowing it.

A display of TR7 components was set out in the hotel's Great Hall, and from there the journalists were corralled in the general direction of the test cars. With seventy-five journalists and seventeen cars, it was obvious that there were insufficient opportunities for thorough road sessions, even with both seats occupied in each car, and so the British Leyland PR team waited with bated breath to see what their guests would make of this very different 'TR'.

First impressions were undoubtedly mixed: few people new to the TR7 instantly warmed to its looks (indeed some were positively horrified at the contrast to the classic looks of the TR6), but most testers warmed to the car once they had a chance to explore its road-going ride and handling. First off the blocks were the British visual and audio media journalists, allowing them to send their reports back home, and among them Mike Cook records that John Humphrys of the BBC (nowadays best known for his anchor role at BBC Radio Four's *Today* programme and BBC TV's *Mastermind*) posted a report to camera on the TR7, which was broadcast on the evening BBC1 News bulletin back home in Great Britain.

In his piece, Humphrys drove up to the camera in a yellow TR7 and leaned over the high door ledge to deliver a message that British Leyland hoped the TR7 'was the start of a new era'.

Although the view of the 'folks back home' was undoubtedly of significance, perhaps of more local importance to the Leonia team was the reaction from the local media – in particular the influential people at the enthusiast monthlies, *Road & Track*, *Car and Driver* and *Motor Trend*. Patrick Bedard of *Car and Driver* magazine, who was present at the TR7 press introduction at Boca Raton, remembers his initial reaction:

> JRT earnestly wanted something new after flogging ancient iron for so long. Michael H. Dale was the corporate evangelist for British cars in those days, a perfect guy for the job, a loyalist and hard worker who carried the fire without gloves. Respect for him coloured the press reception of the car. We couldn't laugh at something Dale took seriously.

Mike Dale's response is that he felt the press may have been somewhat taken by all this show of fun: 'they gave us a remarkably kind ride in the press reports. I do appreciate Pat Bedard's kind words about me personally but I think our whole crew were a bunch of characters and we didn't take ourselves very seriously (and still don't!)' Mike Cook was also relieved at the good reaction from the local press:

> Maybe it was coming to Florida in January, maybe it was the hotel, perhaps it was the charm we all put on

to entertain them but the journalists thought the TR7 was okay! They sat through the marketing presentation and technical address and then embarked for a two-hour spin on the most interesting roads we could find in flat southern Florida. In Europe, where the auto scribes had a chance to go for top speed, there was a lot of negative reporting but in North America the praise was muted but overall positive.

Pat Bedard and his fellow automotive journalist colleagues saw the TR7 as a brave move for a company more noted for evolution than revolution: 'The car was a radical turn for a traditional sports car maker, daring in its shape, so radical that you had to pay attention. And it wasn't a bad thing to drive.' Bedard recognizes this might be seen as 'tepid praise', but, mindful of the rose-tinted nostalgia factor, qualifies his comment accordingly:

> The seers and knowers would guffaw if I inflated the rating after all of these years. You have to take the times into consideration. The seventies were desperate days for car enthusiasts; everybody was reeling from fuel shortages and the engineers were still doing new cars by intuition and art, instead of the fast-response computers of today. The TR7 wasn't powerful enough to elevate the pulse rate and it wasn't beautiful enough to buckle knees. It was merely new … and oddly, bravely, radical in a time of ineptitude and paralysis. And it looked like a doorstop, which was fun to talk about.

John Humphrys reports from Florida on the new TR7.

The Man from the BBC

John Humphrys reported on the TR7 from the launch at Boca Raton for the BBC1 nine o'clock evening television news bulletin.

Shot of yellow TR7 driving around what appear to be estate roads at the Boca Raton Hotel and Club. Robert Dougall [BBC newsreader in studio] provides the voiceover:

… launching Britain's sporty TR7 there was perhaps a touch optimistic. Nevertheless, British Leyland hope to sell 12,000 …

Cut to John Humphrys's voiceover; shot of line-up of TR7s, with cars setting off one by one on press test runs:

25 years after the British opened up a brand new export market in the United States, with an MG sports car, they're trying again – this time with the Triumph TR7. In those days – when British Leyland wasn't even a twinkle in Lord Stokes's eye – the American market was wide open, and the British exploited it to the full. Today, it is perhaps the toughest market in the world – and the British have been beaten hands down. So the TR7 means more than an addition to the range: British Leyland hopes it is the start of a new era.

John Humphrys draws up in yellow TR7, leans out of side window and speaks to camera:

The trouble is, Americans aren't buying cars at all at the moment – at least not in the way they used to: sales are down so sharply, 300,000 car workers have had to be laid off and factories closed temporarily throughout the country. The big manufacturers are desperately worried – and perhaps British Leyland should be too.

TR7 TV commercial starts playing and, as a red TR7 emerges from the hold of a plane, the voiceover begins:

It's out to steal the American road …

John Humphrys's voice takes over:

Their commercial: part of the biggest car sales they've ever launched here. They are determinedly optimistic, but everything depends on getting the potential customers into the showroom. The Americans are failing to do that …

Commercial continues, as the TR7 drives into the back of a moving wedge-shaped articulated trailer, and concludes:

TR7 – the shape of things to come …

Car and Driver featured the TR7 on the front cover of its April 1975 issue, with the headline 'TR7: A Major Triumph'. Inside, Bedard was enthusiastic about most aspects of the new car other than the styling. Of particular merit in Bedard's eyes was the interior:

The TR7's strong suit is comfort. The cockpit is spacious (wider than either a Corvette's or a Z-Car's) and the driving position is exceptionally good … the interior of this car is exceptionally well executed

from almost every angle … The TR7 is one of those rare cars whose agreeable nature hits you as soon as you slide into the driver's seat. It just seems to work. And when you slip into traffic on your maiden voyage, you feel like you've been driving it for years. This is altogether something new for British sports cars …

Bedard sounded some warnings for British Leyland, however: he was not impressed by the brakes ('Another trip through the engineering department is required here' was his blunt comment) and similarly the engine and transmission noise did not escape his notice:

> Despite their thoroughness, the engineers overlooked one conspicuous area: engine vibration. Like all in-line, four-cylinder engines, this one shakes. And at certain speeds it sets up very annoying resonances in the body. You can feel them in the floor, in the pedals, in the seat and – worst of all in your ears. As luck would have it, this cacophony reaches a crescendo at 55mph. And it's even worse with the air conditioner operating. All of this can be fixed with careful vibration tuning – and it must be fixed before the TR7 can live up to its potential as a GT car.

Bedard concluded his April 1975 report optimistically: 'more than anything else, the TR7 is available at a fair price. If the engineering department follows up on the few remaining problems – particularly the brakes and the vibrations – this car will be a hit.'

Road & Track was well known for previewing new models with a fairly detailed 'technical analysis', which usually provides driving impressions but for obvious reasons falls short of a fully fledged road test report. The magazine's April 1975 issue carried an appraisal of the TR7 by Paul Frère and Ron Wakefield, in which they began by offering what amounted to almost an epitaph for the traditional sports car. This completed, they explained that the TR7 was 'a complete breakaway from the long line of TR models' and that the rigid coupé top had endowed it with 'a remarkable torsional stiffness of 7,500 lb-ft per degree of twist'. The magazine surmised that a Sprint and a V8 version could follow in due course, and hoped that if the latter replaced the MGB GT V8, the new car could at least be marketed in America, unlike the older MG.

At the tail end of this report John Dinkel had to make do with a half-page piece on his all-too-brief 'driving impressions' gained at Boca Raton. 'We had hoped to have a full test of the TR7 to go with this month's technical analysis of it,' he began, 'but unfortunately a strike in England

Car and Driver *gave over the cover of its April 1975 issue to the new Triumph TR7, which Pat Bedard described as a 'major triumph'.* (Car and Driver)

(what else is new?) prevented British Leyland from starting production on time and the cars shown at Boca Raton, Florida were pilot models.' Dinkel went on to explain that the two cars he had driven in Florida may have looked like the cars that went on sale on 2 April 1975, but that they didn't have all the latest engineering changes: 'Some substandard components were used to get them put together too: so despite what you may have read elsewhere, we believe a full test of one of those cars would be unfair both to the reader and to British Leyland'. Clearly, as we shall see later (page 80), Mike Cook's faith in John Dinkel's tact and decency were not misplaced!

Like many testers, Dinkel did not like the fact that it was almost impossible to see the front of the car from the cockpit, but he was impressed by other characteristics. 'The TR7 has a solid feel virtually unknown in previous British sports cars', he wrote – citing the TR6 as an example. In conclusion, Dinkel said that

> Even though it blazes no new trails in the evolution of the sports car, the TR7 is a modern and refined car that will appeal to the buyer attracted by sports car looks, handling, size and character but turned off by leaky windshields, buckboard rides and ineffective heaters. If the success of Datsun's 240Z is any indication, British Leyland shouldn't have much trouble selling a lot of TR7s at the $5,100 asking price.

What neither Dinkel nor anyone could know in 1975 was that, within five years, inflation and exchange rates would ensure that price eventually doubled.

Meanwhile, the other key element of the sales and marketing process, the dealers, were looking upon the TR7 with jaded optimism; they had heard fine promises before, although they tended to regard those made by Mike Dale with greater respect. Joe Herson was one of the major JRT dealers at the time:

> I do remember attending the TR7 launch in Boca Raton, Florida. After all those years in the business, we had formed some very close relationships with other dealers from all over the United States. In fact, through the National Automobile Dealers Association, we had formed a study group of non-competing British Leyland dealers (dealers that were not directly, geographically competitive with one another) and it was not

unusual for that group to meet in conjunction with the importers' national events. It sticks in my mind that we had scheduled such a meeting at Boca. So we had our own little claque that attended the intro meeting and sat together and gossiped and joked together. Dale and his cohort did a mighty fine job of concealment and obfuscation. Our group in the audience did not know of all the travails and woe that had gone into the get-ready. In fact as we saw the new TR7 from a distance in the audience, we were quite pleased because it was such a departure from what had gone before. It really looked, from afar, that the British had got their act together and had finally arrived in the 2nd half of the 20th century.

Home Runs: The First Extended Press Trips

After the press launch, some of the magazines asked to borrow cars to take on extended journeys in order to form a more detailed impression of the new Triumph. Sadly there were not enough cars that the British Leyland team felt were anywhere near good enough to place in the care of magazines – and there was at least one too many journalists asking. The only solution, according to Mike Cook, was to toss coins; in the event, Leon Mandel, John Christy and Don Fuller got rides home for *Car and Driver*, *Motor Trend* and *Road Test* respectively, but the unlucky John Dinkel of *Road & Track* was told that his car had unspecified problems that could not be fixed owing to the shortage of parts in the UK as a consequence of the strike. It was a case of subterfuge of the type that Conservative Minister Alan Clark would many years later label as 'being economical with the actualité' but perhaps it was also a reflection of the good humour with which Cook knew that Dinkel would receive the news.

Leon Mandel, founder of *Auto Week* magazine and frequent contributor to other publications, wrote up his drive from Boca Raton to his home in Nevada for the July 1975 issue of *Car and Driver*, which was actually two months after the magazine carried its first TR7 road test. His

All Speke TR7s can be recognized by the larger fuel filler cap. (Alisdair Cusick)

Chris Turner owns this immaculate Speke-built TR7, one of the earliest on UK roads. (Alisdair Cusick)

report entitled 'Travelin' On: America Through a Windshield' was, typically of the man, written in the evocative style of a short story. Mandel reported that the Java Green car, 'somewhat fresh because it is a prototype', showed early warnings of problems to come by consuming copious quantities of oil.

Despite his surprise that the TR7 generated relatively little public curiosity on his trip, Mandel was nevertheless taken by the ambience of the cockpit, particularly its comfort and the reassuring green glow of the instruments and switches at night, while outside 'the rush of the wind along the car is like a storm at sea, a blizzard against a house: it provides a reminder of a hostile and unknown outside, reinforcing the feeling of security inside the car.' Mandel conducted his charge from Florida (calling in at Sebring for a bit of sightseeing) through Alabama, Mississippi, Louisiana and Texas within the space of two days.

Matters suddenly came to a head at 6:15 in the morning in northern Texas when, without warning, the engine seized. 'In Possum Kingdom Lake, Texas, puzzled and infuriated by 2,000 miles of anonymity, I am flashed the other side of the bright coin of sports car ownership in the '70s – a phenomenon that has become commonplace currency in this country over the past two decades', Mandel wrote.

Mandel was soon on the phone to Boca Raton, where, he wrote, 'the twelve remaining TR7s sat being admired by the convened dealers who had been flown in from all over the country'. On the receiving end of the call was Mike Cook, who handed a note to Mike Dale. Understandably, both recall the event with equal clarity. Fortunately a complete engine was available, for as Dale explains, 'Happily, there were a bunch of them in the tent outside taken from the disassembled cars!'

Mike Cook made the necessary arrangements, and the engine was promptly flown in a chartered Cessna to Overseas Motors at Fort Worth, Texas. With a district service manager on hand to ensure that the engine was fitted without delay, the Triumph team was able to get Mandel back on the road the next day: 'I believe we paid for his hotel too!', Dale adds. Pausing at Tucson, Mandel collected his wife from the airport. Mrs Mandel seemed initially impressed: 'She thought I had told her it was not mid-engined. It looks mid-engined enough, she says, and what has British Leyland done, brought in a Mercedes man to design the seats?'

Continuing westwards, the remainder of Mandel's journey was comparatively uneventful, although he recalled a brief encounter with the driver of a Fiat X1/9 – similarly wedge-shaped though, unlike the Triumph, genuinely mid-engined. Following the X1/9 out of Las Vegas, Mandel tried to attract the attention of the female driver using all the tricks in the book, such as pulling alongside and sliding ahead, 'all

Another concept that British Leyland's marketers were keen to stress was the fact that the TR7 offered the most room and comfort of any comparable two-seater sports car.

The bold wedge shape of the TR7 coupé is perhaps at its most striking from the side. (Alisdair Cusick)

in favour of discovering if the driver will notice that this big wedge is somehow different from her car. After ten miles, a reaction: she rolls down her window at a stoplight and tells my wife our right parking light is out.'

Mike Dale readily acknowledges that the swift action of his team in getting Mandel back on the road saved the TR7 from a severe roasting:

> Leon was about the toughest, most brutally honest auto journalist alive at the time. He and I had struck a warm friendship which endured until his death and he wrote a wonderful article on how he was dug out of the predicament rather than castigating us for a major quality problem. It was another of those little crises we enjoyed so much.

Meanwhile, John Christy of *Motor Trend* had an even more eventful trip in his TR7. As Mike Cook recalls: 'Christy was forced against a kerb by a truck during a snowstorm in El Paso and

rolled his TR. The structural rigidity being one of the things about the car that really was top quality, there was surprisingly little damage to the car and none to John.' Later, Christy would write of his experience in his magazine, saying that 'if he had to roll a sports car, he'd rather do it in a TR7'.

Don Fuller, reporting for *Road Test*, had a comparatively stress-free drive from Florida to California in his red TR7, other than a moment in the dark in Mississippi, when the car's misaligned headlamps upset a local driver:

> While cruising comfortably and well over our government's beloved national speed limit, I passed a guy in a Chevy who was doing about 55 or so. He must have thought I had the high beams on; it made him mad, and besides, he had to impress his lady, right? So he immediately got right on my bumper and started flashing his lights. Now I knew the TR7 would do 107 and no more, so it was unlikely I could out-run

The Speke-built TR7s all featured satin-black painted panels at the back, which integrated well with the bumpers (less massive on this UK car than the US specification units, without the integral over-riders). (Alisdair Cusick)

him. And the Chevy was bigger. So I just tensely drove on through the night, until he got bored with his little game, because I had lived close enough to the South for long enough to know that on a rainy night in Mississippi, you don't get out of a funny little foreign car to explain mis-aimed headlights to some dude in a Chevy with a Confederate flag decal on the rear window.

The car that *Road & Track* should have had was a yellow specimen that suffered from a howling rear axle: instead of being passed over to the magazine's John Dinkel, Mike Cook ended up driving himself and his wife back home after the end of the launch – thankfully experiencing a

blissfully event-free trip. John Dinkel, meanwhile, had to make do with his brief session behind the wheel at Boca Raton. When I reminded him of the fate that befell his rivals, and told him of Mike Cook's coin-flipping story, Dinkel laughed that it was obvious he had had the best deal: 'I won!', he said succinctly.

Road & Track's first full test of the TR7 appeared in the May 1975 issue, meaning that the car had two consecutive months of coverage – something that regular advertising budgets would have been hard placed to match. In his report, entitled 'A new direction for British sports cars', John Dinkel and his co-testers were able to assess and analyse the new car in more detail. 'Finally something has emerged from BL's engineering departments', the magazine said, 'and it's only the first of several new sports cars we'll see over the next three years.' In the future, the magazine suggested, 'there will be several new variations on this basic car as well as a new Jaguar sports coupé and, we hear, something new carrying the MG nameplate.'

Dinkel and his colleagues bemoaned (but understood) the lack of an open top but they were, like many fellow testers, very impressed with the interior: 'as soon as you climb into its padded cockpit you know you're surrounded by

Early TR7s featured brushed nylon cord seat facings, which were smart if a little dark in the rather snug interior of the close-coupled coupé. (Alisdair Cusick)

substance and solidity. The dashboard is massive looking, you're sitting low within the car and everything looks, well, heavy.' Interestingly, the *Road & Track* test car did not appear to suffer the maladies of the earlier test cars; Dinkel found the engine 'about average' for a 4-cylinder: 'it runs smoothly, without any annoying vibration periods, although the exhaust resonates noticeably on deceleration.' Dinkel pronounced himself satisfied with roadholding, handling, ride and even the brakes, but at the end of the report he could not help drawing attention to the controversial styling, signing off by saying 'you can't really ask much more … except perhaps good looks'.

The Initial Views of the British Press

We saw earlier how the British TV media reacted to the TR7, their interest undoubtedly fuelled by the unfolding British Leyland crisis rather than any enthusiastic sports car leanings. It would be down to the British motoring magazines to present the more detailed analysis that enthusiasts expected. *Autocar*, *Motor* and *CAR* magazines all reviewed the new Federal TR7 in some detail.

The first British newspaper reports of the TR7 surfaced on 20 January 1975, when The Times announced that British Leyland had unveiled the new sports car 'despite the group's financial troubles'. The TR7, we were told, represented an investment of £11 million and production plans called for output levels between 60,000 and 70,000 per annum. *Motor* magazine's report of 25 January, with the traditional cutaway view, was headed 'TR7 – the seventh son', and told the story in characteristic detail of how Mike Carver and Spen King had engaged with Americans to sound out their views. *Motor* observed that British Leyland's plan of 60–70,000 cars per annum was ambitious, and that the existing MGB and TR6 sold about 20,000 and 12,000 per annum in the USA at the time, '… so the TR7 will have to do rather better than both together. Time will tell.'

By the time of the TR7 introduction, the British monthly *CAR* had already earned a reputation for speaking its mind and readily brooking controversy. In the February 1975 issue, as part of

The European market TR7 press pack from 1976.

a feature headlined 'Enter the '75s', there was a report on the TR7s in Florida under the heading 'Stars-and-Stripes TR'. *CAR* noted the many changes from traditional TRs and quoted Mike Carver, at that time Rover Triumph's Director Product Planning, who had told the magazine, 'I was told very clearly that the TR7 should be a two-seater with a north–south engine and rear-wheel drive for reliability, durability, simplicity and ease of servicing'.

CAR also noted that the styling of the TR7 suggested a mid-engined car but fell short of the promise. The magazine pointed out that Harris Mann had 'come up with the winning sketch: he considered it rather wild, but Lord Stokes, John Barber and Sir William Lyons all liked it …'. This is probably the source of the apocryphal tale that Mann did a wild sketch, only to be shocked when it was chosen. *CAR* clearly did not subject its TR7 to a particularly thorough appraisal, but the magazine liked the interior even if it thought that purists would feel cheated that the TR7 did not have a mid engine. Perhaps the fact that the same magazine had been confidently predicting a range of mid-engined MG and Triumph models in its January 1974 issue could have had something to do with this …

Un-'Speke'-able Quality

With all the pressures on an early launch, and the problems during the lead-in to production, it was perhaps inevitable that the quality of the Speke-built TR7 would be indisputably poor, and so a great deal of effort went into rectifying faults after manufacture and delivery – an expensive and highly unsatisfactory state of affairs. The carefully prepared press cars had given a good initial impression, and a high standard to which production cars could aspire, but in the months that followed all the usual 'Leyland' problems meant that the real-world quality of the TR7s that ended up with customers was universally poor.

'Of course management blamed the workers for much of this, and the British government for dictating Speke as the assembly plant', Bob Burden recalls. However, he was keen to see for himself where some of the problems lay, and soon after the US launch he wangled a trip to visit the Speke factory. 'I wouldn't call it the highlight of my automotive career,' he wryly observes, 'but it certainly helped me to understand some of the quality problems.'

Burden was assigned a young engineer to escort him round the Speke works:

> We stopped at a point in the body assembly process where a front member was being installed. He told me quite proudly that it was called 'Nessie' because of its shape and that it was the most complex pressing in the European car industry at the time. I nodded and said something like 'how interesting', thinking all the time that a) complex is contrary to prevailing manufacturing philosophy and b) we can't even do simple really well, much less complex!

The slant-four engine was mounted well back in the engine bay, which contributed both to balance and crash performance. (Alisdair Cusick)

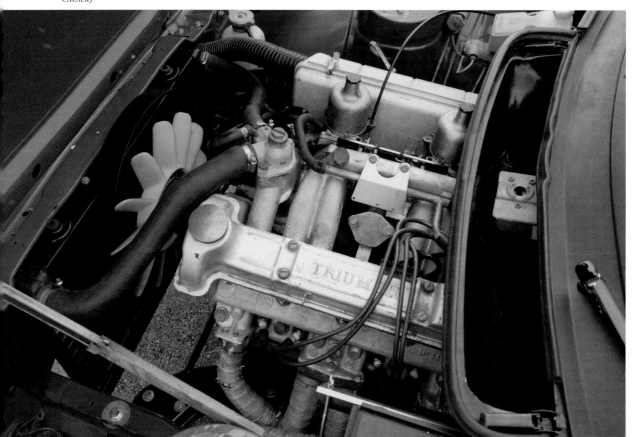

The Speke Cat Pee Strike

Speke was famous in the industry for strikes over seemingly trivial matters, but one that made national headlines in December 1975 was particularly extraordinary. *The Times* reported on 17 December, under the heading 'Cat smell dispute makes 600 men idle', that 'about six hundred men from the Leyland Triumph car plant at Speke, Liverpool, were idle yesterday because of an unofficial strike by 21 workers who complained of a smell caused by stray cats'. The twenty-one men downed tools while cleaners spent forty-five minutes scrubbing and disinfecting the floor. Management agreed to pay the men while this cleaning took place. Once the cleaning had been done, however, the workmen declared that the floor was now wet and too dangerous for them to return to work – so they did what car industry union men did best in the 1970s and called a meeting to discuss the matter. After management had agreed to pay the men for their idle time, they had been told that there would be no extension of this pay for any subsequent meetings, and so the twenty-one men were told they would not be paid any more. So the workmen did the other thing they were good at doing following a union meeting – they went on strike to protest at not being paid. A day later saw all 600 workers in their section laid off, and TR7 assembly had to rely on dwindling supplies of trim in stock. Thus, for a time, twenty-one men and some stray cats wielded power over the whole of Speke production.

This simply 'defied logic' in Burden's view.

The tour continued, and before long Burden reached the point on the assembly line where, in his words, his 'pet peeve was inflicted'. Burden's minder had left him to his own devices in order to attend to more pressing duties, and so Burden found himself free to talk to the men on the line:

One particular worker installed the roof/screen pillar moulding. I asked him why they never seemed to fit right. He proceeded to show me why: first he fitted one flush to the 'A' pillar, and hammered it around the roof line to the rear where there was now a three-quarter inch gap; then he fitted the moulding to the rear of the next car and followed it around to the front – where there was now a three-quarter inch gap. The

compromise, which he demonstrated on the third car, was to centre the moulding leaving smaller but equal gaps at the front and rear. My immediate reaction was that he was demonstrating a problem on what would soon become customer cars, but I let that pass in my quest for enlightenment, and asked him why longer mouldings weren't used. He pointed silently to boxes of moulding around his station waiting installation – all cut to the too-short length!

The stories of Speke are legion. Brian Anderson was one of the men from Canley who made regular trips to the Liverpool factory, which he regarded as a semi-lawless enclave subject to different rules:

I used to go to Speke every Thursday to represent Engineering – it was a real eye-opener! The workforce ruled the roost, and got away with murder. Under the body conveyor there was an area curtained off – and there was a guy under there measuring up people for suits! At the end of the day I'd have a cup of tea with the Quality Manager, and one time I noticed that everyone was wearing leather coats, which it turned out they'd paid £5 each for. He asked me if I wanted one! I said no thanks – and then the next time I was up there, I found that there were no leather coats – there had been a police raid!

Mike Dale also recalls that a special trip organized for US dealers to see the 'home of the TR7' did the business few favours:

The production line was filthy; workers were idly standing around and greeted any female with loud whistles and cat calls and odd parts were scattered in all directions. It was a striking contrast to the orderly production line in Abingdon with its friendly people. They were really committed to MG and it showed. The Triumph workers at Speke clearly gave the impression that they didn't give a damn.

Jeff Herbert joined British Leyland in September 1977, becoming Managing Director of Rover Triumph a few months later and, for reasons that will become apparent later, saw Speke in operation only for a short time. However that brief period allowed a visit to Speke to become firmly pressed on his memory:

> The plant manager at Speke was an ex-Ford Liverpudlian in his mid-fifties – he knew the car industry really well: he was a classic 'car industry man'. There are two things I can clearly recall. One was an effigy of him hanging from the roof, with a rope around its neck, and the second was a group of men standing on the bonnets of cars with their hobnail boots on. The manager just took my arm and gently guided me away, quietly suggesting I shouldn't say a thing! And that was where the TR7 was being built!

Of course, there are always two sides to a story, and there is no doubt that many of the workforce at Speke, given an even chance, wanted to produce a high-quality product of which they could be justifiably proud. Although most of the engineering was driven remotely from Canley, the hard work of building the cars fell to the people in Speke.

Ken Hazelhurst was a maintenance fitter who worked at Speke during the TR7 heydays, and he recalls a particular issue related to the fact that early cars were all exported to the USA, in particular those destined for California:

> In order to comply with the Federal regulations, all these vehicles were set up to run on unleaded petrol, which was virtually unheard of in the UK. Fuel tanks were then installed to store this fuel in the factory, and as each finished car was driven off the production line they were then driven to Liverpool docks, and then on to ships, for passage to America. We were amazed when we were informed that a gallon of this fuel cost £2, an unbelievable price then!

The Shape of Things to Come

Bob Burden credits the US advertising agency PKL Advertising (later Shima/Passberger) for the clever launch marketing concept that played so heavily on the TR7's wedge shape, and the snappy slogan 'The Shape of Things to Come'. Across the border in Canada, the local marketing team

based in Ontario plumped instead for the strapline 'The Magnificent Seven', although much of the publicity literature was otherwise similar to the US equivalents. Burden maintains that:

> Not only was the theme of 'the shape of things to come' so right – if not correct as history would show – for the TR7, it was pre-emptive and attention-getting, which are the hallmarks of good positioning and good advertising. Unfortunately the mechanics of the TR7 did not live up to the promise, but the style did, and that first impression was key.

Burden also credits the way that the TR7 marketing cleverly built on the preceding 'British Racing Green' theme that had been generated for the TR6; the new car was heralded by 'From the Land of British Racing Green – now comes the Shape of Things to Come'. 'That helped to give the TR7 an instant pedigree and a position in the marketplace, while reinforcing the continuity', Burden believes.

The wedge theme carried over into other forms of communication logically and naturally, from brochures and point-of-purchase material to what Burden refers to as 'trinkets and trash': 'I still have a set of cufflinks with their distinctive 30–60–90 degree triangle shape', he explains. 'In short, "Shape" was a total marketing package, and contributed to making the TR7 launch the most successful in Triumph's history and the best year for Triumph sports car sales ever.'

Mike Dale agrees:

> The advertising was really well received. The Shape of Things To Come was cleverly conceived because it not only seized on the car's basic shape to set it apart from its competitors but it allowed us to poke fun at ourselves at the same time. I was always comfortable with the fun aspect, because, after all, these were sports cars and if they aren't fun then why bother! The ultimate expression of this was Ken Slagle's TR7 racecar trailer, which was fully enclosed in the shape of a big yellow wedge.

By the time of the TR7, television was already an important advertising medium and so British

Two contemporary 1975 brochures – one from the USA following the 'shape of things to come' theme, while the other, for Canada, used the slogan 'The Magnificent Seven' – yet the artwork and photography were all the same!

Leyland commissioned some commercials linked to the same theme as the print media. One of the first commercials, featuring a TR7 and a truck with a wedge-shaped trailer, was dubbed 'Cross Country 1 (Truck)'. According to Bob Burden:

> The truck (really a trailer) also appeared in 'Rocket', done the same year. As you can imagine, filming at sites around the US was quite expensive so the running footage was used in a number of commercials including 'Cross Country 2 (Garage)', where the car ended up in a wedge-shaped garage next to a faux Tudor house – the wedge, of course, was the signature device for the theme line, 'The Shape of Things to Come'. In another launch spot, the TR7 emerges from a wedge-shaped factory – I still have the Lionel train with two car carriers filled with Dinky Toy TR7s from that commercial. Another cross-country spot had a wedge-shaped Indian teepee and there was even a spot with a wedge-shaped car wash.

All in all, Burden believes, the TR7 TV adverts were 'a pretty good body of work, but like the car itself, not a home run. Mike Cook and I think it ranks above the TR6 work, but below the Spitfire stuff. Funny how ad agencies can really nail one product and fall down on others!'

The TR7 in Service: Customers as Development Engineers

We have already seen how development hiccups and delays meant that the launch of the TR7 was a rushed affair, with many engineering and production issues unresolved. As had become the depressing norm for British Leyland, this meant that the customers of early cars – what to a later generation would be known as the 'early adopters' – became unwitting guinea pigs along with the dealers who had to field their grievances.

'I often said that the customer was the test driver' Bob Burden contends,

> but this was only partly facetious. The major weaknesses, like the engine and drivetrain combination, were obvious from the design stage. The poor build quality and the cheap materials were there from Job One. Add to those the problems from the merger and

The TR7, we were told in this advertisement, was 'out to steal the American road' – a tag line also used in TV commercial voiceovers.

The TR7 was also the 'shape of things to come', although quite what H. G. Wells might have made of the TR7, nobody knows …

the problems of Speke. Throw in a somewhat battered and apprehensive US dealer body, and the result was inevitable … However, it was my impression that we were as prepared as we could be under the circumstances. There was a higher energy level and a stronger sense of commitment in the organization.

One of Burden's favourite Mike Dale quotes goes something like 'the British are always at their best with their backs against the wall – and they will go to extraordinary lengths to get to that position'. In Burden's view 'we were in that position'.

By this time the dollar–sterling exchange rate was particularly favourable to British exporters; in March 1976, the pound was worth just two dollars. Many voices in the United States began to complain that state-owned British Leyland was 'dumping' product on their territory, and

undoubtedly price was a major factor in deflecting valid criticisms over quality. Unquestionably, however, what little reputation for quality that British Leyland might have had was eroded in this period despite the level of sales.

Sales Headaches

As far as Mike Dale and his colleagues were concerned, the arrival of the TR7 was crazy business as usual:

The launch at the retail level was the usual BL chaos. The production ramp-up was far behind schedule, parts were at about 60 per cent of the target launch stock, quality problems were reported from dealers as the cars arrived at their dealerships, driver's handbooks were missing and there was an abysmal lack of technical info on fixing the quality problems.

While this pissed off the marketing group in the US, it was pretty normal and we had learned to so thoroughly distrust any information coming from the UK that we had adapted a management style that was highly attuned to crisis. The first budget put together for BL called for production of over 120,000 cars for the US and we really felt the market was there for us to sell them. The UK sent just over 65,000 and about 50 per cent of budget was normal for any of the years in the '70s.

A Distributor once demanded of me that we should send a bulletin out to the Distributors whenever there was a strike. I told him the bulletin would be useless because we couldn't keep up with the rapidity of the labour strife in the UK and he should assume that one, at least, of our five factories supplying the US market was on strike all the time. This, unfortunately, was the literal truth.

The team in the US were essentially Anglophiles and we kept hoping that with each iteration of the UK auto industry we would finally get a handle on how to build automobiles. The TR7 was to prove that our hopes were in vain. An enormous disappointment because, speaking for myself, there were many people in the UK management who I really liked and respected. From Spen King to John Bacchus they deserved to be more successful but were trapped in circumstances over which they had little real control.

The cars started to dribble into the dealers and, while we cut back on the advertising in order to keep our powder dry for when the cars started to flow in larger numbers, it was successful in driving a flood of floor traffic into the showroom. After a couple of weeks of encouraging customer interest we were looking forward to the sales figures at the end of the month but they were an enormous disappointment. In fact, they were shockingly low compared with the number of salesmen's 'ups' and the dealers were not slow in telling us why. Everything from the way the car looked, the performance and the price had rapidly turned people off. The customers simply didn't see what the name Triumph or the advertising had promised and when they were told the price they walked away.

There were a number of issues that rapidly fed back through the dealer chain, according to Dale:

the interior was a remarkable morass of ill-fitting black plastic that masquerades as the facia. Carpets wouldn't stay clipped and the door locks were jamming. Headlights winked at you by only raising one at a time and you didn't get to choose which one. Rattles and squeaks abounded. One dealer used to spray the facia with WD40 to keep the squeaks under control!

Despite the woes, sales of the TR7 were reasonable if unexceptional during the first half of 1976, earning British Leyland useful dollars at a time when home-market sales had slumped. In July the company reported that sales of the three Triumph sports cars on sale in the USA – the Spitfire, TR6 and TR7 – were the best on record, up 25 per cent on the first half of 1975.

As the initial sales euphoria evaporated, and TR7 sales slumped alarmingly, there were a number of consequences. According to Mike Dale, not all of these appeared wholly rational:

In spite of the obvious rejection of the TR7 in the marketplace the UK insisted on raising the price again, pressured as they were by their complete loss of control on costs. This had an obvious effect on the sales rate and on dealer morale. They now knew they weren't dealing with a realistic future.

On 1 December 1976 British Leyland Motors Inc. slashed the TR7 list price by $654 to $4,995 – at the same time as some other importers were raising prices. The $654 price cut included contributions from the manufacturer ($277), distributor ($110) and the dealer ($26).

Joe Herson, a dealer based in Rockville, Maryland, and Chairman of the Leyland National Dealers' Council, thought the TR7 story was symptomatic of what he had come to expect of British Leyland:

Retail sales of the TR7 were never impressive in my memory. And from a quality point of view, early production of British cars has always been very dependable. It's dependably bad; it's going to make trouble between you and your customers. Stuff will go wrong, you won't get any engineering assistance from the maker, you won't get any replacement parts – or if you do, they will still be the bad stuff and it will break or fall off again. And the retail customer will be convinced that the dealer is incompetent, doesn't care and is a crook. With the TR7, this was all multiplied by at least five.

In the quest to establish the root cause of poor sales, enquiries took place on several fronts, including hard questions about the way the car was being sold. According to Mike Dale:

> There was a faction in the UK that believed the TR7's failure was really poor marketing and what was needed was a change in management. David Andrews, then head of BLI, and Sir Ian MacGregor, a BL Board member, were dispatched to Leonia to examine the situation and the strong rumour out of the UK was that they would then decide the fate of the US management. Graham Whitehead and I were the two the investigation was aimed at.
>
> This, frankly, didn't bother me much because I had great respect for David Andrews and his rational approach to business. He was (and I'm sure still is!) an excellent man from every point of view and I felt that if he came to the conclusion we hadn't done our job he was probably right. I certainly knew we would get justice. Sir Ian, we were to find out, was a fitting partner for David.
>
> A list of questions was prepared for David and a friend in BLI secretly got a copy for me so we could be properly prepared. I often wonder whether David knew this and never said anything. It would have been just like him to know and not let on to anyone. He was shrewd and a fine analyst of a situation.
>
> The meeting in Leonia took several hours while we took them through the whole TR7 programme. With our tongue in cheek we finished the presentation with a black and white photograph of the UK TR7 buck on which we had based our forecast and then flipped onto the screen alongside it an identical photo of a TR7 taken in Leonia. The buck was so far from being the vehicle we actually had to sell that the comparison was ludicrous. The contrast between the two vehicles was so startling that the whole meeting burst out in laughter.

> I asked David whether he had any more questions and he smiled, shook his head and folded up the list of questions in front of him. Sir Ian then said to David how it amazed him as he went around BL how many clumps of really competent management existed within the chaos of the company. It was kind of him to say so and made the team feel appreciated. As I have said earlier, I think he was right. Many good people striving in a system which was totally out of control.

In late 1977 Jeff Herbert became the latest in a succession of UK management that the Leonia team saw crossing their threshold from time to time. He readily concedes that the JRT team did a remarkable job despite the odds stacked against them:

> I went to the USA on many occasions. You might ask what influence JRT Inc. had. They did have an influence in that their views were often very different to those in the UK. I used to see Mike Dale and Bruce McWilliams. I remember we were looking at SD1 and we asked them to put together an interior for the SD1 that they thought would have been successful in the US market. The inside of the end result looked to me like a bordello – it was red velour from roof to carpet – but they assured me that that was what the US market wanted – but at the same time I knew that back in Solihull, Rover would never have done it.

JRT tried to impress upon the parent company the quality of the opposition. Herbert recalls driving a Mazda RX-7 and Toyota Corolla during one of his visits:

> They were taking the US market by storm, and JRT were asking me to look at these cars as they were regarded as key opposition. I went there [to Leonia] on many occasions and I think that we failed to listen to them adequately – and that had dated from before I had joined and persisted even after I left.
>
> I think that they did a tremendous job with poorly developed product that was not properly designed with the USA in mind. Nevertheless they shifted that product.

Dealer-Fitted Accessories and 'Special Editions'

In the wake of the TR7 launch, and the disappointing tailing off of sales in the USA, the Leonia team worked hard to find ways to make the proverbial silk purse out of a sow's ear. During this time there were a handful of locally sponsored 'Limited Editions', one being the 'Southern Skies', which included a locally sourced sliding fabric sunshine roof coupled with some decal stripes and badging. Mike Dale led the process at Leonia:

> For the next few months we tried every marketing ploy in the book while Bruce toiled away at trying to give us locally produced kit to improve the way the car looked. Pressure was brought on the UK to make it in convertible form as quickly as possible and the idea of putting the five-speed box in with the strengthened rear axle was put on the table. We argued that putting the five-speed box in would allow a lower first gear and at least get over the initial sluggishness off the mark. It would also cure some of the quality problems with the overall transmission. Wheels were a big issue because the standard ones looked so puny in the enormous rear wheel wells. Bruce found what looked to be a good solution. Spoker wheels were in fashion and we could change the look plus try to fill in the wheel arches to make it look a little more like a sports car.

Mike Cook was not convinced that those 'spoker' wheels really looked the part: 'I thought they were like Conestoga wagon wheels', he says, referring to the chunky wooden wheels used on the wagons of America's pioneers in the nineteenth century. However, good idea or bad, fate would eventually intervene. Dale recalls that the production rate of the wheels – first seen on the TR7 'Victory' Limited Edition, announced as a celebration of the TR7's early motor sports prowess (*see* Chapter 6) - was slow, 'and we had quality problems with them from the start. Welds broke and they went rusty really quickly. The company finally went bankrupt.' Back in Coventry, Mick Bunker also remembers those wheels: 'They sent some samples back to us to seek our approval and we ran the standard fatigue test – and found they were fine. The production wheels, however, had disastrous fatigue levels; when we got them to the laboratory, we found they were of an inferior material.' The wheels were eventually the subject of one of many official TR7 recall campaigns.

To celebrate successes in SCCA racing, Bruce McWilliams helped concoct the TR7 'Victory Edition', which was heavily promoted and sold reasonably well. The wheels proved disastrous, prompting an official recall.

Things to Come for the Rest of the World

For British sports car fans, during 1975 and much of 1976, the only time they would see the TR7 was by reading about it in specialist magazines, in the occasional television report or through seeing the serried ranks of cars waiting for export at the docks. Production problems meant that the launch date outside the United States kept slipping. On 19 May 1976, however, their wait was finally over, for that was when the European specification TR7 was introduced.

Illustrating the frustration these delays caused, Leonard Setright, the epicurean wordsmith, began his much-delayed first report on the TR7 for the June 1976 issue of *CAR* magazine (in an article unpromisingly titled 'Lousy Icing, Lovely Cake') as follows:

> My first drive of the TR7 was to have been a big one, an epic journey across Europe, timed to coincide with the opening of the Paris show last year [September 1975] when the car was due to be introduced to the European market. The trip was postponed: since its original release to the USA market in January 1975, the TR7 had done so well that Leyland were inclined to keep feeding it to the Americans for a little while longer, so the European launch was postponed to the 1976 Geneva Show [March 1976].

Setright thought that the delay would give him more time to plan his trip:

> I was quite happy until there came the news that the European launch of the car had been delayed again, and that the trip could therefore not be timed to coincide with the Geneva Show either. Now, after the Americans have kept me waiting while they bought £24 million worth of the new Triumphs, the car is coming onto our market at a time that does not seem to coincide with anything, and I have been suffered to celebrate the fact in a 180-mile half-day jaunt around southern England.

One could almost hear the acid sizzling on the page.

Although at a cursory inspection the European version of the TR7 looked little different from the Federal one, closer study showed that a number of welcome changes had been made. Most noticeable was the use of substantial three-piece bumper units, without the heavy reinforcement demanded by US legislators. This meant that both front and rear bumpers were not only much less heavy, but they also projected less; the rear bumpers of the European cars also did without the curious large 'overriders' that projected from the rear bumper of the Federal specification TR7. In place of the side marker lights of the US cars, British Leyland fitted rather cheap-looking black plastic trim pieces. Removal of the strangulations of Federal emission equipment released 15bhp, up to 105bhp from 90bhp. In most other respects, however, the first European

As well as the home market, the spring of 1976 saw a push into the European market, as exemplified by this French magazine advertisement. 'Bon Sang – ne saurait mentir' roughly translated means 'pure-bloods [thoroughbreds] cannot lie'.

John Olliver worked at the Henlys British Leyland dealership at Ashford, Kent, between 1975 and 1981 and sold many TR7s, such as this one seen at the showroom. 'The TR7 was okay but not a brilliant seller, the MG and the Spitfire were more popular' he says. 'Occasionally, if we had a TR7 which was sticking (unsold) I'd get a special paint job done which used to do the trick. I remember the guy's wife who bought the one dressed up in Red White & Blue asking me not to do another!' (John Olliver)

market TR7 looked fairly similar to the early US market cars.

The summer of 1976 was a busy time for British Leyland, for in addition to unleashing the European TR7, the company unveiled its exciting Rover 'SD1' saloon. Sharing the heady optimism in those early post-Ryder days, British Leyland Chairman Sir Richard Dobson told *The Times* in May that his dream 'would be to see Leyland so profitable that its shares could again be distributed, perhaps under a different government, perhaps under a similar one, to the general public as a worthwhile investment'. Meanwhile, however, to make life easier for the coupé TR7, the MGB GT was withdrawn from left-hand drive European markets in June 1976, and the MG MGB GT V8 was killed off in anticipation of the 'TR7 V8', leading to cries of foul from MG fans.

The UK embargo date for the Euro-spec TR7 was 19 May 1976 but, as *Motorsport* commented in its June issue, the fact that the TR7 had already made its rally debut made something of a nonsense of this reporting restriction. The magazine had hoped to have a full road test for its readers but had been told by Leyland Cars that there was 'insufficient stock' to accommodate a proper UK magazine road-test schedule: 'we had to be content with a 200-mile run into Wiltshire in company with 19 other TR7s and 38 more journalists'.

Motorsport headed its report 'Triumph TR7 – sports car or two-seater saloon?', providing a comprehensive but ultimately lukewarm view of

the new Triumph, comparing it to the RS2000 Escort, which the writer thought was a natural rival for the tin-top Triumph. 'All in all we were left a bit cold by this new two-seater. It felt characterless, largely because the road holding and handling were too good for the performance. Hence boredom. In most respects, it felt like a good saloon car.' The *coup de grâce* was the conclusion that the TR7 'might prove a good ladies' car, but until more powerful versions are available, the true enthusiast might look elsewhere'.

Motor subjected a UK-specification TR7 to a full road test for its issue of 11 September 1976. The precis at the start of the test report began 'Startling styling heralds the "new era" among

---

What Did Giugiaro Say?

According to a popular, but apocryphal, story, the designer Giorgetto Giugiaro came upon the TR7 at one of the major motor shows and looked at it quizzically. He then moved round to the opposite side and exclaimed with mock horror, 'My God! They've done it to the other side as well!'

This is one of those stories that seems to have become part of popular folklore, but Giugiaro, who was then at a personal high (his VW Scirocco and Golf designs had just gone on sale to widespread acclaim), seems to have forgotten the incident. I did check, but Barbara Gemetto of his office told me that 'Mr Giugiaro … unfortunately doesn't remember what he said when he saw the car for the first time!'

Famous footballer Kevin Keegan was given a TR7, the most stylish sports car for an up-and-coming 1970s sports hero. He is seen here at Canley; BL's Mike Akers is at the left and Canley plant manager Fred Young is at the far right, while Keegan is second from left. Keegan signed the photo, which is now in the possession of Fred Young's son Cliff. (Cliff Young)

Leyland's sporting cars: the TR7 is like no TR before.' *Motor* found quite a few things to like about the TR7 – in particular its spacious and well-appointed interior – but it did not warm to its 'lack of refinement, unpleasant gearbox and poor visibility'. The magazine achieved a top speed of 111.2mph (179km/h), which it applauded, but the other performance figures were rated as unexceptional, in part a consequence of the four-speed gearbox, which was described as 'one of the least pleasant aspects of the TR7'.

The magazine's complaints were not just about change quality but also about what it thought was a strange choice of ratios and a tendency for the transmission to whine. 'Most of the faults can (and should) be overcome with a little more development', *Motor* suggested, and the magazine awarded a coveted five stars to the TR7 interior. Summing up, *Motor* concluded that, along with the Princess and Rover 3500, the TR7 represented 'the spearhead of the future of Leyland, and a bright future at that'. The TR7 also, the magazine suggested, 'really makes the MGB GT look thoroughly old-fashioned'.

The 1977 Model Year

In the autumn of 1976 – in time for the US 1977 'Model Year' - the TR7 finally got a decent

gearbox: the new LT-77 five-speed unit and stronger back axle were shared with the new Rover 3500, and the new improved drivetrain was therefore more than up to the task of dealing with the TR7's 2-litre engine. At first, the new unit was an option but before long became standard fitment for the Federal markets – this move meaning that a shortage of available units precipitated the temporary withdrawal of the five-speed gearbox from other markets.

An early clue to the problems comes from the minutes of the Rover Triumph Advisory Board in April 1975, when UK sales were anticipated in October, but in the event it was a whole year before the UK version of the TR7 went on sale. At the meeting,

> doubts were expressed concerning the 5-speed gear-box being ready for the UK launch in October. Mr Carpenter stated that unless adequate supplies of

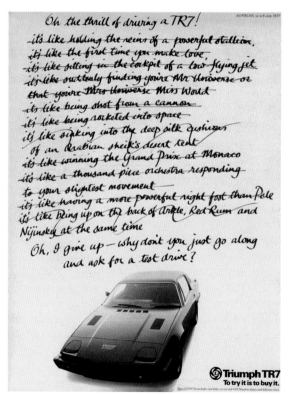

'To try it is to buy it' is the message in this advertisement from the summer of 1977.

vehicles fitted with the 5-speed gearboxes could be guaranteed, he would prefer to do without at the initial launch. Mr Carver said that a month's supply should be ready by October.

As so often was the case, promises were made upon which others failed to deliver.

Road & Track tried a TR7 with the new gearbox for its June 1977 issue and was clearly in favour of the change. 'The original TR7 4-speed gearbox has been discontinued as of the 1977 models and we don't lament its passing because the 5-speed is vastly superior,' the magazine said, adding that the new unit 'mates so well with the engine's characteristics, giving the 5-speed snappy driveability that was lacking with the 4-speed'.

A number of other improvements were introduced at the same time as the gearbox changes. The rear suspension was lowered by an inch (25mm) as a response to criticism about the tail-

Gearbox and Final Drive Ratios

	Old Gearbox	New Gearbox
1st	2.65	3.32
2nd	1.78	2.08
3rd	1.25	1.39
4th	1.00	1.00
5th	—	0.83
Final Drive	3.63:1	3.90:1

Contemporary automatic transmissions

Final Drive – auto	3.27:1	3.08:1

high attitude of early cars, and tyre sizes were widened from 175/70 HR13 to 185/70 HR13. New silver full-diameter plastic wheel trims looked a little more like the genuine alloy wheels that the American marketing people really wanted. Meanwhile, California-market cars now gained an additional carburettor as an effort to better commonize all US-bound cars (cars for all fifty states now featuring catalytic converters), although needle and distributor differences still marked out cars destined for the Golden State. Inside the cockpit, bright red or green tartan plaid seat facings replaced the sombre nylon cord, the new material being described by *Motor Trend* as 'like hotels use to cover their furniture'.

Despite the comment about the seat trim, *Motor Trend* liked the new improved TR7, describing the $5,849 base-price TR7 in its road test of December 1977 as 'the best thing under five figures to come out of England for years', a slogan that British Leyland proudly picked up for a rash of advertising. Unfortunately, around the same time that *Motor Trend* was appearing on US news-stands, there were storm clouds brewing across the Atlantic.

Michael Edwardes and the Strike at Speke

The coming of Michael Edwardes as chairman in November 1977 caused little stir in a nation

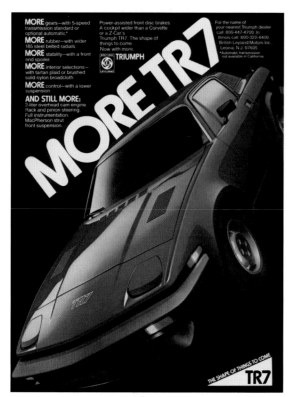

US advertising made much of the improvements to the 1977 TR7 – still built at Speke.

The 1977 TR7 prototype at Canley, with the new silver polycarbonate full-diameter wheel trims, which looked a bit more like the alloy wheels the car arguably deserved. (Norman Rose)

The bold tartan seats introduced for 1977. (Alisdair Cusick)

by now used to the ongoing soap opera that was British Leyland. The effect of his arrival, however, would soon be felt throughout the company, for Edwardes's no-nonsense business focus allowed him to scythe his way through to the furthest reaches of the corporation. A slightly ominous greeting from the TR7 was the news, broadcast exactly a week before Edwardes arrived, that there would be a major recall of 5,000 of the Speke-built cars sold in the USA during 1975 and 1976 in order to replace defective accelerator cables.

Under Edwardes's leadership, no stone was to be left unturned when it came to commercial decisions, and the substantial overcapacity at the Speke assembly plant – endemic in most of the company – made it a prime candidate for closure. However, as we saw earlier, Speke was also a breeding ground for determined militants who had never been tackled by management and had allowed the assembly plant to become a hotbed of dissent. The four-month strike that began on 1 November, the same day that Sir Michael Edwardes took charge of the company, only served to help seal the factory's fate.

As the Speke strike entered its fifth week, *The Times* carried a news item on Tuesday 6 December 1977 headed 'Triumph output worth £33m lost in manning and work levels dispute', which reported that already production of 10,000 cars

During 1977 there were early thoughts about a future facelift for the TR7, exemplified by this 'TR9' sketch by Rover Triumph designer John Ashford. (John Ashford)

with a showroom value of £3,000 apiece had been lost.

It did not take long for clues to Speke's fate to leak out to the press; the *Sunday Times* of 8 January 1978 reported: 'Speke's TR7 is regarded inside Leyland as a disaster. How the company came to launch a hardtop model aimed at North America, where drivers want an open sports car, remains a mystery.' Less than a week later, *The Economist* was hinting that 'Mr Edwardes may have had the nod from Mr Callaghan to play it tough. The government is known to want a solution to the Leyland problem wrapped up by early spring.'

By 13 February 1978 production losses at Speke were being put at £100 million and the British Leyland Director of Personnel and Administration, Pat Lowry, commented to *The Times* that 'with the TR7 having been out of production for so long, selling it in a competitive market would mean virtually starting from the beginning – with the added disadvantage of the model's history'. Several commentators were suggesting, by this stage, that the TR7 was doomed.

When the announcement came two days later, on 15 February, that Speke was to close as part of a plan to cut back overall manning levels across British Leyland by 12,000 personnel, many in Liverpool refused to believe it – including the local managers. But, as Edwardes records in his book *Back from the Brink,*

the decision to close the Speke Number Two assembly factory was the first test of the new Board's resolve, for there was no enthusiasm for closing it among the veterans of the management team. On any commercial consideration the Speke plant had to be a prime candidate for closure … yet the decision was bitterly

John Ashford's sketches were, in common with those of some of his colleagues, translated into scale models. The result was rather neat if less bold than the original. (John Ashford)

Life at Speke: Home of the Militants

The Speke factory had earned a reputation for militancy, but was this justified? An insider's view comes from Ken Hazelhurst, who feels that a combination of weak management and infiltration by outside elements contributed to much of Speke's problems. He concedes that:

> Speke was certainly perceived by the public as a hotbed of trouble. Together with a large proportion of the workforce just wanting to hold onto a steady reasonable job – of which I include myself – there was a large number of politically motivated people, many operating under the guise of Trade Unionists, who were hell-bent on causing trouble at the slightest opportunity. The general public were never aware of the strife which existed within the two factories. The Workers Revolutionary Party were almost always present at car park factory meetings, distributing rabble-rousing literature and in some cases taking part in 'show of hands' voting.

Hazelhurst claims that these were seldom people employed by the company. Another faction that helped foment disputes was the International Socialists:

> A colleague with whom I worked was a shop steward for our section and he would often attend meetings or discussion group get-togethers of any shop steward or interested parties, held at a pub close to the plant. These meetings did not involve any members of management, but were solely for the workforce stewards and their associates. My colleague attended most of these meetings before beginning his night shift rota and would then make his way into the plant, which was a mere couple of hundred yards away. Many times he would arrive in work quite badly marked about the head and face. Having dared to question some of the issues discussed, he had been quite badly beaten for his efforts. For his part he never once, to my knowledge, shirked from attending these meetings.

In Hazelhurst's opinion, the most amazing aspect of the Speke factory and the way it operated was simply how it operated at all:

> When I started work for Standard Triumph in 1969, I had previously been employed by Ford Motor Company at its Halewood Factory [now Jaguar]. The difference in the two cultures was to say the least extreme. Apparently, this soon became common knowledge in the locale and as Triumph began recruiting for labour, many applications were received from Ford employees seeking a somewhat easier work experience!

Hazelhurst recalls a time he was leaving the plant on his way home one Sunday:

> As there was only one entrance and exit at the factory, when it rained most people who worked at the end furthest from the main gate would walk through the paint shop in order to keep dry. As I passed by a clocking station I noticed that one person had clocked two cards. This was also seen by a supervisor who had been walking behind me. The supervisor told the offender to destroy the card and nothing further would be said, whereupon a shop steward piped up, 'Do that and not one car will be produced here tomorrow'. The absent person whose card was being clocked would have been paid 16 hours pay as the rate for Sunday was double time, while not even being on the premises that day. On another occasion an operator was caught smoking inside a spray booth while leaning over a 45-gallon drum of cellulose thinners. The paint shop staff immediately walked out on strike when the offender was sacked. The management then rescinded the sacking to a suspension. Following this the supervisor who had caught the man smoking was threatened that his car would be 'seen to' in the company car park. From that day on until the factory closure, the supervisor was allowed to park in the senior management car park, which was in a much safer position well inside the complex.

A photograph mocked-up with some prototype alloy wheel designs. (John Ashford).

opposed inside and outside the company, not necessarily because it was felt to be wrong. Many managers were simply convinced that the closure could not be delivered, that the Labour government or the unions would make it impossible to implement.

Ray Horrocks, Chairman of BL Cars from August 1979, confirmed Edwardes's claim: 'On one occasion, I spoke to the guy running Speke – woefully over-facilitized – and I told him that we were going to shut it. He said 'How do I know you're telling the truth? I've been told that before – and I made a mistake the first time of telling the workforce.'

The next day, 16 February, *The Times* said that 'Leyland has actually been saving itself money by not making the TR7', a view that Alan Edis confirms was, at times, perfectly true. That same evening, Prime Minister Callaghan faced a barrage of questions at a meeting of the Parliamentary Labour Party, including allegations that the government had authorized the closure. Callaghan denied the accusation, and explained that Michael Edwardes had been appointed to 'be in charge of Leyland' and that he 'deserves our backing'.

With the closure of Speke No. 2, which finally shut its doors on 26 May 1978, came the consequent need to move the TR7. Although the logic had been questioned internally, it was also tested by some highly placed people, as Edwardes recalled in his book:

Before the public announcement of the Speke closure we advised the Department of Industry through the NEB. Subsequently the Prime Minister, James Callaghan, asked to see me together with the Industry Secretary, Eric Varley, and Sir Leslie Murphy, representing the NEB [National Enterprise Board]. We did not require the government's approval for the closure, but we felt we should fully explain the logic of the decision, particularly as this was the first major car factory closure in Britain for many years. For half an hour I was closely questioned by the Prime Minister, who was extremely well briefed on Speke. Then he asked a question which made it clear to me that our

Sir Michael Edwardes

Getting Away With Murder: More Tales of Speke

It is difficult to imagine the remarkable goings-on at Speke in a modern context, but the stories are legion. Take, for example, the story of the meat safe. Peter Wilson, who was responsible for engineering liaison between Speke and Canley, takes up the tale:

The windscreen on the TR7 was bonded to the steel body – one of the first in the UK – adding to the structural strength of the bodyshell. The bonding used a special Bostik 'sausage' of adhesive known as Solbit [*see* Chapter 3], which was a long cylindrical extrusion with a copper wire in the centre of the adhesive. The glass and the frame were both primed with a special primer, the 'sausage' was put in the screen aperture, the screen was pushed into place and a 12-volt electrical current was applied through the copper wire for about 20 minutes to heat up and cure the adhesive. Each car had a set of leads which came down from an overhead 'bus-bar' that moved along as the car progressed along the track. Unfortunately the Speke workforce weren't always that good at sticking to processes – and so on a bad one, if you braked too hard, the screen might come out!

Now the Solbit needed special handling, and had to be stored at a low temperature. The twin tracks were elevated about eight or nine feet off the ground and underneath was a storage area for parts to be brought out and up to the line using a forklift truck. The plan was for refrigerated trucks to deliver the Solbit adhesive to a six-foot long by five-foot wide meat fridge, which was large enough to have storage shelves inside. Bostik's lorries would arrive and decant their load into the meat fridge. On the first day, Bostik duly arrived and delivered the adhesive. At the time, I'd be up at Speke from Monday until Thursday, coming back on the Friday. The next morning after the load of adhesive had arrived, I was walking along the production line and there was something of a ruckus going on. The fridge had gone completely and there was the adhesive all stacked on the floor! How this massive fridge got out without being noticed, goodness knows; it must have been an inside job! That fridge was never found – we had to get a new one!

Then there was the saga of the missing batch of TR7 coupés discovered mouldering in a car park two years after they had been built: 'We used to store cars at Speke airport. In 1978 we found about thirty cars – which had supposedly been shipped to North America two years before – lying on their bellies, minus wheels, all covered in two years' worth of grime!'

There was also the fracas over the colour of screwdriver handles:

We used both Pozidrive and Phillips screws at Speke, and so we used specially colour-cordinated screwdrivers, which had blue handles for the Pozidrive and red ones for the Phillips. One day there was an altercation with a foreman, who said that he wasn't going to use a screwdriver with a blue handle when his colleague down the line had one with a red handle; he said he was a Liverpool supporter (and so wanted red) rather than an Everton supporter (blue)!

Wilson adds that it was 'common knowledge' at BL that Speke:

was the best factory in the company for pilfering; they'd learned the art on the docks! We were introducing a facelift at Speke in 1977 and it involved fitting radios as standard. We used to have 'worker participation' meetings – the shop steward or plant convenor sat in on that. When we said we would be fitting radios, the shop steward's eyes lit up like torches. He soon knew all about the special security arrangements that we were going to introduce – and of course, large numbers of radios were soon disappearing out of the factory!

Perhaps the craziest story of them all comes from Ken Hazelhurst, working at Speke:

To illustrate the relaxed nature of our working environment, the following tale was typical of what went on. To be fair to the people who actually produced the cars, those of us employed in the Engineering department and other support activities did have much more freedom than the average guy on the production line. At one point in my career with BL, I worked in the maintenance workshop, which was sited remotely from all the car production facilities – quite a large building, but split into sections to facilitate numerous tasks. Two workmates, one of whom was a complete nutcase, were always cooking up some crazy scheme or experiment. Steve, the madder of the two, spent many months manufacturing boomerangs made from plywood, all obtained from the joinery shop housed in the building, with some degree of success it must be said.

Another madcap scheme involved building a canoe, with the intention of sailing it on a pond at the rear of the building. Now this pond was full of all varieties of wildlife, mainly insects such as dragonflies, their size being so large I have still not seen any to equal them. Families of Mallard ducks, rabbits, hares and skylarks all lived at our own 'Safari Park'. One day Steve decides he is going to build a canoe in order to get closer to nature. This he eventually did while situated only a stone's throw from the management offices. This vessel was, as I recall, approximately ten feet long and over three feet wide. All the plywood was 'borrowed' from the joinery section, although they didn't know it at the time. The canoe did work and would support two men. Following this success, Steve then obtained two air-conditioning fans from a Stag, together with the necessary power supply, namely a car battery to drive them. This set-up was also successful. The empty bay where the construction of the canoe was carried out was eventually used to house a number of prototype Lynx body shells and spot-welding equipment destined for manufacturing that model, which as we now know would never materialize.

case was won. It turned out to be a prophetic doubt: 'You have said that your new Board will always act in a business-like way and will not make decisions that are not commercially sound. Surely on that basis the TR7 sports car should be scrapped and not transferred elsewhere.'

Edwardes went on to remark, 'Now he may have said this with tongue in cheek, but as things turned out, he was absolutely right'. Nevertheless, the TR7 final assembly was moved to Canley, and body assembly to Swindon, although some press work remained at the Speke No. 1 factory – for the time being at least. Edwardes saw the outcome as a turning-point in British Leyland's fortunes:

In the event the predictions of doom and gloom and all-out warfare over Speke proved groundless. The workforce voted to accept the closure terms and managers who had warned the Board that plant and equipment would not be allowed through picketing mobs, watched the equipment being loaded and transferred peacefully and quickly to Canley and elsewhere. The Speke closure was a test of the new Board's determination to carry through difficult and painful actions, and from that point onwards it dawned on employees and public that there was a positive determination to get the business into shape.

Meanwhile, Pat Lowry reiterated his statement to *The Times* by telling the workforce:

By reason of the model's severe lack of profitability and the amount of money which would have to be spent in re-establishing the model in the US market,

it would be a prudent commercial decision to discontinue the TR7 completely. Instead however we propose to reduce the fixed cost base by transferring assembly from Liverpool to Canley.

The Speke No. 2 closure resulted in 3,000 redundancies and, as the *Liverpool Echo* reported, 'Production of the controversial wedge-shaped sports car – designed to conquer the American market – will continue at Coventry but for the Liverpool car men the dole queue looms, with only a limp Leyland golden handshake to soften the blow.' As well as the loss of livelihood for the Liverpool workforce, the closure also led to the cancellation of two projects, the TR7 Sprint and the 'Lynx', that might have allowed better use of resources. (For the story of those two projects *see* Chapter 5; for the TR8, which had entered pilot build at Speke, *see* Chapter 8.)

In his book about the closure of Speke, commissioned by the Transport & General Workers Union and written in the immediate aftermath, Huw Beynon remarked: 'So the Speke No.2 plant is closed … meanwhile a new track is being laid at the Swindon works, body production of the TR7 is planned for the autumn and Leyland are recruiting labour. Just now, in Liverpool the clever money doesn't hold out much hope for the No.1 plant at Speke.'

Beynon's words were indeed prophetic: within two years Speke No.1 was also out of use, both factories were sold off and the people of Speke suffered a further blow when the big Dunlop factory in the town also closed its doors in 1979. It is very doubtful if the initial investment required for Leyland Speke was ever recouped. Norman

A clever UK marketing theme contrasted a bright red TR7 with a similar hue Ferrari.

Rose illustrates the problem of a remote chain of command and the problems of recruiting and training staff:

> One of our engineers from Canley, Aubrey Cole, would spend three days a week at the Speke plant. One day he was walking along the line when he saw a man applying adhesive sound-deadening pads to the toe-board. The man carefully placed the pads and then proceeded to hit them vigorously with a lead hammer. When questioned as to why he was doing this, the reply was 'the packet says "impact adhesive" – so I'm impacting it'.

The Move to Canley

With the decision to close Speke No. 2, but to continue with the TR7 and at least some of the planned derivatives, it was obviously necessary to

find a new home for the corporate sports car. Despite the tentative suggestion in 1971, the option of moving the TR7 to the MG factory at Abingdon does not seem to have been seriously considered this time: undoubtedly the substantial investment required, the controversy of usurping the MGB and the mismatched relationship between Austin Morris and Rover Triumph were felt collectively to outweigh the loyalty of the Abingdon workforce. The decision was therefore taken to move TR7 production to the established but ageing Triumph plant at Canley. The overall responsibility for this task was given to Jeff Herbert, recently appointed Managing Director of Rover Triumph.

The news was heralded with some celebration at Canley, for as recently as August 1976 there had been a plan to cease all car manufacture at Canley and turn the plant over to engine and transmission production, ending fifty years of Triumph car building in Coventry. Under the worker-consultation in place at the time, a by-product of the Ryder report, this plan had depended upon union cooperation – and the company got none. With memories of this threat still fresh in their minds, the men at Canley were even less sympathetic to the plight of their comrades at Speke than one might have expected.

The change to TR7 production, while reducing infrastructure, meant that there would be more carting around of components than before, one of the things that consolidation in one place had been originally intended to address. The projected production levels for the TR7 at Speke, however, had proved unrealistic. For a time Speke No. 1 continued a decreasing involvement, but the responsibility for body pressing and body assembly moved to a brand new production line in Swindon's 'B' Building, which until recently had also built the Triumph 2000/2500 'Innsbruck' range. The bodies were painted, trimmed and assembled at Canley. However, for Triumph enthusiasts there seemed cause for optimism as it appeared that the Triumph sports car, created in Coventry, was at last coming back home.

'I made the Canley Plant Manager [Fred Young] responsible as Project Manager for the

Leyland's Mini Dynamo: Michael Edwardes

British Leyland was dominated in its early years by the charismatic figure of Donald Stokes (*see* Chapter 1), but once the company came to the brink of destruction, and the Stokes era came to an end, there was something of a vacuum at the top of Britain's biggest indigenous car maker. In the wake of Lord Ryder's report, a well-intentioned but severely over-stretched management, largely drawn from within the company, did its best to wrestle with an organization that seemed to veer further and further away from reality. There were many reasons for this, going far beyond what is relevant to the TR7 story, but a key underlying theme was a dichotomy between the workforce and the management, underscored by the continuing rise in militant unionism. With a left-leaning, union-friendly government in power, and the world economies in turmoil due to the oil crisis of 1974, the task of any management board was arguably a tough one: for those at the head of a nationalized company it was almost impossible. Things had looked promising in the spring of 1976, when a new Managing Director, Sir Richard Dobson, arrived from British American Tobacco to take over, but the clandestine tape-recording of some racist remarks he made at a private function put paid to him in October 1977.

By late 1977 the combination of further strikes and the realization that Ryder's plans were unaffordable had already led the National Enterprise Board (NEB) to believe a new direction was needed for Leyland. They found what they were looking for in the form of Michael Edwardes, the forty-seven-year-old South African head of Chloride, who was already a member of the NEB and had quadrupled profits during his tenure at the battery maker. It did not take long after his arrival for Edwardes's no-nonsense style to become apparent: he was not a man to suffer fools or to tolerate plan-wreckers. Before his first month was out there had been the first of many changes in British Leyland's structure, which rapidly cascaded from the board of management (slashed from thirteen to seven directors inside a fortnight) down through the ranks of middle managers. Edwardes set out to recapture the ability of managers to manage and hunker down for an unprecedented change of policy towards the more militant union elements. The strike at Speke was one of the first such trials of strength and the outcome set the scene for what would follow.

Unsurprisingly, views on Edwardes's tenure at British Leyland are mixed, for while he regained management control over the company, he also presided over major dismemberment. The latter process could be seen as overdue, a task that had been deferred again and again by previous managements, but the fact that what had been the world's fourth largest car maker eventually contracted to almost nothing was not – in simplistic terms - the happiest of long-term legacies. While Edwardes was in charge, however, British Leyland and all who worked there certainly experienced an exhilarating ride.

Jeff Herbert (in dark suit and striped tie, to the left of the car) greets the first TR7 off the line at Canley. (Jeff Herbert)

Jeff Herbert: Rover Triumph's Last Director

Jeff Herbert was born in Newport, Shropshire, in July 1942 and studied production engineering at Loughborough University. At Perkins, a common 'breeding ground' for rising talent that would later see service in BL, he had risen to the post of Director of Manufacturing by his early thirties. He eventually joined British Leyland in September 1977, at the tail end of the so-called 'Ryder era' and just two months before Michael Edwardes took charge. He explains that he was recruited initially, within the context of the Ryder plan, as 'Director of Product and Plant Engineering': 'Under the Ryder plan, the government was proposing to spend an absolute fortune. My job, in essence, was to buy the kit to make the cars and to organize the production aspects'.

Not long after Michael Edwardes arrived in November 1977, major changes began to sweep through the company and before long the thirty-five-year-old Herbert, like many other young managers, found himself in a new role: Managing Director of Rover Triumph within Jaguar Rover Triumph (JRT). As we shall see later, the problems of the Speke factory were an early challenge that both Edwardes and Herbert would tackle, but the Liverpool operation was only part of Herbert's responsibilities:

Canley was a very old plant and little money had been put into it over the years; Solihull was the mainstay for Rover Triumph. Strangely enough I also had Powertrain responsibilities for Land Rover. Mike Hodgkinson ran Land Rover, Bob Knight ran Jaguar and I ran Rover Triumph. My [extra Powertrain] role was to be responsible for the running gear of Land Rover, and Mike's was to build the Land Rovers. I guess part of the reason was geography: there were three or four old Rover plants like Acocks Green shared between Land Rover, Jaguar and Rover Triumph – so the decision had been taken to keep them all together under my control.

Life inside British Leyland was certainly arduous for anyone tasked with reasserting managerial authority. Looking back from a period of relative industrial calm, it is easy to forget how fraught factories were in the 1970s. Herbert, in common with other senior management, found that developing the product was but a small part of their day-to-day activities: 'Literally 75–80 per cent of my time was spent on employee relations. You weren't spending time on making a better product, sales and marketing, quality and so on – you were spending time just trying to keep the people working. The Motor Industry today is so different – as is the whole employment relations situation'. Contemporary studies have shown, for example, that a similar manager in the German car industry would typically have spent barely 5 per cent of his time on employee relations, and the remainder on making a better product. The contrast is striking.

Rover Triumph as an entity would eventually cease to exist (for reasons covered later) and, with his area of responsibility seriously eroded, Herbert would move on to pastures new: 'I essentially left BL when Rover Triumph became no more as it got sucked into "Volume Cars" along with Austin Morris.' Herbert's resignation was announced at the beginning of August 1980. For the time being Harold Musgrove assumed the role of chairman of both Austin Morris and Rover Triumph. Herbert moved on to join Arnold Weinstock at GEC: 'That was an interesting time too. Later, in 1982, Sir Michael Edwardes left too. Thereafter we worked together in some other companies – sometimes with Sir Michael as Chairman and me as Chief Executive.' Now semi-retired, Herbert is able to look back on a successful high-flying career – with the part of it spent at British Leyland like an apprenticeship at the school of hard knocks.

move, and we did it to time and to budget', Jeff Herbert recalls. Production started in October 1978, coincidentally the same month that the first clandestine meeting took place between British Leyland and Honda officials. There was little doubt that bringing the TR7 to Canley helped ease the path of various quality and manufacturing changes that meant that a 'Canley' car would become known for its superior build quality. According to Herbert, these changes manifested themselves reasonably quickly: 'In the

eighteen months that followed many things got a lot better – silly little things that had been problematical, like the paint staying on the headlamp pods!'

In fact there were other problems with those distinctive headlamp pods apart from the matter of paint staying on them; Speke-built cars featured electric motors that were inadequately resistant to water and it was hardly an uncommon sight to see a TR7 with one headlamp erect and one hidden, giving the curious impression that the car was winking at onlookers. The move to Canley provided an opportunity for some re-engineering of this and other problems, but that did not stop the need for a recall at the end of January 1980 for all 18,400 Speke-built TR7s sold in the UK up to that time for 'attention to the headlamp lifting mechanism'. Similar recalls took place in the US market.

Many detail improvements were introduced to coincide with the switch to Canley – around 200 changes were made, according to Jeff Herbert – including improvement to the sealing of the headlamp motors (to deter the ingress of damp and dirt), improved seat upholstery and the application of more comprehensive anti-chip paint coatings on the sills and in the wheelarches. The most obvious visible change, however, was the deletion of the 'TR7' graphic decal from the nose in favour of a bulky circular laurel leaf decal with the 'Triumph' name in the centre. It was undoubtedly a good idea to differentiate the 'new' cars from the old, but to some this one change was seen as a detraction rather than an improvement.

It seems that the closure of Speke No. 2 did not immediately sever the TR7's connection with Merseyside entirely, for some pressing work still took place at Speke No. 1, although this declined with the transfer of most of the press-work to the former Pressed Steel Fisher plant at Swindon. As we have seen, bodies were built on a brand new dedicated TR7 line at Swindon and then shipped by road from Swindon to Canley, where they were painted, trimmed and assembled. Obviously this was less efficient in many ways than the former arrangement at Speke, but then 'efficiency' was always a relative term at British Leyland, which still had a surfeit of plants and production capacity.

From Speke to Swindon: Moving the Press Tools

David Nicholas of Pressed Steel at Swindon became involved in moving the TR7 from Speke. He recalls his amazement at the quality of the relatively new facilities at Speke: 'They had some lovely facilities – Terrazzo floors, stainless steel rest-rooms, light and airy – a beautiful place to build cars.' This was quite a contrast to many other car assembly factories in Britain at the time, although Nicholas adds, however, that the facilities were in a pretty dishevelled state when he saw them, 'covered in muck, and lanolin everywhere'.

Soon after the decision had been made to close Speke, Nicholas was summoned to see

TR7 Premium Limited Edition

In January 1980 BL announced that there would be a limited edition version of the TR7 coupé for home-market consumption. *Motor's* issue of 12 January 1980 carried the news that this would be limited to production of 400 cars, all finished externally in black with either a gold or a silver side stripe (based on the decal intended for the TR7 Sprint). 'Extra equipment' included as standard would include a sunroof, alloy wheels, halogen headlamps, a front spoiler and a push-button radio, while inside the trim would be to 1980 specification, with a choice of navy or tan vinyl trim and co-ordinated plaid fabric panels to the seats. The dashboard would be grey in place of the previous black, and we were told that the trim was the same as would be available in the forthcoming UK version of the TR7 convertible, due for launch in the spring. At a retail price of £6,100, this limited edition was subsequently marketed as the 'Premium', and a genuine TR7 Premium is undoubtedly quite a rare car nowadays. Effectively, the Premium was a 'warm-up act' for the changes that would be introduced to the whole TR7 range once the convertible version (described in Chapter 7) went on sale in the home market in the spring of 1980.

A pre-production TR7 Premium (with gold wheels) sits on the field behind the Canley site where the earlier 'Bullet' and 'Lynx' models had been photographed some years earlier. (John Lloyd)

Chris Turner owns this immaculate (and rather rare) TR7 Premium. (Chris Turner)

The TR7 Premium previewed the lighter grey dashboard introduced across the TR7 range in the following months. (Chris Turner)

Swindon Plant Director Les Lambourne (an ex-MG Abingdon manager):

> I was told to go up to a meeting at Coventry. When I got there, it was announced that they were going to move the TR7 away from Speke. We then realized, because there were some people there from 'Group' at Longbridge, that we were going to do the bodies at Swindon and send them to Canley.

Pressed Steel rose to the challenge. 'We got that job into production at Swindon two months ahead of schedule, and with a huge – and I mean huge – quality improvement, and that was with the existing materials', Nicholas remembers with some pride. The first step in this process was for Nicholas to visit Speke and establish the scope of the task:

> The first day I went up to Liverpool, I found when I got there that they had welded the gates up. There was a picket line, and I got out of my car and went up to explain that I had been asked to come to a meeting. They told me to go to a pub across the road, where I was told that I would find one of their union officials.

So I drove over – this was about 9:00 in the morning – and I went into this pub and asked for the guy by name. I was directed into a room, and there was the Works Committee, all sat there. I walked in and asked for this fellow – 'that's me,' he said. I explained that I was coming to a meeting. Now by that time they knew that the place was going to close, so he asked me what I was there for. I wouldn't tell him any more than the fact that I'd come for a meeting. He said, 'You see that chap over there – go and say you're going in. You'll have to leave your car' … I walked into the factory and my first port of call was the gents, where there were a couple of chaps in white coats, standing at the stalls. One turned to the other, and said, 'Watch out – here come the body-snatchers!' – typical Liverpool humour.

At Swindon a brand new body line was established for the TR7 in 'B' Building, and for a time Pressed Steel was producing both MGB and TR7 bodyshells, albeit from different buildings. The transfer from Speke to Canley was clearly a success, although the switch had not been without some casualties, as will be explained in the next chapter.

5　The Lost Family: Lynx and Sprint

Failure to Launch: The Shape of Things that Never Came

From the vantage point of the beginning of the 1970s, the Triumph TR7 appeared – at least to its supporters – to have a glorious future ahead of it. The Speke facilities were mapped out to become the new Corporation's mainstay of sports car production and, as we have seen, fantastic sales volumes were forecast for the largely self-sufficient pair of Liverpool factories. Similarly, the slant-four engine had been developed to receive a cleverly designed 16-valve cylinder head, with four valves per cylinder operated, against the prevailing convention, by a single rather than twin overhead camshafts. Although the Dolomite started life as Project 'Ajax III', the 16-valve version had its own project name. Thus it was that Project 'Swift' (Alan Edis's first Triumph Product-Planning project) saw the car that had begun as the front-wheel-drive Triumph 1300 stretched to its ultimate iteration when equipped with this new engine – driving the rear wheels – in the form of the Dolomite Sprint.

The Dolomite Sprint and its worthy but more staid Dolomite brethren both earned steady sales, while the Sprint performed gallantly in motor sports against the contemporary first-generation BMW 3-series opposition, but the fact remained that, even when the TR7 entered production, the Dolomite was living on borrowed time. The 'SD2' project, intended as a Dolomite replacement, had been abandoned (*see* Chapter 3). It could be argued that as the prospects for a true Triumph-engineered 'new Dolomite' evaporated, the justification for keeping both the Triumph slant-four and its technically brilliant 'Sprint' offshoot also began to fade. (In the closing days of the TR7 story, the slant-four would also be targeted for euthanasia; *see* Chapter 7.)

TR7 Sprint

In the early gestation of the TR7, many of the problems on the horizon were unforeseen, and product planners and engineers were considerably enthused about the prospect of fitting the Sprint engine into a version of the TR7 to be known, hardly surprisingly, as the 'TR7 Sprint'. The transplant was fairly easy to make – the higher-performance TR7 would need the five-speed Rover Triumph gearbox, uprated brakes and other changes necessary to cope with the increased performance – but beyond that, in typical British Leyland fashion, the trim and options list would be broadly as per the 'base' model.

With the principle established, and marketing plans in hand, the TR7 Sprint moved inexorably towards production, with the pilot build of a series of pre-production cars (alongside their 'TR7 V8' siblings) between February and October 1977. Surviving records are incomplete, but it is likely that the work was split between the main Triumph Engineering facility at Canley and the production facilities at Speke. Martin Smith is adamant that the cars were actually built on the line as '8 valves':

Some if not all of these cars were definitely converted at Canley from 8-valve to 16-valve; I believe the

The TR7 Sprint was one of the tragic 'might have beens' of British sports car history; many at Triumph actually preferred the performance characteristics of this car to those of the more powerful TR8. Robert Turner is the lucky owner of this rare and immaculate pre-production TR7 Sprint, one of very few still on the road. (Alisdair Cusick)

The sides of the TR7 Sprint were supposed to have received this striping treatment, designed by John Ashford, had the car gone into production. Instead the stripes were adapted and used for the TR7 Premium Limited Edition shown in the previous chapter. (John Ashford)

intention was to track build the cars as 16 valves but the Speke unions wanted added bonuses for dealing with 'non standard' cars. At some point I remember returning from Speke with a boot full of unused 16-valve parts like exhaust manifolds. I don't think we ever found the Sprint engines that were dispatched up there!

Meanwhile, Triumph stylist John Ashford had developed a special side-stripe for the TR7 Sprint, which in modified form would later appear on the TR7 'Premium' limited edition (*see* Chapter 4).

Various people have attempted to establish exactly how many genuine Triumph-built TR7 Sprints were assembled: the general consensus is that somewhere between fifty and sixty were produced, all fixed-head coupés with a special 'ACH' commission number prefix and engine numbers of the form 'CH - - - E'. As has happened before in British Leyland, sales and marketing and service literature began to be prepared, and a driver's handbook was printed.

There were few significant differences to the standard TR7, other than the use of uprated TR8-style front brakes and a different exhaust manifold. Many of the first batch of cars were originally destined to be press cars and, according to TR7 Sprint enthusiast Graham Fountain, many of these Speke-built cars were completely retrimmed at Canley to avoid embarrassment to the company at the hands of the press. That is something else confirmed by Martin Smith: 'If it was a "press car" it would also have been completely stripped, and repainted (one way to tell a genuine press car is that the turret tops would have been "smoothed" with filler), then rebuilt meticulously.'

Testing was done not only in TR7s but also in converted Triumph saloons, since, according to Bryan Reynolds, 'I remember that they still had a number of Triumph 2000 cars running with TR7 Sprint running gear during the mid-'70s'. This certainly matches the entries in the Triumph 'X' Register, which record a number of cars as 'Bullet/ Innsbruck' – Innsbruck being the code name for the Triumph 2000/2500 range.

In the event, however, the crisis at Speke caused the TR7 Sprint project, along with other variants, to become stuck in an unfortunate limbo from which the production cars never emerged. The delay also conspired against the engine in terms of market expectations and North American emissions requirements, as Mike Dale explains: 'The next shoe to fall was the four valve. It died and wiped out a model option for us.'

The fact remains that the failure of the TR7 Sprint project was truly a tragedy, for an enormous and expensive programme of work centred on its development, with fuel injection a key element, and later – as described below – an attempt to salvage something through a cost reduction programme. Triumph engine development engineer Martin Smith remembers the project well:

> I worked on the Sprint EFI engine, originally destined for SD2: it gave good power and was emissions-capable for North America. The inlet system for SD2 used slide throttles (like a race engine) and was a very nice package. The first TR7 Sprint-engined car featured electronic fuel injection or 'EFI' (Bosch system) and had a matt black paint job; it was Engine Development's 'hack car' by the later '70s – it disappeared in about 1978/79; we think it was 'liberated' by someone in Experimental! I had the keys for it on my desk, which was a cause for embarrassment and some searching 'questions' by Corporate Security!

Later, there was a conscious effort to cut the costs of the Sprint engine, in the form of the 'Redco' or 'reduced cost' programme. Martin Smith feels that this could have drastically changed the fortunes of the Sprint engine and possibly Triumph as well:

> It corrected the head bolting/sealing problems and would have been a superb engine which would have competed well with the Cosworth BDA. When it was scrapped, we, as a department, raided the prototype stores and hid the engine bits in the roof spaces over the engine test beds and above the false ceilings in the engine development offices. Security were ordered to search the Fletch North buildings shortly after the axing of TR7 to search for hoarded parts – such were the levels of paranoia.

Smith says that the Sprint-engined TR7 was ready to build and all the parts were 'track side' when it was killed off:

> Apparently the Marketing department killed it because the 0–60 acceleration times were identical to the 2V engine with little increase in top speed. The

Badging on the TR7 Sprint was commendably simple.
(Alisdair Cusick)

problem with looking at 0–60 times is they do not give an accurate picture of a vehicle's 'on road' performance. Zero to any speed is a question of initial traction and the TR7 was undoubtedly 'traction-limited' by its rear axle design, hence Lynx's torque tube axle design to contain 'axle tramp'. The real test was the 30–50, 50–70 times and here the Sprint was significantly superior to the 2V engine and even challenged the TR8's abilities. Certainly, if we were going 'off site' the preferred vehicle to 'borrow' was a Sprint TR7 over all others and that includes the TR8.

Peter Wilson, also at Triumph, was similarly fond of the TR7 Sprint and, after the press cars became surplus to requirements, ran one (a Java Green car, SJW 547S) as his own 'management plan' car:

At the changeover in July 1977 (to the new common underframe) we built a batch of thirty TR7 Sprints. The marketing people said that there wasn't enough performance difference between the two-valve and the four-valve cars. Now up to about 4,000rpm that perhaps was true, but above 4,000rpm the TR7 Sprint was an entirely different animal. It just goes to show you that decisions were being made by management people who probably only drive their cars below 4,000rpm in any case – they were hardly qualified to judge!

In Wilson's view, the TR7 Sprint 'was the best of the bunch – and that includes the TR8!'

Jim Johnson of the TR Drivers' Club is another TR7 Sprint enthusiast who has not only catalogued the surviving cars, but himself owns an interesting car that was once used for development for the proposed Japanese-market variant of the TR7 Sprint. He noticed that it had some unusual shields on the underside, which Martin Smith explains were special to Japan:

Japanese regulations required 'grass shields' over the exposed underfloor exhaust piping, as well as thermocouples on the exhausts which 'lit' a dash warning light and buzzer when exhaust pipes went over 800 degrees Celsius – these were designed to prevent grass fires by people pulling off the highway onto long dry grass. At the time Japanese emissions regulations were

Kas Kastner's TR7 Turbo

Although Kas Kastner had left Triumph and branched out on his own, he did not turn his back on Triumph completely, maintaining an interest in improving the performance of 'classic' Triumph sports cars. He also made a couple of further brief forays into the 'Shape of Things to Come':

I did a turbocharger installation on a TR7 from my private company Arkay Inc. (turbo specialists). In fact I delivered this car to the Triumph offices in New Jersey from my shops in Hawthorne, California, driving in fine November weather and despite the maddening 55mph driving speeds across country. Only one speeding ticket, which was surprising. The car was really fast. I became well acquainted with the TR7 on that 2,800 mile drive. The heating/ventilation into the cockpit was the best I'd ever had. In the cold November days, I had the heater on my feet and the open air ventilator on my head and shoulders. Perfect. But, the interior was crushingly bad. Pieces of every nature fell off, peeled off and split or ripped. With the turbo power, though, it was great fun to drive quickly. I had a nice 95–100 mile an hour run from Las Vegas up through the hills and mountains to Wendover, Utah, and managed to elude the Law Officers a couple of times. I delivered the car to the head offices of BL and never drove another TR7. With TR8, my involvement was even shorter by a bunch. I was commissioned to gather a large group of hot-rod inlet manifolds for V8 American engines and ship them to the engineering department for evaluation. That's it. I left the company and my direct factory connection.

quite lax (similar to European standards), but they still had these quirky 'grass shields'!

According to Martin Smith, a Sprint SD2 engine even found its way into a Spitfire:

This was a 'Saturday morning car' and used a large-car rear axle in a box section cage with full coil over dampers and four-link rear suspension; chassis department were trying out ways of improving the Spitfire's notorious 'swing axle' design, a powerful chassis development car was therefore required. It was a lethal weapon! But it was great fun to drive as there were

Alongside the more familiar Stag, John Lloyd and Les Moore championed this fastback proposal, which could have preceded the later TR7-based Lynx. Financial constraints killed this project. (John Lloyd)

few cars around that could get near it. I remember leaving a 'tuned' 3-litre Capri standing on a drive to Northampton one day. I'm sure the driver never knew what the car really was!

Nowadays less than a dozen TR7 Sprints are believed to have survived, and of those only a few, such as Robert Turner's immaculate Tahiti Blue car, have been restored. Private TR7 Sprint conversions (and garage conversions such as the 'TR7S' referred to in Chapter 10) were not uncommon when the TR7 remained current, and for a couple of years afterwards, but the more popular conversion by far has always been the V8 engine transplant.

Wrong Direction or Blown Opportunity? The Lynx

Right from the very beginning of Triumph's proposals to replace the TR6 there had been two complementary strands involved. As well as 'Bullet' – the open-topped two-seater (*see* Chapter 2) – there was to have been the closely related two-plus-two coupé codenamed 'Lynx'. Pitched slightly upmarket of the Bullet, Lynx was intended to cater for the sports car driver who started a family, needed more carrying space or whose tastes had simply evolved. If he or she

needed any more space, they could later graduate to a Triumph saloon such as the Dolomite, 2000/2500 or their replacements. Naturally Lynx would be well placed to tackle the growing opposition from Japanese manufacturers and would provide a back stop in the event of any legislative problems with open cars.

In the event, although both models and full-size vehicles were built, the fate of the original pre-1971 Lynx was tied to that of the contemporary Bullet and so, when the latter project died, Lynx – subsequently known colloquially inside Canley as 'Lynx Mk.I' – went with it. The immediate task faced by Rover Triumph was to get the definitive TR7 into production, and look again at the idea of a two-plus-two once the ball was rolling. Of course, once the decision had been made to make the TR7 a fixed-roof coupé, the case for the Lynx was arguably weakened, for the TR7 could do battle against the two-seater Japanese and European coupés. Even so, by the beginning of 1972 work was already underway to style a new generation of 'Lynx' using the Harris Mann Bullet as a starting point and with memories of the plea for a '2+2' that Spen King and Mike Carver had picked up in the USA in 1970 still fresh in the mind.

At an early stage in this process, the Lotus Elite and Reliant Scimitar GTE appear to have been

Triumph's Tragedy: The Beautiful but Ill-Fated Stag

The purpose of the Lynx project was as much as anything to replace the Triumph Stag, a car that many saw as a potential Mercedes rival, but which a combination of factors saw condemned to an early grave. The roots of the distinctive Stag two-door came from a Michelotti exercise to build a show car. Instead of being shown, this was hijacked by Triumph's Harry Webster to form a new model to sit above the classic 'TR' line. The Stag was closely based upon the Triumph 2000/2500 saloon range, but along the way it gained a new Triumph-designed V8 engine based on the slant-four unit developed for Saab. This unit began as 2.5 litres but grew to 3.0 litres and offered the potential of an exciting 32-valve version using Sprint technology. The Stag was a good-looking and versatile four-seat grand tourer with a choice of a soft top or removable coupé hardtop, and it also featured an unusual roof bracing structure aimed at compensating for the combination of a lack of a fixed roof and a generously proportioned passenger compartment.

The Stag was launched with great fanfare in June 1970, and was seen as a means of boosting both Triumph and British Leyland's image. Sadly, however, the unique Triumph V8 engine proved to be its Achilles heel and plans late in the day to replace the Triumph unit with Rover's 3.5-litre V8 came to nothing, although running prototypes and styling models were certainly built. Les Moore also produced a very attractive proposal for a fixed-roof fastback version – appraised in some detail by Bruce McWilliams in August 1969 – which could be said to have formed inspiration for the later Lynx, but it eventually became impossible to sustain the Stag in the US market, from which it was withdrawn in 1972. The car remained in production (in relatively uneconomic volumes, but with many minor improvements) for sale elsewhere until it was finally discontinued in 1977, by which point it was generally assumed that the Stag would be replaced both in the showroom and on the production line by the new 'Lynx'.

There was a final postscript to the saga, with a study to resurrect the Stag about eighteen months after it went out of production, but using the Rover V8 engine. Peter Wilson says: 'We built a couple of prototypes in Canley. But then we discovered that some of the tooling had already been lost and so it became uneconomic to proceed.'

considered as potential role models for the Lynx. The Lotus was a fairly boxy wedge-shaped coupé with an upright tail, while the GTE was a reasonably successful Ford V6-powered two-door sports estate fitted, in common with the Lotus, with a glass-fibre reinforced plastic body. The Reliant featured a fairly generous load space and an almost vertical glass tailgate, and it had carved out a niche for itself, mostly in its home market. There appears, however, to have been little evidence – or research – to support the notion that this type of vehicle would find a ready market in North America, but Rover Triumph persisted with a project that clearly held the potential, if successful, to expand output at Speke.

The work on what would become the 'definitive' Lynx began at the end of 1971, when Triumph's design studio was still an independent entity. According to Norman Rose, Triumph's Chief Body Engineer at the time, this new version was known at the factory as 'Lynx Mk.II', although there is little evidence to suggest that this was anything more than convenient shorthand by the engineering staff. Rose recalls that the first efforts had tried to retain the TR7 front wings, with fairly disastrous results from an aesthetic viewpoint.

Designer John Ashford had produced a brown pastel rendering of a side view of Lynx, which he pinned up on the studio wall. One day the rendering caught the attention of Spen King during one of his regular visits to the studio: 'He saw it, said he liked it and said he would bring Bill Davis in – Bill being the Managing Director at that time – and so the two of them came in a bit later on, and they both said they'd like to see it as a 0.3 scale model'. Within a matter of weeks, the model was ready. Around that time, however, 'Rover Triumph' was formed; the merger brought with it Rover's David Bache as overall design director:

David Bache didn't know that my model was being done at that time – he was just taking over. The Solihull studio were doing the 'SD1', but David Bache was obviously now overlooking both studios. Anyway, he didn't know that Spen King and Bill Davis had

John Ashford shows the author his original styling sketch that led to the Lynx.

asked me to produce my 0.3 scale model. He didn't see it until it had been finished and painted. Then he just happened to notice it and said 'oh – that's impressive' – possibly thinking to himself 'we can't show that!' I explained that the rendering had been viewed and that they'd asked for the model to be done – so he didn't make any more comment.

David Bache is widely credited as being the genius behind many Rover shapes, but in truth he was, like most studio directors, only as good as the work that his team produced. He also had some slightly eccentric ideas on what a new sports car needed for the new decade. 'Dave Bache and Les Moore both did their own models,' John Ashford explains:

David Bache said that the car wouldn't sell – particularly in the American market – if it didn't have opera windows, because that was the fashion that had come out with some of the American cars – although it wasn't a very long-lasting fashion. They were horrible, really – I didn't like them and I didn't think it was right. I thought that in America, if the Americans were buying British sports cars, they wanted to buy something that looked British rather than a copy of what the Americans themselves were doing. They could buy their own cars with that sort of feature. So I didn't think that David Bache was right about that at all – and I don't think that Spen King did either.

John Ashford's sketch was on display in the studio when it was spotted by Spen King and Bill Davis. (John Ashford)

John Ashford's sketch was used as the inspiration for this three-tenths scale model in March 1972. (John Ashford)

The nose of the Ashford Lynx proposals featured wraparound indicator lamps and 'concertina' bumper sections. (John Ashford)

Nevertheless, the time came when senior management were scheduled to come to the studio to view the various Lynx models. David Bache seems to have set out to quash the Ashford model, created without the benefit of the Rover designer's input. 'My 0.3 scale model was put behind a curtain', Ashford explains. Adding that he felt, in his words, 'a bit bolshie', he decided his model should not be so easily overlooked:

> so, just before they came in for the senior management viewing, I pulled it out from behind the curtain just at a point where it would have been too late to have hidden it again. It was on a table, so I simply had to push the table out into view. So they looked at it – and they said they liked it.

Perhaps irritated at having lost out, David Bache initially tried to kill off Ashford's design in favour of his own squared-off version with those 'opera windows'. There then followed, according to Ashford, 'a stand up row between Bache and Spen King, the latter eventually directing Bache to accept the chosen version'.

Lynx in the Wild: The Car Takes Shape

In translating John Ashford's basic design to meet his own requirements, David Bache made a few changes to the Ashford shape, perhaps the most noticeable being his trademark concave side fluting, as seen on the Rover SD1 and later on the Austin Maestro. According to Ashford, Bache had a pet theory to support his liking for side flutes:

> He said they had beneficial effect on the moving vehicle 'in yaw'. It was also Bache who insisted on the 'flip up' on the roof above the rear screen (to the ruination of airflow). If you look at the rear of Lynx you can see what looks like an embryo spoiler sitting below the rear screen. This was not a spoiler but a moulding to protect the paintwork when loading items into the boot (and also the spare wheel which had to be removed through the hatch with the risk of inflicting the owner with a hernia). This moulding is where the spoiler should have been.

John Ashford: Father of Lynx

John Ashford, 'stylist of the Lynx', photographed in the sole surviving prototype at the British Motor Heritage Museum in November 2006. (Alisdair Cusick)

Did Michelotti do all the design work for Triumph? You might be forgiven for thinking so, for the Italian stylist is rightly given the lion's share of the credit for Triumph's styling renaissance in the 1960s. However, although Triumph unquestionably owed an enormous debt to the Turin maestro, there was nevertheless a small but dedicated team at Canley that carried out the majority of the practical detailed work. Headed by Les Moore, the design team was rarely more than a dozen strong, and that included studio management, stylists and modellers.

From late 1968, John Ashford was part of that team, and he would go on to become in effect one of Triumph's last stylists. Interviewed by Moore and Chief Body Draughtsman Arthur Ballard, Ashford had come from Rootes via Ford and Lucas. Ashford had started his working life in architecture, but answered an advertisement at Rootes's Humber Road studio in 1958, where among other work he made the first 0.3 scale clay model of what would become the Hillman Imp. In 1961 he moved to Ford, where he was part of the teams that styled the Mark I Cortina, Transit and the D-Series truck.

I left there at the end of 1963 and went to work at Lucas Industries at Shaftmoor Lane, mainly involved with the lighting section, doing lamps and so on – fog lamps and whatever. We also used to go out to smaller manufacturers like Morgan and Lotus – and AC and Alvis were still going in those days – and helped them to work out any problems they might have with styling.

One of Ashford's designs at Lucas was the famous Lucas 'Square 8' fog and driving lamps seen on cars as diverse as the Rolls Royce Silver Shadow and Shelby GT-500.

The small team at Triumph had to deal with everything from a mundane door handle to complete body proposals and facelifts. Among the latter were projects such as the Spitfire Mk. IV and the GT6 Mk. III. John Ashford did much of the exterior work on both of those: 'the rear end style of those were taken from Michelotti, but the front end was actually all Triumph – Les Moore did some of it and I did some too. The Mk. IV Spitfire was more grown-up looking: it probably wasn't as "cute" as the earlier ones.' Other bits of Triumph design claimed by Ashford include the distinctive Spitfire IV pressed steel wheels. 'As far as I know, this was the first pressed steel wheel with a plastic centre section that was retained by the wheelnuts,' Ashford says, adding that it was adopted by Formula Ford racing cars.

In the spring of 1972 Rover and Triumph were merged, and design responsibility fell under Rover's David Bache:

John Ashford in the small Canley design office back in 1969. (John Ashford)

We shipped over to Solihull – that was while Lynx was being developed, although a lot of the styling work on Lynx stayed at Canley. I moved over to Solihull, but as Lynx stayed at Canley I was going backwards and forwards between Solihull and Canley, to carry on with the project. I was one of the first to go in 1974 to Solihull; the rest didn't come over until around 1975/76. Then they shut down the old Triumph studio and everybody was amalgamated into the Rover studio under David Bache.

It was John Ashford – with direction from, first, Les Moore and then David Bache – who designed the Lynx. Afterwards, Ashford was one of those who provided models for the 'Broadside' (*see* Chapter 9). He survived the various purges that took place when studios merged and, along the way, contributed to many other programmes, notably the Montego Estate and the MG Metro Turbo wheels and rear spoilers, and was responsible for the neat underbonnet layouts of just about every Rover Group product until he retired in 1999.

Around the same time as the Ashford Lynx, Rover Triumph's incoming design supreme, David Bache, also dabbled with Lynx designs, as did Les Moore. Judge for yourself how successful this effort might have been. (John Ashford)

Eventually a reasonably happy compromise was reached that featured elements of the Ashford and Bache designs. (John Ashford)

Work progressed on the final model, although this was complicated by the move of the former Triumph Styling personnel to the Rover studio at Solihull. The actual Lynx was eventually finalized and it moved into the stage of going to tooling. 'The Lynx Mk.II was completely engineered in the Triumph Body Engineering department, with tool design and manufacture by Austin Morris body division – the old Pressed Steel – with the intention that production would be at the Liverpool plant', explains Norman Rose. Already at this stage, by the summer of 1974, just as British Leyland was suffering its crippling financial problems, five prototypes of the Lynx had been built and some testing had been undertaken at MIRA, but 'then the whole project was frozen in mid-1974 for approximately twelve months due to the economic crisis that British Leyland was experiencing'.

In the wake of the Ryder Report, according to Rose, in mid-1975 the Lynx 'became the first project to be reactivated [by 'British Leyland Ltd'] and was planned for pre-production in the autumn of 1977'. From an engineering point of view,

> Lynx 'Mk.II' used the main floor, dash and engine compartment from TR7, as well as the bonnet and front panel. It had new wings, doors, roof and windscreen and a new underbody. Mechanically it used TR7 front suspension and engine/gearbox mountings, but it had a different rear suspension based on that of the Rover SD1.

The wheelbase was longer – by eleven inches – which allowed the fitment of 'occasional' rear seating. According to Rose, 'full engineering and safety sign-off had been achieved and tooling was almost completed'.

Bruce McWilliams remained resolutely unconvinced by the Lynx all the way through. Thinking of the 1969/70 offering, McWilliams states that:

> At the beginning, the Lynx was an ungainly, primitive effort – hardly surprising, given the limited resources of the Triumph design organization, then run by Les Moore. When Spen King came on board at Triumph, I quite forcefully pressed my criticisms of Lynx, to which he responded in a number of ways helpful to its appearance.

Ironically, as the photos show, it would seem that the quirkier changes arguably came on David Bache's watch.

Part of the problem with the new version was the understandable decision to retain the front

This fascinating photo shows the full-size 'model stack', intended to form pattern guidance for the toolmakers, seen here at Pressed Steel's Cowley plant. (John Ashford)

The tailgate of the Lynx comprised a large glazed opening. (Alisdair Cusick)

The high lip of the tailgate necessitated a plastic spoiler that doubled as protection against light damage from heavy objects being lifted into the luggage compartment. Note also the retention of the large US-market rear over-riders. (Alisdair Cusick)

end of the TR7 more or less intact, a principle that lasted to the end. Even those who disliked the side or rear aspects of the TR7 tended to agree that the sleek front end, with the pop-up headlamps, was a successful design aspect, but the problem was that the nose was if anything too familiar and easily associated with the TR7. Family resemblance is all very well, but it can be a curse as well as a blessing – an obvious example being the MGB and MGC. This meant that the dynamics of the TR7's rising wedge would inevitably be lost in translation to a longer fast-back coupé, and so it was a challenge to make the Lynx hang together aesthetically. However many would feel, at least based on the work by John Ashford, that Lynx could have been successful – even if it might have been more warmly welcomed in European than North American markets.

By the autumn of 1977, with concerns from the North American office presumably sidelined, most of the tooling had been completed (at a cost said to be about £10 million). Although the intended launch date had slipped slightly to 1978, it still seemed that British Leyland (aided by the prevailing dollar/sterling exchange rate) would soon achieve the much needed production volumes, with the 'TR7 Sprint', the 'TR8' and the 'Lynx' (the latter possibly as an 'MG') all programmed for production. Production targets would therefore be achievable in theory, even if there were mixed messages about customer demand in a key market. The reasoning behind the 'MG' badging was, according to Alan Edis, a consequence of the long-running debate about branding that kept running in the background: 'the MGB GT had shown a market acceptance for a 2+2 MG and Lynx might have fit that segment'.

Mike Dale was horrified by Lynx when he saw a finished running prototype:

It was so badly realized that we wanted to opt out completely and this led to a clinic on the West Coast, at which a potential customer remarked that it looked as though it had been designed by three separate designers who had never met. The rear wheels had

The Lynx was intended to add the benefits of occasional two-plus-two seating to the TR7 family. (John Ashford)

incredibly large gaps at the top of the wheel arches, and when we pointed this out, Alan Edis, the project planner, remarked that it was only a showroom condition! I really liked Alan, and still do, but it was the kind of remark that showed how far removed we thought the BL management was from the realities of competing in the US market. At the clinic we put large weights in the rear to disguise the problem but the car was so bad it didn't help. Lynx died at that clinic.

From his point of view, Mike Dale felt that the clinic had been a waste of time because it seemed clear that nobody would want to buy the Lynx as shown:

However I was wrong because it was the only thing that stopped the UK from actually building the monstrosity! The company who ran the clinic told me they were the worst results they had ever seen in a car clinic in the entire industry. There was a large gap in

attitudes between myself and the UK management over things like this. No enmity (on my part at least!) but I had earned my early living as a retail salesman and that coloured my view of what was saleable and what wasn't. I was completely convinced we had a disaster on our hands.

Alan Edis concedes that the Leonia people never liked Lynx, but he defends it: 'I have to say that my view of that clinic was rather different; I didn't feel that the customers and comparison vehicles were necessarily the right ones; we certainly needed to attract the right type of customer.' Edis thought that the clinic may have been flawed as a result:

I don't think that the Americans quite understood the concept we were trying to push, but if there was a fault, it was with the British management. North America had enough to contend with on the TR7, but I still think that Lynx could have had a market in the USA and that it could have been successful. But it never did have the support from the Leonia management and so that all became rather self-defeating. The North American management had certainly had tough times – particularly with the fluctuating dollar/sterling rates – and they had had to make moves to deal with this. In that context, it is understandable they were not convinced.

Bruce McWilliams, like Mike Dale, remained unmoved:

My views on Lynx continued to be vociferous and negative, and ultimately a climactic summit meeting was organized at the Elephant House at Longbridge to hear them out. It was short and final: Dick Perry presided, and Spen King, Graham Whitehead, I and a few others attended. Dick began by asking if I believed the car to be saleable, and I said absolutely not. Then there was a sort of sucking-in-of-breath sound, and Dick said something to the effect that that was it, Lynx is cancelled. And so it was. The meeting, which lasted all of about five minutes, was immediately adjourned.

To some, the views so forcefully expressed by Mike Dale and Bruce McWilliams may seem

Sideways on, a Lynx prototype – bearing 'MG' badges – at, arguably, its most elegant angle. (John Ashford)

The 'MG' badging is evident in this showroom shot of a prototype Lynx. (John Ashford)

The unique alloy wheel design for the Triumph Lynx. (Alisdair Cusick)

harsh: when you study the sketches and models – and even the studio photographs of the penultimate MG-badged Lynx – there are hints of a sleek coupé that perhaps might have been successful. Dale agrees that there is some gap between John Ashford's 0.3 scale model and the end result:

> It is a fine example of how the wrong decisions were made based on a model buck where the wheels fit the wheel arches and the body panels look as though they were intended to be together! The fundamental problem was that production simply couldn't put the designer's ideas into practice.

The translation from idea to execution had certainly been a tortuous journey, as John Ashford readily admits: 'Lynx – all the way through – was hot and cold – it wasn't always in favour. After all, it was even revived after it had been cancelled! And finally it was cancelled again permanently.'

Closer appraisal of the Java Green-painted running prototype certainly reveals some elements that might seem ungainly or a little crude, particularly in the context of some of the contemporary Japanese and European opposition, and of course a large V8-powered 2+2 coupé was some way from the sports car ideal that Dale and McWilliams really wanted – particularly if it was intended to wear an MG badge - and could

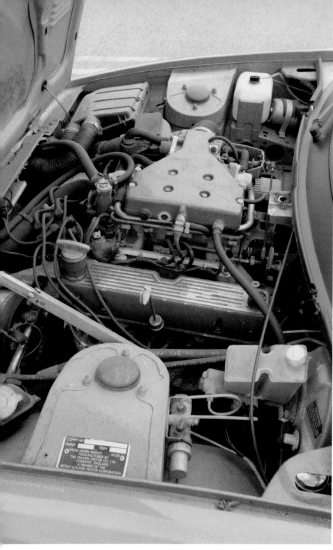

Like the TR8, the Lynx would have utilized the Rover V8 engine, as seen in the surviving prototype. (Alisdair Cusick)

The rear seats of the Lynx would have offered the chance for British Leyland to have extended its sports car repertoire. John Ashford's scale model can just be seen on a shelf in the background. (John Ashford)

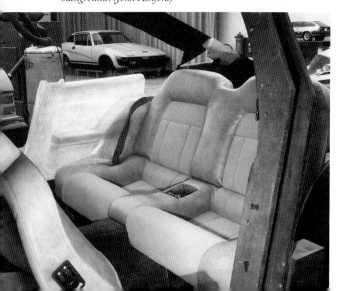

have become something of an albatross in the critical US market.

When he examined the prototype during the photoshoot at Gaydon, Harris Mann noted how the rain channels stood much more proud of the roof than those on the TR7 Coupé – possibly, he suggested, because of fabricating difficulties when the prototype was being built. This was probably one of a number of minor details that could have been resolved had the Lynx moved closer to production, where it would have shared production facilities with the TR7. Apart from the detail issues, however, it could be argued that the changes that David Bache wrought on John Ashford's design detracted from rather than enhanced the end result; sadly Bache is no longer here to defend himself, having died on 26 November 1994.

In fact this very prototype had been 'walked through' the Speke plant by Peter Wilson back in 1977: 'I organized the paint trial of the Java Green car, now at Gaydon. It was painted at Liverpool and we had to run it right through the factory, down the line, to ensure that it fitted the various jigs and didn't snag on fixtures or anything as it moved along the line'.

Looking back on the Lynx, Bob Burden, a sales and marketing colleague of Dale and McWilliams, concedes that Lynx might have been given a warmer reception outside North America:

> Sadly to my mind the design is like a reflection of BL – bits and pieces from here and there flying loosely in formation to who knows where. I will admit that my view may be coloured by American taste: hatchbacks have never been popular here and we are ever so slowly coming round (in 2007) to the concept of a small sporty station wagon. But at that time, I would have voted 'NO' based on the design alone. Add to that the fact that the TR7 wasn't exactly a resounding success, and it would have been a loud 'NO'.

Jeff Herbert arrived on the scene late in the Lynx project; he could see its limitations but would later try to find a way to utilize some of

Compare these contemporary black and white images, dating from April 1976, with the colour images taken for this book: the TR7 heritage is obvious. (John Ashford)

its better aspects. Like Alan Edis, Herbert's view is certainly less damning than those from North America. 'I thought the Lynx was quite a nicely balanced car,' he says. 'Of course there were still some people who had hopes of it happening but in reality I think it was already dead by the time I came.' A key reason by then was a shortage of funds: 'many of the older people within the company had been educated in the engineering field whereas many of the newer people were more economically educated and could see that the company didn't have enough money. The Ryder Plan had seemed to offer unlimited cash, but that idea soon became discredited.'

One point that Triumph enthusiasts often fail to recognize is that the 'Lynx' title was by no means guaranteed as the production name for the big coupé. Just as the Daimler 'Dart' became the Daimler SP250 in production, owing to the fact that Dodge already had the US rights to the Dart name, the fact was that 'Lynx' was already registered by Ford Motor Company, which – having already used the 'Cougar' name on its Mustang-derived Mercury brand 'personal coupé' – planned to use the name on a smaller model that emerged in 1981 as a variant of the Ford Escort, replacing the previous Ford Pinto-derived Mercury Bobcat. There is no certainty that Ford would have been willing to cede the domestic US rights to the 'Lynx' name, although barely three years after the TR7 was discontinued, the by then moribund Mercury 'Montego'

name was effectively sequestrated by Austin Rover for its Marina replacement (it is now back on a Mercury product).

Museum Exhibit

Over the life of the Lynx programme, there were a number of running prototypes. According to Bryan Reynolds, 'Lynx No 2' (a red car) was around at 'Fletch North' when he arrived in 1974 and was totally rebuilt during the late 1970s at great expense. It had an unfortunate end: 'on its first night shift around the Cotswolds durability route, on its very first outing after the rebuild, it was written off by the durability driver!' Reynolds, who still works at Land Rover, remembers his involvement with the Lynx with

Colour coordinated bumpers were considered – even if not exactly colour-matched. (Norman Rose)

The dashboard of the Triumph Lynx was more or less identical to that of the TR7, although the different style of the interior door trims and the more luxurious seats are a visual clue to the big coupé's identity. (Alisdair Cusick)

affection: 'at the time they looked so cool to a teenager. The build of No 15 stands out to me as it was the first ever full prototype build I was part of – and I have been involved in hundreds since then.'

The final survivor of the Lynx programme is the green-finished running prototype (X905), which normally resides at the Heritage Motor Museum along with some other fascinating Triumph prototypes. This Lynx prototype has formed part of the British Motor Heritage collection from the Trust's inception, and was set to form part of the display when the collection set up home at Syon Park in West London (prior

to the move to Gaydon) at the end of 1980. However, as so often is her wont, fate intervened. Ian Elliott, Public Relations Officer at British Leyland, explains what happened:

I had taken Rob Golding, then motoring correspondent of the *Birmingham Post*, into Solihull to interview David Bache. It was while walking outside the Studio that we had one of those PR nightmares – the Lynx prototype was being loaded into a covered wagon, and of course Rob spotted it and insisted on having a look. David Bache, who was always a bit of a loose cannon in PR terms, was completely relaxed about this (in fact thinking about it, he may well have been

The rear luggage compartment and rear seating of the Lynx were well upholstered, even if the forest of beige draylon is a hallmark of the 1970s. (Alisdair Cusick)

The commission plate of the only Lynx prototype known to survive, X905. (Alisdair Cusick)

The only surviving Triumph Lynx prototype is this green specimen, preserved at the Heritage Museum in Gaydon, Warwickshire. The styling in simple terms could be described as a blend of TR7 and Rover SD1. (Alisdair Cusick)

having a bit of deliberate mischief!) Back in David's office, he produced photographs of the Lynx, and offered one to Rob to take away and publish. This wasn't the sort of ad-hoc way I would have wanted to reveal such a story, but David was a very senior Director of the company (reputed to be one of the few with an individual contract outside of the standard management grades), and wasn't going to be put off by a mere PRO.

When Elliott delicately questioned the wisdom of encouraging an article that would make it rather obvious that British Leyland had buried yet another sports car project, he was assured that 'the car was going to go on display at Syon Park anyway, so there was no problem'. Golding, of course, was delighted, and the photo duly appeared next day in the *Birmingham Post*. Elliott continues:

All hell broke loose when Harold [Musgrove] saw it. As piggy-in-the-middle for the umpteenth time, I nearly got fired myself! With the benefit of hindsight, I don't think it was so much the revelation of the Lynx that caused the eruption as the fact that David had taken a unilateral decision to reveal it. Relations between David and Harold were steadily deteriorating at this time, leading towards a final explosion in the Longbridge 'Elephant House' Styling Studio in 1982, when an exasperated Harold summarily fired David.

At Musgrove's insistence, the Lynx prototype was covered up and hidden away from public view, and in fact it did not go on public display for many years afterwards. Readers may interpret that in whatever manner they feel appropriate.

6   Motor Sports

Motor Sports and the Shape of Things to Come

By the time that the TR7 came along, the tradition of British sports car racing was already a firmly established part of the motor sports scene on both sides of the Atlantic. However, although it might have seemed an obvious benefit for the UK and US motor sports exponents to pool their expertise, the fact was that both factory and private team endeavours on either side of the Atlantic tended very much to plough their own furrows. This was partly a consequence of the different racing traditions – circuit races like Sebring and the full season of Sports Car Club of America (SCCA) races dominated the North American scene, while in Europe there was much more of a focus on rallying. Furthermore, it is a truism of any organized sport that the locals tend to know not only all the rules, but also how far it is possible to bend them. Largely as a consequence of this, the TR7 motor sports story is, with a few exceptions, one of two continents going their own ways.

Unquestionably all the factory-supported TR7 (and later TR8) motor sports efforts had a common goal of raising the credibility of the controversial Leyland sports car, but different ways were adopted in North America and Europe to achieve this. In the USA and Canada, the sight and sound of mighty V8-engined race cars is not much of a novelty: for those markets, the appeal of the petite Triumph had everything to do with the exotic attraction of a European sports car. In beleaguered Great Britain, however, the TR7

– and even more so the TR7 V8 – had a different sort of exotic appeal: the distinctive (and unique) rumbling sound of the fabulous V8 engine on the RAC Rally and other events cheered those who had almost lost hope that Great Britain could hold her head up in just about any field of endeavour. With heroes like Bob Tullius and John Buffum in America, and Tony Pond in the UK, Triumph enthusiasts in the late 1970s at last felt they had reason to keep the faith.

Racing the American Way

US efforts stemmed from an early assessment of the 'Bullet' by Mike Dale and his colleagues at Leonia. Dale's first impressions were not particularly favourable: 'when we looked at the engine from a racing perspective it became even clearer what a mediocre piece of equipment we were getting from a performance angle. We struggled mightily with it but were never able to make it provide any real horsepower or torque.' Racing had long been a key part of Triumph's US marketing effort – and Dale was a strong defender of motor sports in the face of opposition from colleagues who doubted its virtue – but even so, at the beginning the TR7 did not look a promising prospect to take over from the ageing but nevertheless successful TR6.

According to Dale, 'the TR7 was not responding well at all. The basic engine was sound but we had to work from the standard cylinder head and, while this may have been well designed for emissions, it certainly didn't lend itself to producing power.' In order to tackle this, the various

The Group 44 Inc. Triumph TR8 was tested in the Lockheed wind tunnel – at a cost of around $600 per hour. (Bob Tullius)

US race teams were encouraged to look to their own expertise; in Dale's view 'the UK technically was a long way behind the racing scene in the US so was unable to help'.

Despite the supposed promise of its modern wedge shape, the US team were further disappointed with the way the body behaved at high speeds out on the track: 'aerodynamically the car was a joke', Dale says:

> Ken Slagle, a close racing friend of mine and National Champion SCCA driver in a Spitfire, was trying to develop a competitive TR7. It was handling really badly at high speed and, in order to investigate the airflow, Ken and I fitted lines of tufted wool on the trunk and rear window then drove it round the banking at Pocono. I sat backwards on the floor without seat belts and a helmet taking pictures out the back while Ken drove the car at high speed round the oval. Between the ride, noise and dust flying around the cockpit it was quite a ride.

This process – crude but effective – confirmed Slagle and Dale's suspicions:

> The results showed the airflow, as we had expected, was actually moving backwards over the trunk [bootlid] and up the window creating lift … it was so bad that at the beginning of a straight the car body would be roughly where it was at rest, and by the end of the straight the car body was several inches higher.

This prompted Group 44 Inc. to take the later TR8 to the Lockheed wind tunnel at Marietta, where it became clear that the car was actually generating 400lb of lift at the rear at speed:

> A huge spoiler was put on the car to cure this but the best we could ever do was reduce the problem to zero lift. Once the aerodynamics were brought under some semblance of control, the overall handling was excellent because the basic suspension layout was fine and we were able to substitute lightweight bumpers for the safety bumpers on the standard car. These bumpers were a great detriment to the standard cars' handling because the body overhangs were large and, once the car lost any kind of traction, they acted as pendulums.

Ken Slagle says that his team, Slagle Racing, tried lots of things to try to improve the aerodynamics: 'One idea was a specially designed fuel cell container that reduced the high pressure under the rear of the car a bit, but the car really needed a big spoiler like Group 44 ran on their Trans-Am cars to help the problem (which would have slowed the car down even more!)' In the end, Slagle's problems with the coupé would be rendered redundant by the adoption of an open-top car, by which time the motive power was V8 rather than four-cylinders. The TR8 (including the Lee Mueller and Ken Slagle cars) is covered in greater detail later in this chapter.

Bob Tullius politely toed the corporate publicity relations line for a contemporary advertisement, where he was quoted as saying of the TR7 – presumably tongue-in-cheek – that 'obviously the aerodynamics of its shape are hard to beat', but in reality he agrees with Dale on the TR7's deficiencies:

Bob Tullius: Triumph's Racing Ambassador

Bob Tullius is a larger-than-life American racing hero who started as he meant to go on, and never looked back. He was born in Rochester, New York, on 12 July 1936. As a college football star, he was once asked to try out for NFL's Baltimore Colts. His first racing experience came in 1953, driving his 1937 Ford Coupé on oval tracks. Early in 1961, while working for Kodak, he armed himself with a Triumph TR3, joined a drivers' school and graduated by winning the race at the end of the course. Hearing that Standard Triumph was preparing to provide a brace of the new TR4 sports cars to favoured drivers, Tullius tried to persuade the company to do the same for him, but was initially unsuccessful. Disappointed but undaunted, Tullius simply went away and, driving his old TR3, proceeded to out-point those who had been given the TR4s.

Bob Tullius, one of the best North American motor racing exponents Triumph ever had. (Bob Tullius)

Before long Triumph decided that Tullius was clearly a talent worth nurturing, and so Mike Cook was given the job of despatching a new blue TR4 to him. A race soon after at Lime Rock saw the Tullius TR4 finish promisingly in second place, but at Lake Garnett, Kansas, Tullius had the misfortune to crash head on into a tree while avoiding track debris. As Tullius told *Classic Motorsports* magazine: 'Triumph was not happy when I called to tell them I needed a new car. They declined to supply another one.' Tullius turned to his friend Ed Diehl who, according to Tullius, took a single door from the previous car, bought two wrecked TR4s and, Frankenstein fashion, created one good car from the useable parts, all inside three weeks. This car, raced by Tullius and Diehl, went on to score a steady stream of successes that belied its mongrel origins, as Tullius told me: 'In the Diehl built car in 1962 I won the SCCA National Championship and Ed Diehl won the N.E. SCCA Division Championship.' After a successful season in SCCA races, Triumph decided to let Tullius take over one of the Kas Kastner ex-Sebring TR4s, and Tullius rewarded Triumph's generosity by winning two national championships, including the first American Road Race of Champions at Riverside International Raceway in 1964.

By now Tullius, the part-timer, wanted to move into racing full time, and so he gave up his day job and established himself as Group 44 Inc. in the town of Falls Church, Virginia, in March 1965 with partners Brian Fuerstenau and Dick Gilmartin. Fuerstenau had first met Tullius as a teenage mechanic in 1963 and swiftly became the engine guru at Group 44 Inc. The new team – a 'group' that took the key part of its name from Tullius's race number – set out to create a trio of race cars so that each of the three could compete in a full race season. Tullius had prior experience of dealing with Quaker State Motor oil, whom he persuaded to become the principal sponsor of Group 44 Inc., and who also funded a smart team transporter for the team in the distinctive white and green livery. After a year Gilmartin left the team. For a time Group 44 Inc. dabbled with a Dodge Dart race car, as Tullius recalls: 'The Dodge/Chrysler program produced a significant win at the Marlboro 12 HR. in 1966, the first American car to win the event, also a victory in the first Trans-Am event ever in 1966 at Sebring'.

However, it would be Tullius's enduring relationship with Triumph and latterly British Leyland that would bring him the most enduring period of success, culminating in the exciting Jaguar race cars of the 1980s and '90s. Lawton 'Lanky' Foushee joined as the chassis counterpart of Brian Fuerstenau after he met Tullius at the 1971 Paul Revere 250 race. Within ten years Group 44 Inc. had outgrown its Falls Church premises; on 1 February 1975, just days after helping with the TR7 launch in Boca Raton, Florida, the team moved to new premises at Herndon, also in Virginia, and two miles from Dulles International Airport. The new shop had four times as much floor space and would allow the Group 44 Inc. operation to expand to accommodate MG, Jaguar and Triumph race programmes, while increasing the company's contract and research business. During 1975, while waiting for the TR7, Group 44 Inc. raced only one Triumph, a TR6 piloted by John McComb. This car would go on to win the 1975 class championship and be acquired by actor and race driver Paul Newman. Group 44 Inc. remained in business for twenty-five years, competing in SCCA Club Racing, IMSA GTP endurance events and SCCA Trans-Am pro races and notching up some 300 victories. Nowadays Tullius focuses on his interest in restoring Second World War fighter planes, but maintains fond memories of his time behind the wheel of the TR8.

Bob Tullius's Group 44 Inc. TR8 at his Florida premises: still a very purposeful looking motor car after more than two decades. (Bob Tullius)

The TR7/8 was never meant to be a race car, but we forced it to be an excellent race car through the talents and ingenuity of Brian Fuerstenau and Lanky Foushee. The first indication we had that it didn't want to be a race car was the factory appeared not have done any aerodynamic testing. I'm certain it had never been in a wind tunnel, or, if it had, they ignored the result.

Nevertheless, despite these teething problems, the Americans persisted with their efforts to make a racing car out of the TR7 that met their own requirements.

Work on Group 44 Inc.'s first TR7 race car project began in November 1975, just as that year's SCCA race championship was drawing to a close: the team knew that the TR6 would be a hard act to follow, a fact that would later be proved rather dramatically the following season. Meanwhile, however, in the closing months of 1975 the plan was to have the first car ready for testing in mid-March 1976, which called for an intense period of preparation in the run up to Christmas. During the final two months of 1975, the Group 44 Inc. team stripped out the donor car, modified the bodyshell and installed the obligatory roll cage. During the Christmas

holiday, the body was painted in the new corporate Group 44 Inc. colour scheme of white and green, and the New Year saw work on the engine and suspension get under way.

MacPherson strut front suspension was a major change from the TR6 set-up, but the mechanics set to, adapting and reinforcing the springs and anchorages as necessary to bring them up to race standards. At the rear, ace engineering guru Lawton 'Lanky' Foushee removed the standard TR7 upper trailing links and replaced them with a tailor-made single upper arm over the differential, and two additional lower trailing links to supplement the standard lower arms. With the aid of a Panhard link, the rear axle was firmly controlled against unwanted wayward movements. Koni double-adjustable shock absorbers were used with bespoke springs. Front brakes were BL Special Tuning units, although at the back standard brake units were merely upgraded with competition shoes and larger wheel cylinders. Brian Fuerstenau, with three personal SCCA National Championships under his own belt, succinctly explained this rear brake philosophy to *Road & Track*, saying 'you can't really use 'em hard on most race cars'.

Brian Fuerstenau (with glasses) and Lanky Foushee were two of the key members of Bob Tullius's Group 44 Inc. team. (Bob Tullius)

Just as they had shown countless times before – not least, as we saw earlier, at the TR7 launch, when they had stepped in to save the day for Mike Dale and his colleagues – the Group 44 Inc. team showed their ability to meet tough targets and had their SCCA Class 'D' TR7 race car ready for the end of March. Bob Tullius took it out for the first time in anger at the Charlotte Motor Speedway on 28 March 1976, following track testing the previous day that had allowed Brian Fuerstenau and 'Lanky' Foushee to fine-tune engine and suspension, respectively.

The race was a good opportunity to measure the new car against one of the key competitors of the day, Jim Fitzgerald, in his Datsun 2000, and there were some entertaining changes of lead between the two out on the Charlotte circuit. At the end of the race, it was Tullius who took the chequered flag, giving the Group 44 Inc. TR7 a maiden win. The following month the same car, now officially wearing the British Leyland/Quaker State sponsorship, took to a damp circuit at Lime Rock on 24 April. Wrestling the car into the lead, Tullius held first place and won again,

with a fifteen second lead. It was a promising beginning. Wins followed at Bridgehampton, New York (the SCCA National) on 16 May, Pocono Raceway (Long Pond, Philadelphia) on 6 June and Nelson Ledges in Warren, Ohio on 13 June.

While Tullius oversaw the east coast effort, BL Inc.'s good friends on the west coast, Huffaker Engineering, ran a TR7 out of their California premises, with Lee Mueller driving. The latter car, resplendent in silver and wearing number '8', saw some really close racing with the ex-Group 44 Inc., John McComb title-winning TR6 of actor-turned-race driver Paul Newman, wearing number '75', in particular at the traditional end of season SCCA 'run off' at the Road Atlanta circuit. Mueller (in TR7) and Newman (in TR6) diced closely for most of the race. Newman eventually won, with Mueller snapping at his heels a mere 0.84 seconds behind in second place. It was perhaps not quite the result that BL either expected or secretly wanted, but it undoubtedly served as a platform for some good publicity for Triumph! Sadly, Lee Mueller passed away in

Always a highly visible hallmark of the professionalism of the Group 44 Inc. team was their impressive tractor-trailer combination in full Quaker State/Group 44 livery. (Wayne Ellwood)

2001, but his son John is understandably proud of the Mueller racing legend and is keeping the family flame alive through his own career.

The series of race successes that the TR7 secured during 1976 were used as an excuse for the first North American 'limited edition', the TR7 Victory Edition (*see* Chapter 4), while a celebratory advertisement for the TR7 had a subtly altered strapline that proclaimed: 'TR7. The shape of things that win'.

During 1978/79 attention began to turn towards the future promise of the TR8. The first North American race challenger to switch over was Lee Mueller, who drove his Huffaker-built TR8 to its first win at Sears Point in April 1979. Others followed, the chief among them being Bob Tullius, whose legendary TR8 exploits are covered later in this chapter.

The European TR7 Programme

At around the same time that Bob Tullius was developing his first racing TR7, British Leyland back in Great Britain had also started the process of developing a European competition programme.

Successes in rally and circuit races were trumpeted by Jaguar Rover Triumph as 'The Shape of Things that Win'.

Ken Slagle

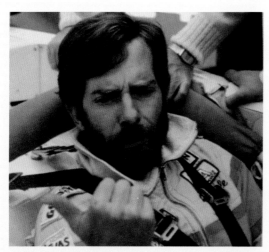

Ken Slagle. (Ken Slagle)

The passenger in Ken Slagle's TR7 flies the flag at Nelson Ledges on a victory lap. (Ken Slagle)

Ken Slagle was one of those front-line race car drivers for whom motor sports was supposedly a spare-time activity, and yet mere mortals would wonder how this pastime squared with the day job. 'I worked "full time" as a Systems Engineer for IBM, and racing was "just a hobby"!', Slagle confesses, adding that 'Slagle Racing' primarily consisted of his wife (also with a full-time job), Slagle himself and their three young children who, as he sweetly puts it, 'provided hours of slave labour, and were a big help'.

Slagle was a loyal Triumph racer from the mid-1960s right through until some years after Triumph sports car production had passed into history. He ascribes the birth of this racing relationship to an accident in the snow with his road-going TR3B:

> The frame was bent and the insurance company 'totalled' the car. I bought it back and fixed it to compete in the Pennsylvania Hillclimb Association, which conducted about eight hillclimb events in central Pennsylvania. After winning the championship in 1966, I went to a Sports Car Club of America (SCCA) driver's school at Marlboro, Maryland, and met (my hero) Bob Tullius, who took an interest in my car (which I'd prepared using a 'Triumph Competition Preparation Manual', written by 'Kas' Kastner, the Triumph Competition Manager).

With this promising start, and encouraging words from his hero, Slagle went on to race in SCCA 'Regional' races, followed by 'National' races in 1968 and 1969, and went to the Daytona American Road Race of Champions ('runoffs') in 1969:

> By then, I'd attracted a bit of attention from Mike Barratt, the East Coast Competition Manager for BLMI, and Mike Cook, the Advertising Manager (who also raced a TR3 in hillclimbs and road races). They offered me an opportunity to buy the 1300 Spitfire that Brian Fuerstenau and John Kelly had raced for Group 44 in 1968 and 1969.
> This was the beginning of a long association with the North American arm of BL.
> I raced three different Spitfires in SCCA racing and won the 'F-Production' National Championship at Road Atlanta in 1975 (1500 Spitfire). That winter, my wife (Janet) and I were visiting Mike and Mary Dale and Mike suggested that I needed more of a 'challenge', since I'd had such a winning season in the Spitfire. (I'd been trying to talk Mike into helping me buy the Group 44 TR6, but he didn't want me to compete against the factory TR7s with a better car.)

Slagle credits Mike Dale as talking him into what turned out to be a long, hard job of trying to make a 'silk purse from a sow's ear', adding ruefully that this was something Dale did several times over the next few years. Ringing in Slagle's ears at the outset were pearls of wisdom he had recently picked up from the late racer Mark Donahue (1937–1975), who had sagely opined, 'you can't make a race car out of a pig, but you can make a damn fast pig.'

Slagle Racing got hold of a TR7 body and some parts, and started building their new race car. 'I had no idea what a long, uphill battle we were in for!', Slagle claims:

> After several months of getting the roll cage fabricated, building moulds for body parts, etc, I started working on engines. Fortunately Group 44 was well ahead of me, and showed me quite a bit of what they'd done in the chassis and engine development areas. (Brian Fuerstenau and 'Lanky' Foushee were both very open and answered all my questions, but it became obvious that if I didn't ask the right question, I didn't get the information!)
>
> Over the next several months, we spent a lot of time using a friend's engine dyno and working with cylinder head ports on our airflow bench. Our first season (1976) was really tough. We had trouble with rear axles breaking (a wheel comes off the car!), the rear drum brake self adjusters would tighten as they got hot to the point that you couldn't turn the wheels when you stopped in the pits.

Slagle barely qualified for the runoffs that year, finishing behind Bob Tullius.

> Over the next couple of years, I got the TR7 to be a reasonable race car, but still had memories of how much fun the 1500 Spitfire had been! I qualified on the pole at the runoffs in Road Atlanta in 1977 and 1978, but the car was too heavy for the tyres we could fit, and I had problems with the tyres 'going off' in the later stages of a race and would finish third or fourth. We were classed with the Lotus Super 7, which was much nimbler, and could draft the bigger cars on the straights and pass under braking (the roles were reversed for us with the TR8, when we raced against the Corvettes, Cobras, and Trans-am cars!).

The public statement that Leyland Cars would be returning to motor sports came in October 1975, with the simultaneous announcement that the opening gambit would be a two-car TR7 team for the 1976 RAC Rally Championship. Leyland had a wide range of vehicles to choose from, but it was entirely logical and fitting that they should kick off with their futuristic new sports car. The team would see the pairings of Tony Pond and David Richards, and Brian Culcheth and Johnstone Syer. Pond in particular would eventually take on almost mythical status through his association with what fans would call the 'flying wedge' and David Richards would eventually become the powerhouse behind 'Prodrive' – but that is getting ahead of the story.

According to Bill Price, leading light within Leyland's Motorsports division (at that time still based at the MG factory in Abingdon-on-Thames), early viewing of the pre-production TR7 at Speke in September 1974 had allowed the opportunity to plan for the development of a rallying version, and the first test session took place on 4 March 1976 at Finmere airfield near Bicester, which had long been a favourite testing venue for the Abingdon men. Leyland had already built up a wealth of racing experience with the Triumph Dolomite Sprint, and it was obvious that this would be put to good use in the development of the new 'Bullet'.

Instead of the anticipated five-speed gearbox, the early TR7 Sprint rally cars featured a Triumph Dolomite Sprint overdrive gearbox with a specially made propshaft. By the end of March a car was ready to show off to the press, resplendent in a strikingly patriotic new corporate Leyland Cars livery of white with red and blue flashes – quite a change from the old BMC Motorsports colours of red with a white roof.

This distinctive cheese-wedge trailer was a common sight at race events across the USA. (Ken Slagle)

The Leyland ST mechanics line up at Abingdon along with Bill Price (in the background). From left to right, they are Martin Reade, John West, Les Bowman and Bill Burrows, the Leyland ST workshop foreman, then Bill Price. On the other side of the car, they are Brian Moylan, Gerald Wiffen and, at the front, 'Fast Eddie' Burnell, who, according to Bill Price, could sometimes show the professional drivers a clean pair of Dunlops. (Bill Price)

KDU 497N, showing off the striking patriotic red, white and blue livery on a white bodyshell, poses outside the Leyland ST building at the MG factory in Abingdon, May 1976. (Bill Price)

The first event was the Welsh Rally of 6–9 May 1976, a matter of days before the TR7 was due to make its European debut, and two cars were entered for Pond (Richards) and Culcheth (Syer) respectively. Early excitement turned to disappointment when the Culcheth car succumbed to overheating problems, and after that Pond lasted a few more stages before also retiring, in this case with zero oil pressure and a very poorly engine. The next event was the Scottish Rally, and the TR7 duo was entered after suitable modifications had been made to the head gaskets and a Broadspeed-designed brace to reinforce the base of the cylinder block. Unfortunately, both cars succumbed during the event: Pond's car retired on the tenth stage with a blown piston, while Culcheth's engine expired the following day, although it had given early notice of its imminent expiry the previous evening.

Next up in the calendar should have been the Jim Clark Rally, but, with the strong evidence of something fundamentally wrong, it was decided to miss that event and focus on being ready for the Burmah Rally. Suitably modified, with suspension upgrades as well as improved engines, the cars started promisingly although Pond crashed out on the first stage. Culcheth survived unscathed, and achieved a reasonably respectable, but unremarkable, sixteenth place overall. Bill Price says that Brian Culcheth had been asked to ensure that the car should 'get to the finish, whatever you do!' in order to give the sponsors some assurance that the new TR7 could at least finish an event. That improved fortunes were coming became clearer when the cars competed in the Isle of Man – with the benefit of the five-speed 77mm Rover gearbox for the first time – and helped Leyland Cars secure the Manufacturers' Team prize, Pond and Culcheth finishing in third and fifth place respectively, while a Dolomite Sprint came in ninth.

Less successful for the team was the next outing at Northumberland's Lindisfarne rally: Pond finished ninth and Culcheth retired. There then followed the 'Castrol 76', in which the duo came in third (Pond) and eighth (Culcheth, in KDU 497N) before the focus turned to the

Triumphant Hero: Tony Pond

Tony Pond seen on the winner's rostrum, champagne bottle suitably uncorked and in the process of discharging its contents, at the end of the Rothmans Rally Manx Stages in May 1980. (Bill Price)

In an era when great European rally drivers seemed inevitably to have Scandinavian names, Tony Pond was an exception to the rule, and someone whose success on the circuits made him a hero of British motor sports fans. From promising beginnings in a Hillman Imp in 1967, Pond developed a fondness for the products of Chrysler UK as well as Leyland – often eschewing the potentially more lucrative contracts that he undoubtedly could have secured elsewhere. His loyalty was just one of many traits that endeared him to motor sports fans and British manufacturers alike. In 1974 Pond entered the World Rally Championship arena behind the wheel of an Opel in the RAC Rally, but for many (not surprisingly, Triumph fans among them) one of the early highlights of his career was his association with the TR7 and TR7 V8. In later years he would drive Vauxhall Chevettes, Lotus Sunbeams and the MG Metro 6R4 with distinction – the latter arguably leading to the highpoint of his career, when he came third in the 1985 RAC Rally – but it was his exploits in the Triumph that made him almost a household name.

Tony was all things to all men: a brilliant driver, an excellent development consultant, a consummate gentleman with time for everyone and, despite his often reserved nature, he had a wicked sense of mischief. I once had the exciting experience of being 'chauffeured' round Castle Combe in a car that Tony's company had been working to improve. In the rear seat of the car was a Japanese lady journalist, whose face remained inscrutable throughout the experience but whose white knuckles said a great deal when we emerged from the car afterwards. Tony continued to provide a highly regarded service to his old friends at what had become Rover Group, and then MG Rover. He had a memorable reunion with his old TR7 V8 warhorse in 1998, but sadly he succumbed to pancreatic cancer, aged 56, on 7 February 2002.

Just occasionally a photographer is on hand when something catastrophic occurs – such as here, on the Glen Kinglass military road during the June 1976 Scottish Rally, with Brian Culcheth airborne as his engine explodes; parts of it are visible through the smoke beneath the car. This car had already had one illegal engine swap: the replacement clearly fared little better than the original unit. (D. J. Berry, courtesy Bill Price)

John Buffum is handily available – as a spectator – to lend a hand at the February 1977 Mintex Rally to Brian Culcheth/ Johnstone Syer in OOE 937R, which went on to finish seventeenth overall. (Bill Price)

RAC Rally. An entry in the intervening period at the Raylor Rally actually gave the TR7 (KDU 498N) its first overall UK victory, a cause for celebration and increased optimism. The RAC Rally was a further mixed blessing: Culcheth overcame serious damage that necessitated a new gearbox to come in ninth overall, but despite some exciting dices with Pentti Airikkala's Escort earlier in the event, Tony Pond's car eventually came to grief and was forced to retire.

The second season for the TR7, 1977, saw Tony Pond and Fred Gallagher competing in a single TR7 (KDU 498N) at Belgium's Boucles de Spa Rally on 7 February. The conditions were pretty dreadful on this 500-mile event, but Pond and Gallagher wrestled with their car, fitted for the first time with rear disc brakes, to produce the TR7's first international win. The weather was hardly better in the Mintex International: Pond finished in third place (KDU 498N again) while Culcheth and Syer in OOE 937R recovered from an off to finish in seventeenth place. The Tour of Elba saw Pond in a new car, OOE 938R, while Culcheth/Syer piloted KDU 497N. Pond finished third, but Culcheth was forced to retire.

The 1977 Welsh Rally saw both entries fail to finish: Pond due to an early crash and Culcheth due to major oil loss in the closing stages. Next up was the Esso Lombard Scottish Rally, with Pond/Gallagher (OOE 938R again) and Culcheth/Syer finishing in second and ninth places (and winning the Team Prize). This was followed by a further foray across the Channel, with an entry in the 24-hour Ypres race, although sadly neither car crossed the finishing line. Also on the continent, but in France this time, Culcheth brought home his car to fourth place in the gruelling Mille Pistes Rally. The West German Hunsruck Rally saw more bad luck for the team when both cars failed to finish. Nearer to home, the 1977 Isle of Man Rally saw Pond's engine give up the ghost, but Culcheth drove extremely well to secure a very respectable second overall in the face of some fine opposition.

The 21ème Tour de Corse (5–6 November) was another event of mixed fortunes, with Pond's gearbox failing and Culcheth/Syer finishing in eleventh owing to a slipping clutch. Culmination of the rally season as usual was the Lombard RAC Rally (20–24 November); for this event Leyland Cars pulled out all the stops, entering a four-car team, inducting new team members Markku Saaristo with co-driver Ian Grindrod (driving SCE 645S, a car built by Safety Devices of Newmarket). Pond/Gallagher finished in eighth position and Saaristo/Grindrod managed thirty-seventh after rolling their car. Brian Culcheth/Johnstone Syer retired with a broken wheel. So ended the first two seasons of the TR7 rally programme – something of the proverbial 'curate's egg' – but Leyland had a new weapon up its sleeve for 1978, the Rover V8 engine, the story of which is told below.

Rallying in America

Although circuit racing continued to be the primary interest in North America, by the mid-1970s there was a growing interest in the rally scene prompted by the established long-distance rallies that had developed in Europe and led to international jaunts that generated worldwide interest. Alongside the SCCA was the North American Rally Racing Association (NARRA), which was the brainchild of David Ash, with an excellent racing and marketing pedigree of his own. Ash had become a good friend of the Leonia people through his MG racing exploits at Sebring and his job as advertising manager for one of the leading US distributors of British cars. More recently, Ash had been editor and publisher of the highly acclaimed SCCA magazine *Sports Car*. At the time that the TR7 came on the scene, however, Ash had moved on to set himself up as an agent and promoter of North American motor sports talent.

Under Ash's wing was John Buffum, a highly talented American 'pro-rally' driver who had cut his teeth in European rallying before returning to the USA, where he had demonstrated great prowess behind the wheel and started his own business, Libra Racing, in the early 1970s. It was not long before Ash was on the phone to Mike Cook and John Dugdale at Leonia, making a pitch for Buffum to drive for Leyland. As Cook explained in his book *Triumph in America*: 'David's pitch was simple: Pro Rallying is just beginning in North America, and the first manufacturer to get involved will get the publicity benefits. Winning is the way to get publicity and hiring John Buffum's Libra International team is a guarantee of winning. NARRA offers the best series.' Cook was impressed by this show of confidence, and it took only a couple more meetings with Ash and Buffum for the Leonia team to be won over.

In order to get the TR7 rallying effort under way as quickly as possible, Leonia ordered a pair of TR7 Sprint rally cars direct from the Motorsports division at Abingdon, for delivery by April 1977: these were much like those of the UK rally effort, although they were naturally left-hand drive. One car would be for Buffum and his co-driver (his ex-wife, Vicki Gauntlett), while the other was intended for the Canadian driver Walter Boyce. In the meantime, Buffum and 'Vicki' (as she was always referred to in official placings) continued to score driver and co-driver championship points by winning events like the Rallyist Borax Bill Memorial and 100 Acre Wood in their Porsche 911.

TR7 16-Valve Rally Engine

From the outset British Leyland had intended that the 'Sprint' version of the slant-four engine (as marketed in the Triumph Dolomite Sprint) would be offered in a 'TR7 Sprint' (*see* Chapter 5). It therefore was entirely logical that the motor sport version of the TR7 should use basically the same engine. Naturally, the rally specification version of the Sprint engine was some way removed from the 'cooking' version seen in the road-going Dolomite Sprint. Twin Weber 45 DCOE carburettors fed through a Don Moore-developed inlet manifold and, aided by a Don Moore camshaft and Janspeed extractor exhaust, power output was 220bhp at 7,000rpm. At first, this fed through to the driven wheels via a Triumph four-speed gearbox with Laycock overdrive, although before long the sturdier Rover 77mm five-speed was adopted. It was a promising start, and would undoubtedly have helped the marketing effort for the road-going TR7 Sprint version originally planned for 1978, but when plans for such a model evaporated – and indeed as the long-term future of the Triumph Sprint engine came into doubt – then the existence of the Rover V8 unit, promising a power output of 300bhp at the same 7,000rpm, made the choice of substitution for the 3.5-litre unit a foregone conclusion.

Eight wins in the first season for the TR7 rally car brought John Buffum the SCCA Championship and the North American Cup.

The TR7 debut was at the NARRA Olympus Rally in Tacoma, Washington, on 23–24 April 1977, followed a fortnight later by the NARRA Rim of the World Rally at Palmdale, California (7–8 May). Buffum had a patchy start to his association with the TR7, however, failing to finish four of their first events, but he more than made up for this by winning all but one of the next seven – events such as La Jornada Trabajosa at Bakersfield, California (24–26 June 1977) – helping him secure first place in the SCCA Pro Rally championship and the Canadian equivalent.

In Canada, at the Rally Critérium du Québec (14–18 September 1977, and part of that year's World Rally Championship) Buffum finished in fourth place behind two Fiat Abarth 131s (driven by Salonen/Markkula and Lampinen/Andreasson) and Roger Clark/Jim Porter in a Ford Escort RS. The 'Press On Regardless' Pro Rally Championship event at Houghton, Michigan, took place on 5–6 November and saw Buffum and 'Vicki' finishing in third place.

Buffum began the 1978 season, now with his new regular co-driver Doug Shepherd, as he meant to proceed, winning the Rallyist Borax Bill Memorial at California City, California (18–19 February) and the next event, the 100 Acre Wood at Rolla, Missouri (4–5 March). The Susquehannock Trail Pro Rally at Wellsboro, Pennsylvania, on 10–11 June was another clear victory and the

Sunriser 400 Forest Rally at Chillicothe, Ohio (23–24 September) saw the pair finish in third place, followed by second at the Nor'Wester Pro Rally at Issaquah, Washington, on 7–8 October. At that same event, at which Buffum's lead in the 1978 championship became virtually unassailable, John Smiskol and Walt Krafft were just behind him in a Datsun 260Z; in 1979 they would compete in a TR7.

Buffum decided to sit out the Valvoline 20 Mule Team Stages (Bakersfield, California; 13–15 October) but he was determined to try for an event win at the 1978 'Press On Regardless' (4–5 November). Buffum achieved his objective, taking overall victory at this particular event he had been coveting for nine years. The last event of the season was the Nevada Rally at Las Vegas, Nevada (19–21 November), but Buffum again stayed home, his championship already won.

It was an encouraging start, but Buffum was already evangelizing about the TR7 V8, having gained some experience of Leyland Motorsport's new weapon through some invitation drives in Europe.

V8 Power: The European TR7 V8 Rally Programme

Just as the fact that the V8 engine would fit under the bonnet of a TR7 was one of the worst-kept secrets in the British motor industry, so it was obvious that the TR7 motor sports programme could move onto a whole new plane with the all-alloy Rover powertrain. The funny thing was that for marketing reasons (the sales people wanted to shift TR7s from the showrooms) coupled with the embarrassing delays with the production V8-powered TR7, Leyland people insisted to the bitter end that their new motor sport contender should always be referred to as the 'TR7 V8' rather than the obvious 'TR8' name that was just as much a poorly kept a secret. Development of the first TR7 V8 rally car took place using KDU 496N as test vehicle, with development input by Tony Pond.

Homologation of the TR7 V8 was expected for 1 April 1978, but this meant that regular TR7s

John Buffum

*John Buffum, pictured in 1979 (*Road & Track*)*

John 'JB' Buffum (born 4 October 1943) is rightly celebrated as the most successful United States rally driver, with a total of 11 national titles and 115 victories under his belt. His interest in the sport began back in 1964, when he agreed to navigate for a friend in an MGA; within three years he was winning events in his own right. After college, Buffum joined the United States Army as a mechanical engineer and found himself posted to Western Germany. It was during his stay in Europe that Buffum first witnessed World Rallies and, smitten by the prospect of participating, he bought himself a Porsche 911T in which he competed locally and internationally within Europe, finishing in twelfth place at Monte Carlo in 1969. Early in his career his 'press-on' style led to him being given the nickname of 'Stuff 'em Buffum'.

Upon his return to the United States he made a name for himself in the early days of the emerging sport of Pro-Rallying, driving Mini Coopers and Ford Escorts (both something of a novelty in North America). This brought him to the attention of David Ash. By that point, Buffum and his ex-wife Vicki (they divorced in 1974, but stayed together as a rally team) had been rallying together in a Porsche 911 since 1975, and were fresh from winning three North American rallies, gaining the NARRA national championship, and only narrowly missed doing the same at the SCCA championship. Buffum remained loyal to the Triumph TR7 and TR8 rallying effort right through until BL pulled the plug late in 1981: his talents were clearly coveted by others, and he went on to further success with the seminal four-wheel-drive Audi Quattro before semi-retirement from driving in 1988. His business Libra International is still active, however, and builds and prepares cars for third parties, building on an unrivalled North American rallying legacy.

had to be used for the first couple of events. All the cars had been subjected to a cosmetic makeover for the new season: in place of a white bodyshell with blue bonnet/sides and red flashes, the new livery was a red bodyshell, still with broadly similar blue detailing but white flashes in lieu of red. KDU 497N and OOM 512R were converted to V8 power, while a new car during the year was SJW 540S. The TR7 V8 made its official debut at a memorable event, the Texaco Rallysprint, held in Wales and shown on BBC television, giving Leyland's new rally weapon maximum exposure. Tony Pond did not disappoint either the crowds or the audience back home, finishing a very respectable second to the Ford Escort RS of the all-conquering Hannu Mikkola.

Good fortune seemed to shine for the TR7 V8 when Tony Pond and co-driver Fred Gallagher secured an impressive victory at the Granite City rally in Scotland, although there was a portent of problems to come when gremlins struck during the Welsh Rally and forced the car to retire. The 19th Esso Lombard Scottish Rally (3–7 June) did not seem much happier, for Pond's car rolled over, fortunately without significant injury to the occupants. The European debut for the TR7 V8 was at the 24-hour race at Ypres, and Pond did not disappoint in front of the Belgian crowd, leading from the start through to eventual victory. The event, along with some of the subsequent successes, was later immortalized in a publicity film, *Sporting Triumphs*. Back home in England, Pond drove the car in the Borders Rally, finishing a reasonable fourth following a puncture early in the rally. Next up was the Burmah Rally: as well as Pond competing, John Buffum also had an opportunity to drive a second car. Pond retired partway through, but Buffum stayed the course and finished an honourable eighth.

Next up was the Ulster Rally. Despite the promise of an early lead, engine problems put

The new livery – still patriotic, but based on a red base instead of white – was also associated with the period of British Airways sponsorship and the move to V8 power. Note how the Leyland ST sign over the door has faded in two years since the photo seen earlier! (Bill Price)

out driver Derek Boyd, with Fred Gallagher as his co-driver. Two factory cars were entered in the Manx Rally: Tony Pond and Fred Gallagher in one, and Derek Boyd driving with Roy Kernaghan navigating. Pond romped home in an impressive first place but the Boyd/Kernaghan car expired with engine trouble when the oil pump drive belt failed, leading to the engine running on its bearings. In the subsequent rally report in *Motor* magazine, headed 'The Triumph

of Man', Pond unwittingly gave a public hint of the tensions in the Leyland camp when he made a point of how he felt he had been vindicated in insisting upon an entry in the Isle of Man: 'at the start of the year I told them that there were two rallies which we must concentrate on because we could win: Ypres and the Manx. They weren't convinced – but now we've got them both'. In an interview for *TR Action*, Pond told Steve Redway of the failure of the dry sump pumps to get oil from the boot-mounted sumps to the engine, so causing oil starvation and eventual bottom end failures.

Meanwhile, in North America, John Buffum had a chance to try a TR7 V8 at the 6ème Critérium Molson du Québec rally (13–17 September 1978), and this helped convince him that the forthcoming TR8 would be essential to his future rally programme. At the same event, Jean-Paul Pérusse/Louis Belanger in their Triumph TR7 finished in fifth place with a time of 5hrs 36mins 56secs. Although he was not able to gain points in the TR7 V8 in Quebec, Buffum would hardly be alone in his enthusiasm.

Despite lessons learned at the Manx, oil-feed troubles continued to haunt the TR7 V8 on the Lindisfarne Rally, as Pond was forced to retire with engine failure. Derek Boyd fared no better on the Cork Rally, although in his case

The distinctive 'British Airways' livery of the Simo Lampinen car. (Jeff Herbert)

The Lombard RAC Rally of November 1978 saw a team of three factory TR7 V8 cars; this is SJW 533S, wearing number seven, and piloted by Tony Pond and Fred Gallagher, who failed to finish due to an accident. (Bill Price)

it was transmission failure that ended his drive. An unpleasant experience on the Tour de Corse led to both cars entered (Pond/Gallagher and Therier/Vial) being forced to retire after losing all their gearbox oil, both cars mysteriously having 'lost' their gearbox drain plugs. This was put down to sabotage in the *parc fermé*, but the culprits were never apprehended.

The Lombard RAC Rally (19–23 November) saw a three-car entry with, for the first time, British Airways sponsorship demonstrated by the airline's logo emblazoned across the bonnet. First up was Pond/Gallagher, while the other cars were driven by Simo Lampinen and Mike Broad, and Norwegian John Haugland (better known as a Škoda rallyist) with co-driver Ian Grindrod. Lampinen eventually retired, but Pond finished fourth (behind a trio of RS Escorts) and the Haugland/Grindrod came in twelfth.

Before the second year of the TR7 V8 programme Tony Pond left the Leyland Team for Talbot, where he had some good drives in the Talbot (née Chrysler) Sunbeam Lotus. There were undoubtedly worries within Leyland about the future of the V8 sports car programme, for the Speke crisis had seen the introduction of the road-going TR8 delayed indefinitely. Production of the TR7 had only recently been transferred to its new home at Canley, yet by the turn of the year there was still an air of uncertainty.

Nevertheless, the largest number of factory cars yet were working the circuits in 1979, including TUD 682T, TUD 683T, SJW 540S, SJW 546S, SJW 548S and the by now almost 'veteran' OOM 512R. In the Mintex Rally, Per Eklund and co-driver Mike Broad drove through thick snow to finish an impressive second overall. The first major event, as usual, was the Welsh Rally, which saw the car of Simo Lampinen and Ian Grindrod finishing in twelfth despite a collision. Derek Boyd and Fred Gallagher had a nasty experience in the Galway Rally when a major crash hospitalized Gallagher. The Rallysprint concept was repeated in 1979, although this time the TR7 V8 had to make do without the popular draw of Tony Pond. In the event, however, Per Eklund proved to be more than adequate a substitute as

Jean-Luc Therier in his TR7 V8 during the Boucles de Spa in Belgium, February 1979: the car eventually retired with distributor problems. (Bill Price)

Derek Boyd was driving the Chequered Flag TR7 V8 SJW 533S in the Galway Rally in February 1979 when he crashed heavily into a stone wall. Co-driver Fred Gallagher was seriously injured and was helicoptered to hospital. Bill Price says that the car was found to be 6in (150mm) narrower as a consequence of the impact. (Bill Price)

he wrestled the car to an impressive win over the mighty Stig Blomqvist's Saab Turbo.

Next up was the Esso Lombard Scottish Rally. All three of the current cars were entered: Per Eklund (co-driven by Hans Sylvan) finished third and Simo Lampinen thirteenth, but Graham Elsmore had the misfortune to be forced to retire when his engine boiled. August saw better fortune for Elsmore as he won the Peter Russek Manuals Rally, a Welsh event that had evolved the previous year from the Tour of Epynt. Venturing nearer the Arctic Circle, the Leyland team entered a pair of cars in the Finnish 1000 Lakes World Championship Rally. Wisely using the

36-year-old Simo Lampinen is seen here passing under a bridge crowned with spectators during the August 1979 '1000 Lakes'. When the Finn experienced distributor problems, Bill Price met him out on the stage and passed him a replacement rotor arm. Unfortunately, later problems led Lampinen to entrust his car to some Finnish mechanics who had little or no experience with the V8 firing order, and his rally ended. (Bill Price)

talents of Scandinavian drivers Per Eklund and Simo Lampinen to the full, Eklund – in a car with an experimental Pierburg fuel-injected V8 set-up – overcame engine bay heat problems to finish a reasonable eighth, while Lampinen's car eventually expired with engine ancillary failures. This event was also the first time that an ex-MIRA engineer, Richard Hurdwell, was on hand as a new recruit to bring a new slant to the TR7 V8 suspension set-ups.

The Lindisfarne Rally saw Graham Elsmore come home in eighth while the Manx Rally the following month saw Elsmore/Gallagher finish a highly respectable third. Although there had been a plan to enter the TR7 V8 in the Ulster Rally in October, this was dropped the previous month because, as *Motor* put it, 'the combination of the patriotically painted Triumph and the current Irish situation were powerful deterrents that could not be ignored by the team'.

Moving to southern Europe, the San Remo Rally brought no joy for the pair of cars entered for Lampinen and Eklund, both vehicles expiring. Back home at the RAC, Leyland entered a team of four cars, although the results were undistinguished at thirteenth, sixteenth, seventeenth and a retirement for Terry Kaby. Playing out in the background, and undoubtedly on the minds of the team, was the drawn-out saga of the threatened closure of the MG factory at Abingdon, which was also home of the BL Motorsports team.

Welcome news for Triumph fans in 1980, however, was the news that Tony Pond had agreed to return to the Leyland camp, while another British hero recruited to the TR7 V8 camp was the distinguished rally veteran Roger Clark, probably best known for his prowess in the early days of the rallying Ford Escort. Per Eklund remained onboard, helping ensure that the team

Scrutineering on the seafront during the San Remo Rally in September 1979. TUD 683T (on the right) was the TR7 V8 of Simo Lampinen and Fred Gallagher; both this car and the other one, to the left of the photo (XJO 414V, piloted by Per Eklund and Hans Sylvan), retired during the event. (Bill Price)

had credibility with fans and sponsors alike. Also good news was the fact that the much-delayed Triumph TR8 road car was in pre-production, with an official launch in the United States on 1 May 1980 and the promise of European sales to follow, although as the TR8 had not been announced on the UK market the rally cars were still officially 'TR7 V8s'.

For the new season, the main cars comprised HRW 250V, HRW 251V, UYH 863S and TUD 683T (the last of which became JJO 931W later in the year). With the New Year fuel injection experiments were abandoned and four carburettors were adopted instead. Mixed fortune followed the team early in the year: in the 13th Rallye de Portugal Vinho do Porto (4–9 March), starting and finishing in Estoril, both cars retired – Eklund/Sylvan with a fuel pump failure and Pond/Gallagher with engine failure. Per Eklund finished second in the Daily Mirror Rallysprint in HRW 251V, while Pond in UYH 863S retired due to accident damage. The Rothmans Stages Rally on the Isle of Man saw Pond/Gallagher clean up in UYH 863S, aided by eleven-inch wide Michelins on the rear.

A wet Esso Lombard 1980 Scottish Rally in June featured the three teams: Pond/(Gallagher), Clark/(Jim Porter, his regular co-driver) and Eklund/(Sylvan). Pond finished in fourth (beaten by a brace of Escorts and an Opel Ascona), while Clark's car (XJO 414V, in Sparkrite livery) finished ninth. Eklund was forced to retire with, as *Motor* later recorded, 'a large hole in the block of his TR7 V8 at the end of Stage 19'. Returning to Ypres in June 1980 after a sabbatical the previous year, Tony Pond drove TUD 683T magnificently in damp conditions to overall victory, although Eklund had an accident and later his car expired with transmission failure. The 1000 Lakes was next (29–31 August), an event in which Eklund/Sylvan finished third overall, although Timo Makinen retired after running out of fuel between stops. The 1980 Manx International Trophy Rally was an excellent outing for Pond/Gallagher in TUD 683T, the pair vanquishing the opposition for a well-earned overall victory.

The Lombard RAC Rally (16–19 November) would prove to be the final outing for the TR7 V8 under the BL banner. Four cars were entered for the event, one of which, HRW 251V, was driven by John Buffum (with co-driver Ian Grindrod). A wet and slippery first stage took in a scenic run through Longleat, home of a famous family of lions, and, much to the TV commentators'

Testing on local roads in Finland, in the first week of August 1980, ahead of the 1000 Lakes Rally – here with Timo Makinen 'yumping' the car while local volunteers (out of view in this photo) armed with two-way radios kept careful watch for local traffic. After three days of testing with alternative tyres, the final choice was for 15-inch Michelins. The reward for this effort? Third place overall at the September event. (Bill Price)

Towards the end of its factory rallying career, the TR7 was tried with fixed rectangular headlamps, courtesy of the Vauxhall Chevette and Jim Oates at the Cowley body section – as seen here on the Tour of Cumbria in September 1980, with Tony Pond shepherding UYH 863S to second overall. (Bill Price)

Roger Clark drove the Sparkrite liveried TR7 V8 XJO 414V in the October 1980 'Castrol' Welsh Rally, seen here at a service stop. Clark eventually retired with an oil pump problem. (Bill Price)

amusement, Tony Pond (in JJO 931W – effectively TUD 683T – with Fred Gallagher as co-driver) slid off the road and crashed into one of the lions' feeding tables. While the lions made alternative dining arrangements, Pond's car, with a severely modified roof, had to undergo some improvised panel-work.

Undaunted, Pond and his car made a good recovery, despite heavy rain and lashing hail at Kielder Forest, to finish eventually in seventh place. Pond told Steve Redway that the strength of the TR7 roof structure was paramount in 'shovelling' the railway sleepers, from which the pen had been constructed, over the roof, consequently limiting the damage to car and crew. Without such a strong roof the TR7 and its crew would have no doubt been out of this particular rally. Meanwhile, however, Roger Clark (driving what would prove to be his last 'professional' team event, with co-driver Neil Wilson) retired in Wales with oil pump failure; the cars of both Buffum and Eklund also expired.

October 1980 saw the introduction of the new Austin Mini Metro, seen as the best hope of salvation for BL as a whole. By this time, too, the last MGB sports cars were passing down the line at the famous Abingdon factory, following the failure during the summer of the Aston Martin Lagonda Consortium's bid to buy MG from BL. With the end of the line for the MGB and Abingdon, it was also obvious that the Competitions Department would soon be looking for a new home. With the uncertain future of the whole of BL's small–medium sports car programme, the major importance of the new Metro, and the North American JRT sales team's reluctant acceptance that their future fortunes undoubtedly lay with the Jaguar marque, it was perhaps inevitable that the motor sports focus would shift away from the TR7 and towards the new Austin hatchback, which before long would spawn MG-badged off-shoots. At the same time, the opportunity could be taken to 'downsize', 'relocate' and 'restructure' the Competitions Department – euphemisms for redundancies and the injection of new blood.

The formal announcement came in November, and brought with it a cutback in staff from

Alongside the TR8, the TR7 – in convertible guise – continued to do well in SCCA Production Class racing, winning Class 'D' for the 1979 championship in the guise of Lee Mueller, seen here driving his black and silver car No. 11 to victory at Road Atlanta in October 1979. The car was built and prepared by Huffaker Engineering.

forty-seven to thirty and the closure of Leyland ST, the former 'Special Tuning' motor sports arm that sold parts to privateers. The official reasons were financial constraints and a desire by the company to reshape its programme during 1981 in anticipation of changes in international regulations expected for the 1982 season. In due course the new team would become responsible for the MG Metro 6R4. Each of the BL rally cars would go on to have careers of varied distinction, but perhaps one of the more poignant events was when Tony Pond, driving JJO 931W, finished first overall in the Coys Historic Rallysprint at Silverstone in 1998, proving that both the old warhorse and its rider could still deliver the goods almost twenty years on.

One year after the closure announcement, the Lombard RAC Rally of 1981 (22–25 November) saw John Buffum competing in the same car that he had used in the 1980 event (HRW 251V) with British co-driver Neil Wilson, but this time the entry was under the sponsorship guise of Leycare, the warranty and service subsidiary of BL. Sadly the TR8 did not finish, due to engine problems; only 54 of the 151 starters finished the event, which was eventually won by Hannu Mikkola/Arne Hertz in an Audi Quattro, a model that Buffum would soon be rallying with considerable success in North America. HRW 251V was sold off and became the basis of a privateer rally effort in the guise of Mike Gibbon's F.G. Rallying.

TR8: Racing in North America with Group 44 Inc.

With the final arrival of the genuine Triumph TR8 in North America (described in more detail in Chapter 7), the motor sport opportunities in that market for the wedge widened even further, for now British Leyland could encourage direct comparisons with road-going cars available from Jaguar-Rover-Triumph dealer showrooms. Triumph racing activities by Group 44 Inc. had been suspended during 1978, allowing the organization to focus that year on a Jaguar-based racing effort, while others, such as Huffaker Engineering and various privateers, kept faithful to the TR7. Now the arrival of the TR8 gave a valid excuse for a fresh focus on Triumph, and

Key members of the Group 44 Inc. team at the time of the TR7 and TR8 campaigns were (left to right) Glen Sullivan, John Lyster and Jay Fox. (Bob Tullius)

two of the key people to capitalize on this association with the factory were Bob Tullius, through Group 44 Inc., and rally driver John Buffum.

The first Group 44 Inc. TR8 was actually constructed using a TR7 Coupé as its basis, although the transformation involved was so thorough that this is probably only of academic interest. Even so, the six-month build cost in the first half of 1979 was around $85,000. As alluded to earlier, transforming the standard TR7 shape into something that would work aerodynamically on the race circuit was quite a challenge. Group 44 Inc.'s sessions at Lockheed Corporation's wind tunnel in Marietta, Georgia, did not come cheaply ($600 per hour), but Tullius knew it was a necessary investment, as he explained to *Road & Track*: 'the learning experience at a place like that is incredible'. The TR8 was positioned in the wind tunnel in several alignments, including straight ahead and skewed, along with variations in ride height and rake. Eventually the solution involved a deep front spoiler and a massive whale-tail on

the back, providing the optimum compromise between downforce and drag.

As ever, Tullius's trusted cohorts Brian Fuerstenau and 'Lanky' Foushee were responsible for making the TR8 go and stay together. Under the bonnet (hood in US parlance) the normal 3.5-litre engine capacity was stretched to just under 4.0 litres to take advantage of the class limits. The first such engine ran in June 1979. Describing his philosophy to John Dinkel of *Road & Track*, Tullius explained: 'More than any other race car I've driven, this one has a balance and agility that are close to perfect.' Tullius compared the TR8 to the 1977 Group 44 Inc. Jaguar XJS, which had been sidelined to allow the Triumph project to take precedence:

The Jaguar had a lot more power, and you'd go along at 4,000rpm in 2nd, stand on the throttle, and it would light the rear tires. The TR8 is so nicely balanced, you come along at 3,500–4,000, punch it, and it simply moves out. Brian Fuerstenau and Lanky Foushee set it up this way, and its cornering, stopping ability and acceleration are all designed to work in concert. For instance, back in 1977 at Watkins Glen, we went around in 2:06.5 or so with the Jaguar. Now assume we would have gained 0.5 sec over the winter – if you don't, you're sitting around doing nothing – so figure a 2:06 flat for the Jaguar in 1978. The TR8 came out of the box that year, and did a 2:04.9. This is what I mean by balance and agility.

The bodywork was largely glass-reinforced plastic (GRP), using Styrofoam patterns expertly shaped by Group 44 Inc.'s fibreglass specialist, Virginian-born John Lyster. Although the large rear spoiler was fabricated from aluminium, the TR8 in race trim had GRP doors, bonnet, boot-lid and bumpers.

The TR8 made its racing debut in 1979, kicking off with Group 44 Inc.'s single car, bearing Tullius's traditional number '44', celebrating a maiden win at Western New York State's Watkins Glen Six-hour Trans-Am race on 7 July. The TR8 led its field by some ten laps, Tullius and Fuerstenau eventually finishing seventh overall (and the only non-Porsche 935 in the top nine places) at the head of the GT class. The sheer dominance of the GT class by the TR8 led to jealous mutterings from some of the opposition. Less than a month later, on 5 August, Tullius was back at Watkins Glen, winning a 100-mile race in his TR8.

There was similar success on 2 September at Elkhart Lake, Wisconsin, in the IMSA GTO class, with a hardly less impressive second place to follow at the IMSA GTO Atlanta on 22 September. Tullius won yet again on 14 October across the country at California's Laguna Seca Trans-Am event, although he had a hiccup at the Florida's Daytona IMSA '250 Mile Finale' Thanksgiving Day event on 25 November, failing to finish when he was involved in a collision with a slower car while fighting for the class lead with a Camaro. This latter event was a particular disappointment, for in the run-up to the Daytona race Tullius had clocked speeds of up to 178mph (286km/h) at the speedway. Tullius's successes at the Trans-Am events, however, were not welcomed by some of the regulars.

It was 1980, however, that saw the major push for the TR8, with Group 44 Inc. moving entirely from SCCA to IMSA. 'Victory is only a by-product', Tullius declared in a press release issued that spring, 'our aim this season is purely one of development'.

However, the first major World Championship race of 1980, the 19th Annual 24-Hour Pepsi Challenge at Daytona International Speedway (better known simply as the 'Daytona 24-Hours') on 2/3 February, with Tullius sharing the driving with John Kelly and John McComb, saw the car fail to finish, retiring after 171 laps with gearbox failure. Undaunted, that same car was entered at the famous 12-hours of Sebring the following month. Driven by Bob Tullius and new team member Bill Adam (Scots-born but naturalized Canadian), the TR8 finished well, winning its class (GTO) and finishing in sixth place overall – just twenty-three laps behind the overall race-winning Dick Barbour Racing Porsche 935K3.

Canadian Bill Adam co-drove the Group 44 Inc. TR8 on several occasions. (Bob Tullius)

Championship Struggle: Group 44 Inc.'s Move From Trans-Am To IMSA

In 1979 the opposition did not take the Triumph challenge from Bob Tullius lying down:

At the second Trans-Am race (having won the first) the entire field of Camaros and Corvettes threatened a boycott of the race if the SCCA did not do something to keep us from winning, so the SCCA, in their desperation to have a race, demanded we add 400lb to our car, which was not only absurd but where would I get 400lb of anything to put in a race car? I eventually talked them into letting us race that weekend and we would add the weight for the next event. We of course won that event, which added even more fuel to their rage, and with Mike Dale's permission we departed from the Trans-Am for IMSA GTO and were equally as successful there as we were in the Trans-Am! We actually won the Sebring 12 hour GTO class the next year. The only thing the SCCA accomplished was losing the best team and spectator draw they had for the Trans-Am series. As for failures, we had so few with those cars I cannot remember any.

As Tullius explained to *Road & Track* magazine, shortly after the switch to IMSA:

Racing is a business, an entertainment business, if you will, for the organizers. So there always remains the question of one team being in a position of total dominance. But with this TR8 in the Trans-Am series, it wasn't so much a matter of dominance as it was quality of the competition. Our car entered competition at 90 per cent of its development capability; the cars we were running against were only doing 60 per cent of theirs. All you've got to do is look at the specifications and potential numbers of the competition, and look at ours. If you were going to choose a race car to run, which would you rather have: 454cu in, 2,900lb and easy availability of parts right off the shelf, or pick some oddball car with 244cu in. and 2,550lb that no one had ever run before?

Tullius was to have his revenge, however. When he discovered that, on the basis of his two wins during the season, the TR8 could win third place Trans-Am Championship money, he ran the last race of the year at Laguna Seca in mid-October. The car actually complied with class weight restrictions of 2,500lb provided it had a full tank of fuel, but the rules were framed so that this weight only applied at post-race scrutiny. Tullius therefore built up a substantial 40-second lead, pitted near the end to refill and make up the overall weight and went on to win the race and the third place money. The SCCA changed the rule the next year to prevent this from recurring. As Tullius would later tell *AutoWeek*: 'I wasn't going to let those bastards get my money. We won the race, got our money and screwed the SCCA!'

All in all, Sebring 1980 was a very impressive result for Triumph, which also happened to be the highest-ever placing at Sebring for the marque and one that also put it on a par with MG, a marque that had been racing at Sebring from the first race in 1950 but had never bettered sixth at the finish.

Fresh from their Sebring class win, the Group 44 Inc. team returned to base to complete work on a second TR8 for Adam, although this time they used a TR8 'body in white' instead of a TR7 base. Essentially the same basic specification as Tullius's car, although building on the lessons learned so far, the second TR8 would allow the team to avoid having all their eggs in one basket. So focused were they that the team elected to miss the next event on their calendar, the IMSA race at Road

Atlanta, and instead aim for a debut at one of the forthcoming West Coast IMSA events, working their way back across country afterwards.

The first of these West Coast events, at California's Riverside International Raceway, saw the new car sit out the race but remain on hand as a mobile parts bin in case of need for Tullius's car '44'. Tullius and Adam shared driving responsibility in this six-hour endurance event, and appeared to be doing well until transmission problems forced Adam to bring the car in to the pit. It is recorded, perhaps apocryphally, that the operation to remove the transmission, extract the one sitting idle in the new car and fit it into car '44' took exactly 44 minutes. Despite this brave effort, Tullius finished the race in twenty-seventh place and without any points.

An interesting view into the tidy Group 44 Inc. pit area at Watkins Glen in 1980. In the foreground is Jay Fox and at left in the background is Brian Fuerstenau. (Wayne Ellwood)

A week later the Group 44 Inc. team raced both cars under clear blue skies at Laguna Seca, running flawlessly to finish second (Tullius in '44') and fifth (Adam in '4'). Tullius just failed to eclipse eventual class-winner Tony Garcia, but nevertheless stayed ahead of fierce class rival Luis Mendez in a Porsche Carrera.

The last Monday in May is always Memorial Day in the United States, and 26 May 1980 saw the team back on the east coast at Lime Rock Park's IMSA event in Lakeville, Connecticut. By the end of the brace of 45-minute sprint races, which saw a disappointing field of nineteen cars competing, the Group 44 Inc. TR8s had finished second (Tullius in '44') and third (Adam in '4'). At Lime Rock, Luis Mendez in his Porsche extracted revenge for being beaten at Laguna Seca, taking the class victory, but Group 44 Inc. at least had the compensation of knowing it had been a hard-fought race.

The following month Bill Adam was away in Europe, competing in the Le Mans 24-hour race (although the Canadian IMSA Corvette of Douglas Rowe with which he was involved failed to qualify – like the Le Mans TR8 Turbo, *see* below), and this meant that Tullius competed solo

at Brainerd in Minnesota on 15 June. Although he led the race for a while, engine maladies on the seventeenth lap, while he was lying second, prompted Tullius to make the conscious decision to rein in the engine and retire rather than compound the damage. Another month on, the Independence Day (4 July) race at Daytona Speedway – the night-time 'Paul Revere 250' – saw both cars fighting hard in the dark against the Porsche opposition to take first (Tullius) and second (Adam) in their GTP class. Ernesto Soto in his Porsche Carrera was beaten into third place.

Neither Triumph was seen at either Sears Point Raceway (California) or Portland (Oregon), but on 17 August Tullius and Adam in '44' took first in their GTO class (eighth overall) at the 1,000km 'Molson Canadian 1000 IMSA GT Series' race at Mosport Park, Bowmanville, near the northwest shore of Lake Ontario in Canada. The nearest car behind them in the GTO class was the eleventh-placed Porsche of Colombian Mauricio DeNarvaez and American Tony Garcia. Group 44 Inc.'s task was admittedly aided when the fancied contenders Luis Mendez and Mandy Gonzalez, in their Hector Huerta Racing Porsche Carrera, crashed out of the event after

The Group 44 Inc. TR8 at Mosport on 15 August 1980.
(Ron Kielbiski)

The Group 44 Inc. TR8 captured at the same event by Wayne Ellwood. (Wayne Ellwood)

fifty-six laps. Further down the field, at fifth place in GTO and twenty-second overall, were Canadians Peter Bulkowski and Bruce Kulczyk in their white and red TR8 (car number 42), which was partially built up by Group 44 Inc.

The 'Pabst 500' at Road America at Elkhart Lake on 31 August saw a new Porsche Carrera contender, driven by Dennis Aase and Bob Bergstrom, initially give every indication of being the class favourite until engine woes allowed them to be eclipsed by the TR8, which took an easy class victory.

Three weeks later, on 21 September, there was another close battle on the 2.54-mile circuit of the Road Atlanta (Braselton, Georgia) race with both the Porsche and Chevrolet opposition. Phil Currin in his Corvette beat the TR8 into a hard-fought second in the GTO class in the first heat of the two races. The second race was stopped after thirteen laps due to torrential rain and a number of crashes out on the circuit, Luis Mendez in his Porsche gaining the necessary points.

On 30 November 1980 the two-pronged Tullius-Adams powerhouse brought in a convincing first-second (Adam/Tullius) victory at the Daytona International Speedway, bringing a successful season to a close. The four-litre Triumphs were up against some high-profile local opposition powered by big-block Chevrolet V8s – particularly those of Carl Shafer and Craig Carter, who were not amused to find themselves outclassed by the 'limey' sports cars. Meanwhile, Phil Currin's Corvette had a tussle with Tullius's TR8 that led to both cars going in to the pits; Tullius returned but the Corvette retired hurt. The Camaros of Shafer and Carter were suffering too: Carter was forced to retire and Shafer had

to cope with tyre wear problems. Tullius drove like a demon to take the lead on the fifty-second lap, only to find three of his five forward gears had gone. Even so, Tullius kept the TR8 going, allowing teammate Adam to slip ahead to take the win, with Tullius cruising to a noble second. The result helped Tullius finish the season in an impressive second place overall, a year that had also seen Tullius win no less than a third of the fifteen events his team had entered.

Mike Dale was always impressed with the results of Group 44 Inc.'s handiwork:

> They turned the TR8 with its much better engine into a really good racecar. Its short wheelbase made its handling really quick and the Buick V8 provided plenty of torque. They would have won the Trans-Am Championship if it hadn't been legislated out of existence by the SCCA during the season. They did this by placing enormous weight penalties on the car as it kept embarrassing all the American Detroit iron by blowing them into the weeds.

Bob Tullius retains very fond and paternal memories of the racing Triumph wedge:

> The TR8 was mine, I loved it: along with the Jaguar XJS it was the most fun I ever had driving, and as is always the case, you tend to like the car that wins, particularly racing against the Corvettes and Camaros! They didn't know what hit them, they never expected a Triumph of any vintage to be competitive, let alone blow their doors off.

Moving forward to 1981, the Sebring race in March was encouraging, although the relentless pace of development of the opposition was telling. Of course by now Group 44 Inc. had two cars: number 44, piloted by Tullius himself and Bill Adam, and the second car, number 4, which at Sebring was piloted by John Kelly and Pat Bedard of *Car and Driver* magazine. Tullius and Adam came from behind at the final hour to finish in tenth place and fourth in class, while Kelly and Bedard led the class for a while, getting as high as seventh overall position in the eighth hour, before suffering gearbox troubles in the ninth hour that dropped them out of the top ten, but allowed them to limp home to twentieth place.

Patrick Bedard, who had raced previously at Sebring in 1978 and 1980 in, respectively, an Oldsmobile Cutlass and then, perhaps more convincingly, a Mazda RX-7, told the author how he felt honoured to have been invited to help out with one of the Group 44 Inc. race entries:

> Back in my racing days, Group 44 Inc., the US factory team, had entered two TR8s in the Sebring 12 Hours. I co-drove one of them. It was very quick and broadcast wonderful noises (Americans of my generation have a thing about V8s) and made me seem more talented than I was. It broke something after about eight or nine hours, but the drive and the team changed my life in a modest way (for the better). I was quick enough in the Triumph that Tullius called me later to stand in when they needed a third driver in the Jaguar XJR-7 GTP car. I drove for the Jag team through May 1984, when I took a mighty whack on the head at the Speedway and retired from racing.

Sadly, there would be no Group 44 Inc. TR8 at the 1982 Sebring race – or indeed at any other mainstream event that year – for by then 'BL Ltd' had killed the TR sports car, and Group 44 Inc. would soon be turning to the promising Jaguar XJR5. It would be left to others to maintain the Triumph honour on US race circuits. Tullius is puzzled at the approach sometimes adopted at the UK end:

> The Brits never, ever, made any effort to benefit by our efforts either during the Triumph or the Jaguar

days, while in both projects we were significantly more successful than they. They were in fact purposefully secretive as we were purposely open; in both cases they never spoke to us. In fact when Broadspeed introduced their Jaguar program for the European Series at the Geneva Motor Show it was the first time I had heard of the project; they went on to have enormous engine problems while we never had an engine failure. Oh well … the eventual result was that Group 44 Inc. did not participate in any British car company activities after 1987.

A Tale of Contrasts: Comparing the 'Race' and 'Rally' TR8

Bob Tullius and John Buffum naturally developed the TR8 platform in the very different directions of Trans-Am circuit racing and mixed-surface rally driving, but *Road & Track* magazine memorably brought the two strands of TR8 motor sport together at Riverside International Raceway in California for a comparison test in its November 1980 issue. The motor sports credentials of the TR8 were already established well before customers could take delivery of their factory cars, as *Road & Track* observed, 'Ironically, both cars were competing well before the stock TR8 ever made its appearance in US showrooms', pointing out that production delays on the part of British Leyland had meant that even before they tested the production TR8 for the June 1980 road test, John Buffum had already made a name for his TR8 Coupé in the SCCA's Pro-Rally series, and Bob Tullius's Group 44 Inc. TR8 had been transformed from a frontrunner in SCCA Trans-Am racing to an IMSA GTO car.

Buffum's Libra Racing rally TR8 car began life as a bare shell, which was then subjected to three solid weeks of work by two men who prepared it for the arduous shocks, stresses and strains that is a rally car's lot. Panel joints were subjected to the traditional seam-welds, much stronger than the basic production-specification spot-welds, while other parts of the structure were reinforced, including the integration of a specially tailored roll cage (with extensions bracing the

MacPherson struts) and the essential underside skid plate.

At the front end, the ostensibly standard-looking appearance of the suspension was deceptive, for stiffer reduced-diameter dual-rate springs (with an initial jounce rated at 140lb/in, but designed so that the rate increased to 240lb/in as the spring compressed) were matched to specially valved Bilstein shock absorbers, tuned to perform without aeration and overheating problems in the typically arduous rally conditions that the car would find itself. Whereas the road-going TR8, in common with the TR7, made do with simple lower trailing arms together with outwardly angled upper arms in order to cater for all normal road conditions, with Buffum's car (and Tullius's as well) the upper arms were relocated to a fore/aft position and thereby functioned solely as conventional trailing arms.

At the rear end, the rally car benefited from a Panhard rod connecting the right-hand side of the axle to a point on the left of the roll-cage structure. As Buffum's car was set up, *Road & Track* observed, it understeered less than the stock version, but was further from neutral than Tullius's road racer. In addition, testers John Dinkel and Dennis Simmanaitis found that the rally car's long suspension travel offered 'a ride that's much softer than the vision blurring road feel of Tullius' car'.

The contrast between rally and race car suspension philosophies was quite apparent on the two TR8s. 'Whereas Buffum can afford to set-and-forget, Tullius and the Group 44 Inc. crew spend a fair amount of practice time setting up the car's suspension for each particular course,' *Road & Track* reported. The differences also extended to the basic structure of the car too, for whereas the Buffum TR8 retained most of the 'stock' body structure, albeit substantially beefed-up, virtually the whole of the front end of the Tullius car was cut away in front of the firewall, with an extension of the roll cage ('NASCAR' style) instead, thereby providing new strong mounting points for the front suspension.

'Slots in the structure allow strut-tower camber changes, and shims permit slight alterations in caster', the magazine recorded, adding that the front track was reduced by three inches in order to accommodate the substantial 23.0 × 10.5-15 Goodyear Blue Streak tyres fitted to the front at the time of *Road & Track*'s test. Rear tyres at the time were 25.0 × 11.0-15s – like the fronts, mounted on Jongbloed alloy wheels – although

Road & Track subjected the Group 44 Inc. TR8 to a comparison test with John Buffum's rally TR8 in 1979, shortly before the TR8 road cars officially went on sale. (Road & Track)

Tullius would later move to sixteen-inch diameter instead of fifteen. The visual benefit was obvious: the standard thirteen-inch road wheels looked even more ridiculous on the TR8 than the TR7, so that car always looked rather 'undertyred'. However, at that time, wheel sizes greater than fourteen inches were still unusual, owing to the relative newness of low-profile tyre technology.

Both cars logically adopted TR8 rack-and-pinion steering, but they differed in detail. At Group 44 Inc. the rack was shortened and lowered to suit the modified front suspension and to clear the oil pan. Tullius also explored adopting power-assisted steering racing, which had worked well in his racing Jaguar XJ-S, believing 'It was one of the best speed secrets we had; frankly, I think a race driver can be a whole lot neater if he has power steering. We'd have mounted it on the TR8 but for clearance constraints.' For the rally car, power steering wasn't even on the radar.

Braking in both the race and rally cars was taken care of by Lockheed discs, front and rear – all vented on the Tullius car (12-inch diameter at the front and 11-inch at the rear) and vented at the front on Buffum's car (10.3 inches all round). In both cases, there was a facility to balance braking forces between the front and back, but in the rally car the adjustments could be made from within the cockpit. Tullius used a balance bar to fix the balance at around 70:30 front to rear, but the mixed surfaces experienced in rallying meant

that Buffum's braking requirements needed to be adjusted on the hoof. A typical balance at the start of an event would be 40:60 front/rear in the rally car, but as the car could spend much of its time travelling sideways, this would be adjusted during the stage. As Buffum explained to *Road & Track*:

> You play the brake pedal differently, depending on what attitude you want the car to take. Jump right on them, or apply the brakes gradually. Sometimes you turn the bias quite a bit to the rear, then when you get on them it'll bring the rear out to where you control it with the throttle.

The engines of both cars came in for extensive alterations, but again very different in execution. Tullius's car was originally aimed at SCCA Trans-Am events (see above) and so his TR8 engine – developed by Brian Fuerstenau – was extended through the adoption of a longer stroke to 3989cc. Unsurprisingly, this was to slot in at the upper end of the 4-litre class. Tullius explained the logic: 'You never want to run a car at the low end of a displacement class, and we spent a good six months of engine development before that car ever raced.' Fuerstenau added a 1.5-inch thick aluminium girdle sandwiched between the bottom of the block and the oil pan.

The Group 44 Inc. car used a special crankshaft to increase the stroke, and special pistons that gave a compression ratio of 12.5:1. For

Group 44 Inc. TR8 at Sebring

Race Number	Start on grid	Drivers	Top ten position (if applicable) at key points							Finish (O/A)	Finish (GTO class)	No of laps
			6 hr	7 hr	8 hr	9 hr	10 hr	11 hr	12 hr			
1980 SEBRING RACE												
44	21	Bob Tullius/ Bill Adam	10	9	9	7	6	6	6	6	1	230
1981 SEBRING RACE												
4	42	John Kelly/ Pat Bedard	10	9	7	7	–	–	–	20	9	187
44	41	Bob Tullius/ Bill Adam	–	–	–	–	–	–	10	10	4	208

Sebring: The Official History of America's Great Sports Car Race by Ken Breslauer (1996)

IMSA GTO – Final Positions

Position and name	Nationality	Car	Points
1979 GTO	**Winston GTO**		
11. Bob Tullius	USA	Triumph TR8	35
25. Brian Fuerstenau	USA	Triumph TR8	20
1980 GTO	**IMSA GTO Series**		
2. Bob Tullius	USA	Triumph TR8	135
4. Bill Adam	CDN	Triumph TR8	116
1981 GTO	**Camel GTO Championship**		
42. Bill Adam	CDN	Triumph TR8	10
42. Bob Tullius	USA	Triumph TR8	10
88. John Kelly	USA	Triumph TR8	2
88. Pat Bedard	USA	Triumph TR8 / Porsche 924 Carrera	2
1982 GTO	**Camel GTO Championship**		
52. Peter Bulkowski	CDN	Triumph TR8	10
52. Bob Armstrong		Triumph TR8	10

www.wspr-racing.com

shorter 'sprint' events, the engine gave 360bhp at 8,000rpm and 310lb ft of torque at 5,500rpm, but for endurance events the engine is slightly detuned via lower compression to around 330bhp. Fuel injection – via a European TR7 V8 intake manifold – adopted an electronic unit that according to Tullius was 'originally Lucas, with heavy doses of Kinsler and Fuerstenau'.

Unlike the race car, Buffum's car kept the standard TR8 3,528cc capacity, but the engine was a specially prepared Blueprinted unit built with 10.5:1 compression-ratio pistons and special cam and con-rods by Huffaker Engineering. Buffum adopted a Holley four-barrel carburettor, on the basis that this was better suited to rallying than fuel injection. 'There's choking dust to contend with,' he told *Road & Track*, 'I'd be worried about the usual bumps, crashes and bangs messing up the electronics.' Buffum also told *Road & Track* that he believed the power was 280bhp at 7,000rpm with torque of 245lb ft at 5,000rpm. Rather than outright power at the top end, Buffum was more concerned about mid-range torque to give him the flexibility he needed on mixed surfaces.

Road & Track encouraged Buffum to sample Tullius's car at Riverside. Buffum said afterwards: 'Wow. It's got gobs of power compared to my rally car. And, of course, its suspension is a lot stiffer, to the point that it really doesn't roll when you get sideways. Sort of like driving a go kart, although the TR8 traits are still there.' Tullius didn't get to return the favour with a meaningful drive, for the rally car was obviously not set up for the high-speed sections at Riverside.

Both, however, drove the standard TR8 that *Road & Track* had brought along as a yardstick. Tullius said of the stock TR8:

It has a lot of punch at the low end, but understandably it fades pretty quickly above 5,000rpm. As for handling, it's as neat as a pin through the fast corners and switchbacks, but when things get tighter it wants to understeer, and you have to feather the throttle to neutralize it a bit. I like the steering better than my race car's because it's power-assisted. As you know, the Jaguar had power assist, and I'm completely comfortable with it at racing speeds.

Tullius wasn't overly put off by the suspension compromises of the road car:

It doesn't bother [you], because you compensate for it. Besides, I've never really been an advocate of what's called classic sports car handling. I enjoy driving, but I like being comfortable at the same time. I prefer a car that has a compromise, if you will, of ride and handling.

Buffum, meanwhile, said:

> [The stock TR8] handles similarly to all TRs. There's some initial understeer that you can balance by tipping on and off the throttle. Play the throttle and steering wheel together, and it'll go where you want. In general, though, the stock car has more initial understeer than mine, and mine has more than Bob's.

OTHER US TR8 RACERS

Although the highest-profile racers of the TR8 were undoubtedly the professional Group 44 Inc. team, a number of other teams upheld the Triumph honour during and, in some cases after, the comparatively narrow window of its career. Among them was Huffaker Engineering, who built a TR8 coupé, as did Slagle Racing.

After the Runoffs in 1978, Mike Dale found a buyer for Slagle Racing's old TR7 race car (Overseas Motors in Fort Worth, Texas) and offered help with a TR8 project to Ken Slagle, who explains, 'We were given a coupé "body in white" (bare body) and the few stock parts needed to build a race car. It was surprising how little original equipment went into a "production" race car, even then.'

Slagle farmed out the fabrication of the roll-cage and suspension pieces and concentrated on trying to manage that as well as engine development:

> Once again, Group 44 was a lot of help, but since their program had shifted to the professional series, we had very different specifications on engine preparation. I had John Caldwell (a motor builder for several of the Datsun/Nissan racers who had gotten to be a good friend despite our different allegiances) build one engine to get us started, and then took over the engine development program after that. (This first engine was quite 'de-tuned', and I was never sure if that was to have a good starting point for further development, or to keep me from going too fast!)

Slagle raced the new TR8 coupé four times in 1979, finishing second in all four to four different

cars ('but I got hit by the same car in each race!'). Then, right after qualifying at Watkins Glen, came a body blow from the SCCA:

> The car was disqualified from production car racing since not enough cars had been imported into the US to meet the homologation requirements. I was a bit annoyed that we'd gotten 'screwed' over a simple rule, but a bit relieved since the car was not very competitive, and was scary to drive at high speed.

At this point, the new convertible TR7 and TR8 were on the stocks, and provided a new option for racers. Slagle Racing saw this as an opportunity:

> British Leyland (or whatever their name was at that time!) wanted me to cut the roof off the coupé to race the following season when the convertible version would be available, but I refused, saying that we'd learned enough by then to build a much better roadster from the ground up.

The team received a new body in August, and had eight or nine months to build what would be their last race car. Slagle hired a friend to work with him part time: 'Together we did the entire car from the ground up. (I'd always done all my own engine work, suspension design, body work and painting, and so on, but this was the first time that I designed and built the roll-cage, suspension attachments, and so forth)'. Slagle had a good feeling about the new open TR8:

> The car was a dream right from the start! We had enough time to go track testing a few times before the season opened in 1980, and were competitive from the first race on. I actually won the first race of the season at Nelson's Ledges, Ohio, and set a new lap record, but the car was disqualified for being under weight after the race (an error in our addition of the pre-race corner weights!) After that we had a good season, winning the Northeast Division Championship and going to Road Atlanta for the CSPRRC (Champion Spark Plug Road Racing Classic) as one of the favourites for the 'C Production' win.

The other leading TR8 convertible contenders, both with cars prepared by Huffaker Engineering, were the late Lee Mueller, whose distinctively liveried car in black, blue and silver always looked immaculate, and Bruce Qvale (son of the famous West Coast distributor Kjell Qvale). Of course, as well as meeting homologation criteria, the convertible TR8 obviously did not suffer from the coupé's aerodynamic problems.

For Ken Slagle, there are a number of fondly recalled highlights of the 1980 season:

> Beating Paul Newman at Lime Rock, Connecticut, was one of them: Paul arrived at the track on the morning of the race, missed qualifying, and started last. I had the pole, with an 'A Sports Racer' (real race car!) next to me. Just after the start, the ASR bumped me off the road in the first turn and I rejoined the field long after Paul went by, but was able to catch and pass him, winning the race. After the race the guy in the ASR wanted to buy our car!

Another moment recalled was when Joe Huffaker threatened to protest Slagle's car for an illegal carburettor:

> This was after he'd had a peek at it while I was fixing the throttle cable in the pits during a practice session at Road Atlanta. I'd installed 'annular booster ring' venturis from a larger carburettor in the Holly 600 CFM 'double pumper' carburettor that we had to run. It was a legal modification, but one that Joe didn't think of and he didn't know you could actually replace the venturis. We had a good laugh, but a secret was out! (I really liked and admired Joe, and always thought that if he had been able to spend the amount of time preparing and developing a car as I did that I wouldn't have always beaten his 'factory team' Triumphs.)

The end of the 1980 season saw the usual 'run-off' at Road Atlanta, where a number of TR7 and TR8 racers were fielded. Alongside Lee Mueller, racing in both the TR7 (Class D) and TR8 (Class C). there were Ken Slagle, Bruce Qvale, and both Bob Griffith and Dan Pohlabel in TR7s, while Ron Hunter had a

TR8 coupé. Alongside the main race classes was the 'showroom stock' category, which saw a few TR7s competing. Not surprisingly the big attraction for Triumph enthusiasts was the Class C racing, which saw the TR8s up against some strong opposition, in particular defending champion Paul Newman, who had shown up the emergent TR7 of Lee Mueller back in 1976 by beating it at that year's SCCA run-off in his TR6.

Things started badly for Slagle Racing and went downhill thereafter since, according to Slagle, 'our "really good" (about 330bhp) engine failed during practice the day before qualifying and we had to stay up all night to rebuild it using parts from our spare engine. I managed to qualify fourth, just ahead of friend and nemesis Paul Newman, in the Bob Sharp Racing Nissan 280ZX.' On pole position at the start of the Class C race was a veteran Jaguar E-Type, while the Triumphs were in fourth (Slagle), seventh (Mueller), eighth (Qvale) and thirteenth (Hunter).

The race started ominously with what appeared to be a very unsportsmanlike move from the Nissan team, as Slagle recalls:

> At the start, Jim Fitzgerald in a Nissan tried to run Fred Baker's Jaguar XKE [E-Type] off the track. There was a lot of pushing and shoving for the first lap and I sat back hoping to miss the carnage that was sure to happen right in front of me. After several laps, I worked my way up to second behind the Jaguar, but then my rear anti-roll bar adjuster came loose and I got more and more understeer. Finally, Logan Blackburn in another 280ZX got a really good run off the turn onto the pit straight, misjudged the difference in our speeds, and clipped my right rear bumper halfway down the straight (around 125mph). My car snapped left into the tyre wall under the pits, was thrown into the air spinning around several times and landed back in the middle of the track. Fortunately, other than a cracked sternum, I didn't suffer any injuries, but our beautiful car was a mess.

The episode was subsequently dubbed by some witnesses, including Slagle's stepson Roger

Ken Slagle: The Shape of Things that Win

Ken Slagle's loyalty to Triumph was imprinted in the 1960s, and he went on to receive support from the North American marketing wing of Triumph. The colour scheme of Slagle Racing's cars was always highly distinctive:

> The first Spitfire I got to build into a race car after damaging the Group 44 car was yellow. Since we didn't have to hack the Spitfire up a lot to fit large tyres we just left it yellow. Janet liked the yellow, since there weren't any other yellow cars in our class, and it stood out on the track. Every 'Slagle Racing' car after that was yellow (getting 'yellower' with each one). We added an orange stripe on the TR7 and TR8 coupés and had a family 'design competition' for the TR8 roadster. Our two boys, Ed (Slagle) and Roger (Troxell), came up with dozens of drawings, but I finally went with one that I pictured in my mind when I got up one morning. It made the car look like a low-slung sports racer, which was just the effect I wanted.

Another clever tactic was the use of a distinctive wedge-shaped trailer to transport the race cars:

> A couple of British Leyland's first ads for the TR7 were of a 'wedge' pulling into a wedge-shaped garage and going into a wedge-shaped trailer. I asked Mike Barratt if I could have the trailer but discovered that the 'trailer' was mostly cardboard. Mike, however, took up my cause and had a very sturdy aluminium trailer built near their headquarters in Leonia, NJ. They 'loaned' me the trailer for several years until they quit selling Triumphs, when I bought it for $1.00. At first, with the TR7, the trailer's lettering said 'The Shape of Things to Come' (BL's advertising slogan), but later when we had to change the TR7 to TR8 on the trailer, we also changed the wording to 'The Shape of Things that Win' (it had to fit in the available space!)

Mike Dale says that, in his opinion,

> Ken Slagle was the finest private racer/constructor in the SCCA at the time. Not only did he win the National Championship in his Spitfire but also he repeated the effort in his TR8 in 1981. Ken designed, engineered and built this car in a garage next to his home in Harrisburg, Pennsylvania. I remember him buying a book on gas flowing heads and then constructing all his own tools to do it really well. The result was a car that, with him in the driver's seat, established track records all around the north east of the USA and was quite capable on any given day of beating our factory teams. It was a resounding victory for the TR8 at Atlanta in which he took the pole and led for much of the race through to the finish.

An unusual overhead view of Ken Slagle's distinctive TR8 convertible at Watkins Glen. (Ken Slagle)

Troxell, as the saga of the 'Nissan Hit-Squad' and it resulted in stern official words and suspensions within the Nissan camp. The other TR8s were fortunately unaffected, and all finished – Mueller in fifth, Qvale in sixth and Hunter in tenth place. The Jaguar E-Type deservedly won the race. In Class D Production, Lee Mueller in his TR7 finished a very respectable third, beaten only by the winning Porsche 924 and, of all things, a TR6 driven spiritedly by Dennis Wilson.

Over the winter, Slagle and his team worked at rebuilding their shattered TR8:

We grafted new pieces of 'frame' to the body at the firewall, replaced everything in front of the firewall including roll cage, suspension attachment points, strut towers, all the front suspension, radiator, oil cooler, etc. It was almost like building a new car, but really depressing that our car had gotten so badly damaged.

The 1981 season was much better for Slagle Racing, with wins at most of the races they ran. 'In addition, we posted several new lap records despite the addition of a carburettor restrictor plate designed to slow the car down. By then we'd worked out most of the "bugs", and had a fast, reliable, fun-to-drive car.'

The culmination of the 1981 season saw Slagle and Newman up against one another at Bridgehampton Road Race Circuit, New York, on the approach to the end of season run-offs. According to Slagle, there was a plea from the Nissan camp for the Triumph to be deliberately reined in:

Before the race, the Bob Sharp Racing team crew chief had come to me explaining that since they had such a full schedule with Paul's professional races and 'movie time' they had only been able to make four SCCA National Races. Paul had to win at Bridgehampton to finish in the top four of the N.E. Division (I already had the Divisional Championship wrapped up) to qualify for the run-offs. Paul and I talked, he said 'do what you have to do', I replied it was 'just another race', and I beat him on a 'greasy' track.

Slagle covered the Bridgehampton course in 28 minutes 28.350 seconds, breaking the 2.85-mile lap record set by Newman in his Datsun 280ZX during the trials of the previous day. Triumph's revenge on Datsun was sweet, with Slagle's victory over the film star even making the pages of the *New York Times* of 14 September 1981, under the 'shock' headline 'Newman Second in Sports Car Race'. Newman indeed finished

The TR7 and TR8 both became popular vehicles of choice in club events, as in this event in July 1981. (Ron Kielbiski)

The Canadian TR8 GTO: Peter Bulkowski

Over the border in Canada, Peter Bulkowski, then of Ajax, Ontario, raced alongside fellow Canadian Bruce Kulczyk in a Group 44 Inc.-built TR8. Among their early exploits was twenty-second place at the Mosports six-hours on 17 August 1980, the race where Bob Tullius won the GTO class. The car was built for Bulkowski and Kulczyk in 1979 with the aim of racing in IMSA, Trans-Am and Molyslip Enduro races. 'The complete body, frame suspension and wheels came from Bob Tullius's shop in Virginia', Bulkowski explains. Often mistaken at casual glance for one of Bob Tullius's own Group 44 Inc. cars, the Bulkowski/Kulczyk TR8 – racing as number 42 – competed not only at the 1981 Mosport and 1982 Trois Rivières Trans-Am events but also at every Molyslip and Ontario GT race between 1981 and 1984. During 1983 Bulkowski teamed up with Target Racing (David Deacon, Steve Lechnowsky, Drew Fesar and Laurence Polley) to race the Six Hour IMSA race at Mosport, finishing fourth in the GTO class.

Peter Bulkowski still owns the distinctive red and white TR8 he raced in the early 1980s. (Peter Bulkowski)

The Canadian TR8 was sold at the end of the 1984 season, but appeared at the 1985 Sebring 12-Hour race, where it was entered by KJJ Enterprises of Ontario and driven (as number 32) by John Bossom. However, engine failure and subsequent fire put it out of contention at the start of the race. For several years, the car appears to have been in the racing wilderness, but then it resurfaced in July 2000, as Bulkowski explains: 'It was found by Camaro and Corvette racer Al Mason and after only two days of contemplating, I purchased the car back'. The car, however, was in a poor way and 'a complete tear down was necessary – including dip and strip, repaint, rebuild and the replacement of all moving parts. That complete tear down and rebuild took three years – with many hours, including dinners in the Garage. Thankfully, my biggest supporter was my wife, Nanette!' The car made a return to competition at the 2006 'VARAC' Vintage Racing Festival at Mosport, although not without problems: 'coming back to the track was very hard since there were two engine failures relating to the oil pump!' At the time of writing, Bulkowski plans to fix the oil pump problems and aims to be out on the circuits of Canada once more, upholding Triumph honour again.

Peter Bulkowski in his Group 44 Inc. TR8 at Mosport on 15 August 1980. (Ron Kielbiski)

second to Slagle and as a result failed to qualify for the Sports Car Club of America run-offs due to take place on 23–25 October. According to Slagle, 'Paul didn't seem to hold a grudge, but a couple of his team members didn't speak to me for some time, and several SCCA officials told us that attendance at Road Atlanta for the run-offs would suffer greatly without Paul being there'.

Slagle went on to win the race at Road Atlanta,

> but I always thought that Paul would have been very tough to beat there. The race that year was in the rain, and the Jaguar that had won the previous year was gridded next to me (I was on the pole). I got through the first turn first and we made it halfway through the first lap before he was blinded by the spray (water and mud) from my car and went off the track, unable to get back on.

Slagle fittingly won the 1981 Class C championship in his distinctive yellow open TR8, but it was perhaps a bitter-sweet victory, as by now Triumph sports car manufacture had ended: 'It was a great win for us, since just after this race most of my support from JRT ended.'

Meanwhile, Lee Mueller explored pastures new, racing a Mazda RX-7 in GTU class with distinction in 1981 and earning as a consequence a higher ranking in the World Sports Car Championship for Drivers and Makes than Bob Tullius (Mueller ended the year in 15th

place, Tullius in 207th). The whole listing for that year shows that the other Triumph racers with World Championship points – all in TR8s for at least part of their year behind the wheel – were Group 44 Inc.'s Bill Adam (who shared 207th spot with Tullius), Briton William Wykeham (also a racer of and nowadays a dealer for Morgans), Canadians Luc Berhar and Peter Bulkowski (sharing 330th place with several others), Pat Bedard and John Kelly (who had shared the second Group 44 Inc. car at Sebring) both in 355th.

Aftermath: TR7 and TR8 Racing in North America After the End of Production

In 1982, with the TR8 out of production, the Slagle convertible was moved to the GT1 category ('SCCA's way of penalizing our performance in 1981', as Slagle puts it), and finished in fifth place at the 1982 end of season run-off, and was also the leading non-Trans-Am car. In fact, Slagle raced his distinctive yellow TR8 for the next three years in the 'GT-1' class, competing against Corvettes, Camaros, Cobras and Porsches:

> We were allowed to increase the size of the engine to four litres (increasing the stroke), with fewer restrictions in preparation rules. This resulted in about 425bhp, with an engine with forged crankshaft and connecting rods, roller camshaft, roller rockers, 'girdle' on the bottom of the block to strengthen the main bearing caps, larger valves, etc. It was quite a car, weighing in at about 1,900 pounds (but having to weigh 2,150 pounds with the 4-litre motor, which enabled us to ballast it to equal weight front and rear).

Slagle had good fortune in the divisional races, and in qualifying at Road Atlanta:

> but I was always hampered during the races by competing against cars with much more horsepower that could get ahead at the start and 'block' me in the twisty stuff. I finished in the top three or four at the

The Slagle roadster was still racing for some time after the car went out of production at the factory; here it is seen at Road Atlanta in 1984. (Ken Slagle)

run-offs each year, but was ready to get out. The end came at the run-offs in 1984 when a freak rainstorm hit one end of the track causing nearly all the cars in the race to pile up on the outside of a fast turn. I was running in third place at the time, and went off the track, just hitting a rear fender on a car I was lapping, but then all the rest of the field came through and car after car slammed into each other, a guard rail and my car. Fortunately, nobody was killed, but it was quite a disastrous end to my Triumph racing career.'

Slagle raced for a couple seasons after that in the IMSA professional series with Rob Dyson, but then retired from racing. 'We kept the TR8 race cars for 12 or 14 years, trying to sell them once in awhile, but had too much "stuff" for anyone to want everything. Finally, a serious Triumph car collector, Vernon Brannon from Charlotte, North Carolina, called and bought them to take vintage racing.'

The North American TR8 Rally Programme

Just as the V8 engine transformed performance of the TR7 in European rallying and North American racing, so it proved to be a major step forward in North American Pro Rallying. The 1979 season would be the first in which the 'TR8' would be able to compete, although the year did not get off the best of starts, when John Buffum and Doug Shepherd failed to finish at the Big Bend Bash in February at Alpine, Texas. They returned to form exactly a month later, however, by securing outright victory at the Murphy's 100 Acre Wood event at Rolla, Missouri. Buffum sat out the Tour de Forest at Shelton, Washington, in late March, but by mid-year, when the duo competed at the Susquehannock Trail Pro Rally at Wellsboro, Pennsylvania, they had already begun to cement a lead, finishing second on that June event.

Later the same month, the Buffum/Shepherd TR8 won La Jornada Trabajosa (which is, appropriately, Spanish for 'the difficult journey') at Bakersfield, California, and victory was theirs

again two months later at the 'Happiness Is Sunrise' at Coudersport, Pennsylvania, finishing ahead of the second-placed Fiat Brava (Ritmo/Strada) on 11 August 1979, at an event that also saw the former SCCA racer of Jon Woodner/Jerry Hinkle finish fifth in their TR8 (an ex-TR7 rally car converted by Joe Huffaker to TR8 specification). A second overall in early September at the Sunriser 400 Forest Rally at Circleville, Ohio, began to make their championship lead begin to look unassailable, although there was another hiccup in October at the Valvoline 20 Mule Team Stage rally at Ridgecrest, California, when Buffum failed to finish, although Woodner upheld Triumph honour by finishing in third.

A fortnight later, at the beginning of November, the Buffum and Shepherd TR8 failed to finish again at the next event, the 1979 Marchal Press On Regardless event in Michigan – and this time Woodner and Hinkle fared no better. Mid-month at the Mini-Price Nevada Rally at Las Vegas, Nevada, saw another disappointment for Buffum and Shepherd, although the season finisher at the Sno★Drift Rally in Grayling, Michigan, in early December saw the Libra TR8 finish a worthy tenth and secure the 1979 Pro Rally championship.

The first key events of the new season in March 1980 saw outright victory (by 48 seconds) in the 14-hour, 400-mile '100 Acre Wood' and later that month another first in the Tour de Forest rally (an event Jon Woodner did not finish, due to a failure in his back axle). The Olympus PRO Rally 1980 at Olympia, Washington, in April saw another upset: for the first half of the rally, Buffum was jostling for supremacy with New Zealander Rod Millen in a Mazda RX-7. Buffum and co-driver Doug Shepherd had already beaten Millen by close margins in the first two rallies, and the Olympus Safari seemed to promise a repeat. Buffum built up a lead of one minute when Millen's Mazda suffered from vapour lock in the midst of the second stage. The two cars fought neck and neck for the following six stages until, as Buffum told the SCCA PR team afterwards, 'I must have braked at the wrong time. We got into a right hander and just couldn't quite make it.' As a consequence, Buffum's TR8 'ended up sitting on some logs and branches off the road'.

Buffum made up for this in May by winning the Northern Lights, an event that saw Jon Woodner/David Orrick in second. Buffum was running a brand new car only just completed on the morning of the event; meanwhile Millen was absent, spending time at home in California preparing his Mazda RX-7 for forthcoming events on the West Coast. During the event, the bonnet of Buffum's new car sprung loose and flew up into the driver's line of site – just a little inconvenient while driving a high-speed straight. Spectators helped remove the bent bonnet, and then obligingly gave Buffum a push to free the TR8 from the sand. Jon Woodner finished an excellent second, his best result in a PRO Rally. Later the same month, at Chisum Trail at Paris, Texas, Buffum and Shepherd won again, aided by Millen spinning his Mazda into a ditch and losing time.

June saw less good fortune, for Buffum failed to finish at either the Susquehannock Trail or La Jornada Trabajosa. In both cases, it was mechanical woes: at the former, Buffum had a half-minute lead, but when he went into the mid-rally service break, he found the V8 had a broken valve, and decided to retire from the event; at the 'difficult journey' event, it was camshaft troubles that mystified Buffum, 'I don't know what was wrong. It was a brand new engine, well, a new rebuild, and it just didn't work. We think it might be a cam. Everything went bad on the way to the stage, so we just turned around and rolled back to the bottom of the hill.' By now it was already obvious that Buffum's main rival for the championship was Millen in his Mazda RX7.

The TR8 was back on song on 9–10 August at the 'Happiness Is Sunrise' event, although this was followed by a 'DNF' at Mendocino Forest the following month (27–28 September), an event where Jon Woodner also failed to finish. The Lubrilon Big Bend Bash in October brought second overall, which altogether meant

that Buffum started the Budweiser-sponsored 'Press On Regardless', held on 7–9 November 1980, with a narrow championship edge over Millen. Buffum already had five victories under his belt and Millen four, so it was obvious that victory at the 'POR' event could prove crucial. Ten hours into the event, Buffum crashed out in spectacular style, injuring himself and wrecking his TR8 against a tree into the bargain. Millen scored the necessary points to make him even with Buffum, but the Triumph driver now had the sticky problem of having no car to drive. At the same event, Jon Woodner and Jerry Hinkle fared rather better, finishing an impressive second overall in their TR8.

To keep the chance of championship victory alive, a European rally TR8 was airfreighted across in time for Buffum to drive in the next event, the 1980 Sno★Drift Rally, held near Grayling, Michigan, on 6 and 7 December; this saw Buffum/Shepherd finish second in their TR8 behind a Jeep CJ7, while Rod Millen finished down in sixteenth place. Ironically, there was a technical problem with the score keeping, as recorded by the SCCA in their post-script piece:

> an unfortunate timing error may have cost John Buffum the win. Failure to record several times on the final stage caused rally officials to remove the stage from final scoring. Raw scores showed Buffum with a 0.70 minute advantage over Light on the final leg – a margin which would have given Buffum victory.

By the end of the Sno★Drift both Buffum and Millen had five victories and two second places, giving them 500 points apiece: they were truly neck and neck.

The culmination of the season was the Frontier Hotel Nevada Rally in Las Vegas on 20 December, with (appropriately) everything to play for and both contenders gambling on a successful drive. Fortunately for Buffum and Shepherd, lady luck was on their side; as Buffum recalls: 'Millen's Mazda rolled late in the race, thus throwing away the 1980 championship'. This left the coast clear for the Triumph, which finished in second place while another TR8, an ex-Buffum car driven by the Canadian-resident New Zealander Clive Smith finished fourth.

Buffum got the points he needed and secured his fourth SCCA Pro Rally championship (each one in a Triumph), added to which he won the 1980 SCCA/Canadian Auto Sports Club North America Rally Cup, as well as the SCCA and SCCA/CASC Manufacturer's Championship for Triumph. Buffum told the SCCA PR team that 'since next year is going to be a development year for our rally program, we won't be going for the championship … that makes this win all the more important and satisfying.' Sadly that development year never really transpired, overtaken by events at BL.

The TR8 that Went to Le Mans

Outside Triumph enthusiast circles, few people know about the brush that the TR7/8 had with the world-famous Circuit de la Sarthe near Le Mans in 1980. Perhaps this is not too surprising, owing to the comparative failure of the exercise, but nevertheless the story of a car that seemed to promise so much, and perhaps could have delivered in different circumstances, is no less fascinating.

The saga of what would become the last Triumph car to participate at Le Mans began in 1977, in the wake of an exercise in which Leyland Cars sent out TR7s to a handful of motor sports specialists in order to gain feedback on how to make 'the shape of things to come' into more of a flying wedge. One of these experts was Jan Odor of Janspeed, a company well known as tuning experts with a wealth of knowledge that had grown out of Odor's 'apprenticeship' at Downton Engineering, the semi-official BMC Mini Cooper tuning consultant. Odor managed to broker a deal with Leyland that meant that he kept the TR7, and he began to consider turning it into a showcase for his company.

Odor's first idea was to build a Modsports racer with a turbocharged Rover V8 powertrain:

the idea was that this would showcase Janspeed's tuning prowess. The idea of a V8-powered TR7 was hardly novel in itself; according to Alec Pringle of the TR Register, who would be part of a small team of dedicated enthusiasts who supported the Le Mans car: 'not a lot of people know that whilst the 4-cylinder TR7 had been homologated into Class B, British Leyland had also put in the TR7 V8 for homologation before the car had even been built! The "TR7 V8" was therefore homologated in Class C.' For Modsports purposes, the car would need some radical structural surgery, with features such as detachable glass-fibre wheel-arches; to assist him with this process, Odor brought in Neville Trickett, best known as the creator of the chopped-roof 'Mini Sprint' and a handful of kit cars of the 1970s.

Then, as is so often the case in the world of motor sports, someone shifted the goalposts. As Pringle explains: 'all of a sudden the [Modsports] rules were changed, and they canned turbochargers – so Jan had a half-converted car, which he now couldn't use in Modsports!' Perhaps the reasons are easy to see, as Pringle points out: 'the fact was that a turbocharged V8 could clearly have wiped the board with the opposition!' With a redundant Modsports car, Jan decided to switch tack and develop the car for Le Mans. The result was a strikingly styled car with a reshaped roof line, swoopy flared wheel-arches and dramatic spoilers that moved the TR7 into the arena of automotive erotica. 'The design was undoubtedly a rip-off of the competition version of the De Tomaso Pantera,' Pringle declares. 'Jan did a lot of promotion with the bodyshell, but at first it still had no engine in it! In fact, there was no engine until 1979 – and to some extent, the project was stagnating.'

Meanwhile, what had by now been dubbed the TR8 Le Mans Turbo appeared – *sans* engine – on the Janspeed stand at the 1978 Performance Car Show at London's Alexandra Palace, where unsurprisingly it generated a great deal of interest. As a privateer venture without any engineering input from British Leyland, perhaps it is hardly surprising that the makers of the TR7 did not seek any association with the project (indeed, they sometimes went out of their way to dissuade suppliers to participate), but at the time many onlookers considered this lack of corporate involvement or encouragement churlish. However, one person who did step in to try to help was dentist and endurance racer John Sheldon, who put Odor in touch with race-car builders Anglo Dutch American Engineering (ADA).

At ADA, Ian Harrower and Chris Crawford were both seasoned Le Mans campaigners and were keen to race the TR8 Turbo. 'We had raced at Le Mans since 1976 but what we really wanted to do was to race a British production based car – so the TR8 fitted the bill', Harrower says, adding that he and Crawford 'leapt into a car and went down to Salisbury to see Jan Odor about it'.

Chris Crawford had successfully prepared racing Camaros even while he was still an engineering student, and Ian Harrower was an accountant who also happened to be a motor sport nut. 'Chris was the number one mechanic at DRA (Dorset Racing Associates) when I met him', Harrower recalls. The two competed at Le Mans in 1976 in a two-litre Lola. Together they had bought out DRA as the basis of what became ADA, developing a company whose main work was building racing cars for events like Le Mans, but generally for paying customers.

ADA tried to tap into BL but to no avail, as Harrower explained to James Elliott of *Classic and Sports Car* magazine in 1998: 'We did everything to get BL involved – I had a mate who played squash with Michael Edwardes and tried to lean on him, but it was no good'. Alec Pringle

The TR Register was instrumental in getting the TR8 Turbo to Le Mans, as this sequence of the car being loaded for the journey illustrates. (Alec Pringle)

wrote to Sir Michael and received a polite but 'no thanks' response from John Davenport, head of BL Motorsport. Even Bob Tullius was approached but, as he recalls, he was not in a position to help:

> Unfortunately by then BL was in such trouble there was no way they could have been involved. Added to that, the project as outlined was much too complicated for Davenport or the company to fathom, plus an effort to turbocharge the engine would have been a disaster, as few people were aware of the metallurgic requirements of building a reliable unit.

Harrower remembers getting a small plug on the ITV motor sports programme of the day and ruefully recalls the outcome of an attempt to secure sponsorship from Unipart, the BL parts specialist: 'We heard a rumour that a decision on sponsorship was being made between us and John Watson – and history shows, assuming that was true, who got the money!' Harrower is fulsome in his praise for the efforts of Pringle and his TR Register colleagues: 'they got a deal going whereby if you sent in a fiver, you got a tee-shirt; we even had some guy in prison in Glasgow sending us a fiver!'

Pringle continues the story: 'ADA worked on the fabric of the car – putting it right as far as they could, on a very small budget!' Harrower stresses that at this stage Janspeed was no longer involved in the engine work: 'It would have been much better for us if they had been, but we had to work on both the car and the engine; we were basically "chassis" people, and so the engine development was really too much for us.'

Getting an obscene amount of power out of the Rover V8 required a great deal of ingenuity; as the project developed, cleverness was not in short supply, even if funds definitely were. Hillborn Engineering produced a bespoke cast alloy bottom end, which combined a dry sump pan and a cradle to support the main engine bearings. Chevrolet con-rods were fitted, along with specially adapted Cosworth pistons. An initial plan to use a Hillborn injection system proved too costly, and so twin RotoMaster turbos were employed, sucking through twin two-inch SU carburettors. Intercooling was crucial, and the solution arrived at was to use a Freon system to chill the air as it passed through the intercooler. Although this set-up – effectively an air conditioning unit for the engine – was a clever idea, it nevertheless added weight and complexity.

For Le Mans the car would run in the Group 5 International Production Class and, as the engine was turbocharged, it needed modification to reduce the capacity (at the time, although the engine limit for naturally aspirated cars was 5 litres, turbocharged cars were subject to a multiplier of 1.4). Janspeed made the necessary changes by reducing the stroke, but this work and other delays meant that ADA did not take delivery of the car until November 1979, cutting in to development time. Many teams would use the Silverstone Six-Hour race as a 'dry run' for Le Mans, but ADA failed, in the first of many setbacks, to make the event for several reasons including a simple lack of funds. Development continued fitfully; that the car actually made the pilgrimage to France was not least owing to the determination of Alec Pringle and his TR Register colleagues, who provided financial, moral and physical support.

Even at the eleventh hour, fresh challenges were being thrown up as regularly as clockwork: the engine had not been adequately tested, the 'interim' gearbox was a 4-speed Muncie T-10 'bone-crusher' (so called for obvious reasons), the propshaft was bent and some of the wheels and tyres were still en route from England, as Pringle recalls:

> I'd gone to Charles de Gaulle airport to pick up a set of Compomotive wheels – being brought in through Pakistan International Airlines. It was a holiday weekend and the customs officials were having some kind of a drinks party – so we had to persuade them to come out and deal with the wheels; we ended up giving away lots of 'souvenirs' to them!

Charles de Gaulle is on the wrong side of Paris for Le Mans and the weekend holiday traffic was bad:

It didn't help that we were in a two-litre Cortina automatic estate that belonged to John Sheldon's dad, and we were driving in the pouring rain: we did an average of 81mph – speeds at times well over a hundred – with the tyres barely touching the road surface – and all the while [my future wife] Diane was sitting in the passenger seat of the Cortina bolting the wheels together. Unfortunately when we got there, the Dunlop people told us that the retaining bolts were 2–3mm out of alignment – meaning they would have fouled the beads – and so the wheels/tyres wouldn't have lasted the race in all probability. We were not impressed!

Out on the circuit, during the qualifying runs, the damaged drive-train posed some rather distinctive challenges:

> The fact that the propshaft was out of balance meant you had to hold the car in gear with your left hand. The tyres also tended to lift off the rims at high speed: Dunlop limited the recommended top speed to 175. But the propshaft vibrations also meant that you went through bends in the wrong gears. A new propshaft was in the process of being made – by a local firm in Le Mans during practice and qualifying - but it wasn't ready at the start. In the end, we decided to do one show-touring lap and then to floor it. But on the Mulsanne straight you had to ram your elbow into the door aperture! Ian Harrower got 201mph on Mulsanne – probably the only person to drive Mulsanne at that sort of speed single-handed!

There has been some debate over the years as to the veracity of that 201mph figure; while records are inconclusive, Alec Pringle and his TR Register colleagues who were there think it may have been accurate:

> I'm pretty convinced that the car did manage around 200. A bunch of TR guys were on the fastest part of Mulsanne, they reckoned that just once it came past on all eight cylinders, overtaking the 924 Turbos by a margin of a good 30mph. The 924s were running 170–180 tops. One of those chaps recently observed that he could still clearly recall the vibration was

The British Racing Green TR8 Turbo undergoes the rigours of scrutiny at Le Mans in the summer of 1980. (Alec Pringle)

visible to spectators, evidently absolutely terrifying to watch. I'm sure it was!

Ian Harrower points out that it was even more terrifying inside the cockpit than for the onlookers.

The three drivers – Ian Harrower, John Sheldon and John Brindley (the latter a last-minute replacement for ADA man Mike Wilds, struck down by chickenpox) – were obviously unused to a car that was a relatively untested animal, having failed to meet the target for shakedown testing at the Silverstone Six-Hours on 11 May owing partly to the lateness of some of the components. Qualifying at Le Mans, held on the Thursday before the Saturday/Sunday of the 24-hour race, was in a mixture of wet and dry conditions, but even so the TR8 Turbo achieved a respectable best time of 4 minutes 37.1 seconds.

TR8 Turbo Le Mans Car

Body: Steel centre section with bespoke glass-fibre and Kevlar reinforced removable sections front and rear. Integral tubular steel roll cage

Engine: Rover V8 (3616cc) with cast alloy crankcase girdle, cylinder heads with five bolts around each cylinder (as per what had originally been the 'Oldsmobile' arrangement, which differed from the 'Buick' arrangement adopted by Rover, although this was not achieved using Oldsmobile parts) and 'O' rings instead of gaskets. Dry sump oil system designed by Janspeed. Twin Rotomaster 'Turbosonic' S4-104192 turbochargers sucking through a pair of two-inch SU carburettors. Belt-driven ancillary oil pump to significantly improve cooling. Compression ratio 8.96:1

Transmission: Muncie T10 4-speed (original plans had called for a bespoke 5-speed, but this never materialized, supposedly because British Leyland was unhappy about some suppliers supporting the project)

Suspension
   Front: Triumph-based MacPherson struts with Bilstein inserts
   Rear: 'Live' Jaguar axle with 2.77:1 final drive ratio
   Brakes: 12in ventilated discs all round with four pot callipers
   Wheels: Compomotive
   Front 15in diameter, 10in wide
   Rear 15in diameter, 14in wide
   Weight: c. 1,068kg (2,355lb)

The green Triumph was a stirring sight for those who saw it make its brief foray at La Sarthe – but the dream was soon broken. (Alec Pringle)

In the end, however, all the team's efforts would be for naught, for – to the chagrin of the TR supporters – the Le Mans bureaucrats performed one of their characteristic late rule changes, which, by a miraculous coincidence, allowed in the French-entered Porsche of Thierry Perrier and Roger Carmillet, whose time was 4 minutes 37.6 seconds, at the expense of the Triumph; the British car was unceremoniously bumped on to the reserve list with a shrug of the Gallic shoulders. A number of other unpopular moves by the ACO officials that year prompted *Autocar* to suggest rather ominously, in its post-race report, that 'legal repercussions are expected to follow the organisers' treatment of some of these entries'. Ian Harrower says that he doesn't really remember the issues with the ACO, since 'we were really just so pissed off that we didn't qualify'.

Despite the disappointment at this outcome, Pringle is nevertheless pragmatic: 'To be fair, it would probably not have lasted the race, not least because it still had a practice engine.'

Undaunted by the misfortune of 1980, ADA entered the Triumph TR again in 1981. In January they co-opted seasoned Le Mans driver Derek Bell for testing ('he did it more or less as a favour', Harrower says). The car was also entered in the Silverstone 6-hour race in May to provide much-needed testing before Le Mans. At first the car performed impressively, although Derek Bell had said in testing that it still needed a great deal of work. Ian Harrower qualified with a lap of 1 minute 44.7 seconds, a time that would not have disgraced the Porsche 935s. A tale of dubious origin says that Bell confided that the car was underdeveloped in response to a question from a bystander at Silverstone who, unknown to Bell, happened to be one of the potential Le Mans sponsors. It seems that irrespective of the truth of the story, and Harrower had never heard it before, this sponsor's money never arrived.

Here the 'Le Mans' car is seen in the patriotic red-white-and-blue livery for 1982. (Alec Pringle)

Unfortunately the car crashed heavily at Becketts, when John Brindley slammed into a wall just minutes into the race, and the paucity of both time and funds ruled out effective repair in time for the Le Mans race, and so the entry was withdrawn. ADA then acquired the car outright from Janspeed. Racing under the ADA Engineering umbrella at the 1981 Brands Hatch 'Flying Tigers' 1000 Kilometres on 27 September 1981 (the fifteenth round of that year's World Endurance Championship for Drivers), Ian Harrower and Bill Wykeham's race ended when the car spun and stalled on the intermittently damp circuit. However, ADA laid plans for a third attempt at Le Mans in 1982, decking the car out in a new red, white and blue livery and with a provisional entry by Harrower and Wykeham, but the necessary financial backing could not be found, and so the dream of a TR at the Circuit de la Sarthe was sadly laid to rest.

The car appeared spasmodically in various races until in 1983 it was sold to the British Sport Car Centre in West London's Goldhawk Road, where it lingered for a while in the showrooms. Alec Pringle briefly contemplated the chance to buy the car, but passed up:

Peter Nott bought it in September 1985. Janspeed completed the engine development programme, and they put the car together with fuel injection in 1987. Peter never raced the car; however he did take it to Le Mans for a sort of 'demonstration run' where the organizers expected the 'gentlemen' – mostly in their classic GT40s – to parade at a civilized pace. Peter clocked 193.5mph at Mulsanne and the people at Le Mans told him to go away and never darken their doors again: he had been honking past those GT40s, who were travelling about 50mph slower!

Bert Smeets is probably the premier TR7 rally enthusiast extant; the Le Mans car is part of his impressive collection, seen here in his workshop in Belgium. (Bert Smeets)

Subsequently the engine blew up again. It was rebuilt by Rover V8 engine specialist John Eales of J. E. Engineering, and in 2005 the Belgian Triumph racer and collector Bert Smeets bought the car to add to his impressive collection of three ex-works TR7 rally cars. The car is being rebuilt, and there are firm plans for the Le Mans car to race again. However, Alec Pringle, who is still providing invaluable support to Bert Smeets, is cautious in his optimism: 'as ever, it's a money pit. Some things don't change …'

Après Le Mans: The TR8 Drag Car

In the wake of the Le Mans project, there were a couple of spin-offs worthy of mention. John Buckham of Sussex Transmission Engineers commissioned Janspeed to build a second V8

turbo engine for a TR8 rallycross car project he was undertaking. Janspeed duly obliged, although the Buckham car featured a different inlet system, with Dellorto carburettors and a blow-through rather than suck-through turbocharger arrangement. When it ran well, the power was phenomenal, but unresolved problems with the fuel system eventually led Buckham reluctantly to abandon the project. Meanwhile, a second project that took its cue from the Le Mans car was the so-called 'TRS' built by Triumph specialist 'Del' Lines of Weston-super-Mare (*see* Chapter 10).

Finally there was a TR8 'drag racer', which Peter Nott built and is now owned by Alec Pringle's wife Diane. 'There has been some understandable confusion between the TR8 Turbo Le Mans and the TR8 Drag Car – both having re-emerged from years of obscurity in

Diane Pringle is the lucky owner of one of the most powerful TR8 drag racers in existence. According to her husband Alec, 'I've demonstrated the thing, but none of the V8 TR race or rally guys have as yet accepted the challenge'. (Alec Pringle)

2005', Pringle explains. The TR8 Drag Car was built by Peter Nott and Philip Eaves, and Pringle insists that:

> It was, and remains, the sole replica of the LM car … Peter utilized the spare set of Janspeed outer panel-work on a strengthened TR7 tub, as per the original, together with the Le Mans rear wing, and some spare mechanical components. Once again a twin turbo Rover V8 was used, but a later Rovercraft unit of larger capacity and greater power. After a brief competition career, this car too was stored for years before

being rebuilt and substantially evolved by Paul Brackley into its current, normally aspirated, drag racing format. It remains in full race order.

The engine in the drag car is a 4-litre Rover V8, with a wet sump and:

> just about everything internally as extreme as it gets; a 650 Holley double pumper fuels it, with two-stage Nitrous Oxide available, and complex electronic engine management. Best strip times were 10.8sec/130mph, stage 1 NOS, but since then the tuning has been properly sorted. A good strip driver should be able to break the 10sec mark.

The gearbox is a strengthened competition Ford-Cosworth unit with fifth gear removed, connected by a massive competition clutch. At the back end, the rear axle is a narrowed nine-inch Ford, with a 'spool' diff – all by Steve Strange Engineering, evidently as good as it gets in drag circles. Front brakes are also Strange, as are hubs all round, the rear brakes a special Mercedes/Peugeot hybrid. Suspension remains all to circuit racing rather than drag spec, just another anomaly. Wheels are 15-inch diameter and 4 inches wide at the front (with Citroën 2CV Michelin X 135 tyres), and 16 inches to the rear, shod with gigantic Hoosier slicks, a foot and a half wide.

According to Pringle, the interior

> is like something out of an aircraft cockpit. Two seats and harnesses, all the electronics in the passenger footwell, and enough dials and switches to keep any pilot happy. Starting it is like starting a plane: by the time you've switched on the row of above-screen toggles – extinguisher, electrics, water pump, engine fan, dash fans, fuel pumps, ignition, NOS prime, NOS arm, and finally pressed the starter button. Then it's mayhem, and check all the gauges. Steering, pedals and gears are all heavy as hell, and it's extremely difficult to control – I use the term loosely! I've demonstrated the thing, but none of the V8 TR race or rally guys have as yet accepted the challenge. OK until you get to firing-up, then the second thoughts cut in!

7   The Convertibles

Opening Up the TR7's Potential

The fact that the Federal judgement threatened under FMVSS208 (*see* Chapter 3) never came to pass was welcome news for sports car fans, but of course the change of tack was too late to prevent such cars as the TR7 and Jaguar XJS from being launched as fixed head coupés alone. There is little doubt that had British Leyland been in sounder commercial health, without being pitched head-long into the turmoil of public ownership, industry recession, industrial strife and corporate ineptitude, the open derivative that the TR7 badly needed might have arrived sooner than was the case, as Alan Edis explains:

> We didn't get to look at an open version of the TR7 until after the original launch – we still had the MGB in the marketplace, and we had to deal with quality issues first. Many people seemed to like the new look of the TR7 – the comfortable and well-appointed interior in particular – and yet people still felt we needed to have an open version. As the threat of leg-islation had effectively taken most open cars out of the market, it wasn't clear for a while quite just how much people really valued the open top. In the meantime, therefore, we worked on things like good heating and ventilation, air conditioning and a generous sliding roof – but even then, none of these fully satisfied the market requirements.

A full-length folding fabric sunroof had become a popular option in the TR7 coupé. This drew some praise from *Road & Track*, although they did not know that the sunroof aperture reduced the torsional stiffness of the TR7 bodyshell by as much as 50 per cent. So Alan Edis (with Spen King) looked at the possibility of an open TR7:

> We went about this in a very simplistic way; we cut up a brochure photo and with a bit of artwork we quickly arrived at what we wanted. It was a happy thing to find that we could make a handsome looking open version. It quickly became clear it would work – it was definitely doable.

It seems that by this stage serious thoughts about an MG version of the TR7 with different exter-nal sheet-metal had been shelved. This could have been partly because the MGB had been given a second lease of life with a clever facelift of June 1976, which had rectified some of the evils inflicted on it late in 1974 when the 'rubber bumpers' had been grafted on to Abingdon's veteran sports car. As the MG was so obviously based on 'Austin Morris' components, it was kept

The full-size folding fabric sunroof was the nearest that early TR7 buyers could come to an open-air experience. (Alisdair Cusick)

within that part of the company instead of being adopted by the Rover Triumph division.

Perhaps the big change in attitude came during 1975, when British Leyland decided to abandon the premise of badge engineering (renaming the Austin, Morris and Wolseley 18-22 series simply as the 'Leyland Princess'). From then on, for the time being at least, it seemed more likely that 'MG' and 'Triumph' variants on the Bullet platform would have to have more than mere badges to set them apart. Even so, according to Edis, 'naturally, the creation of the TR7 convertible rekindled the debate about whether that ought to be an MG instead of a Triumph!' Indeed, three years later there were reports in the press in 1978 that British Leyland was toying with bringing back dormant names like Riley and Wolseley, but in the event these plans never progressed very far. The idea of an 'MG TR7', however, would subsequently be given one more shot (*see* Chapter 9).

The TR7 had been seen from the start as more of an MGB successor than a TR6 replacement, but by the time that British Leyland began to plan the open TR7, there was recognition that the Triumph might not soak up that part of the 'classic roadster' market that the MGB still served. Instead, there was the view that the MGB could be allowed to soldier on and keep the market sector alive in readiness for the TR7 convertible, after which the situation could be reviewed: if the sports car market remained buoyant into the 1980s, then perhaps the next generation of British Leyland's offerings in the 'TR7/MGB' sector could be carefully targeted to cover both sets of customers with a model – or a brace of models – better able to cater for customer expectations.

Off with its Head: The TR7 Convertible

Once the decision had been taken to go ahead with the open TR7, a prototype had to be built. The first step was taken at the Canley workshop in August 1975 when John Lloyd, Tony Lee and their colleagues were discussing the various US tests, including the suggestion that there was supposedly a loophole in the roof crush regulations to the effect that, if there wasn't a roof, the rules would not apply. 'After lunch, John Lloyd cut the roof off a TR7 to look at it', Tony Lee says. 'We all

The first TR7 convertible prototype, as driven from Turin to Coventry by Tony Lee. (Tony Lee)

agreed that it could look very good and so it was arranged for a car to be shipped off to "Micho".'

Norman Rose explains that as well as cutting off the roof, 'it was necessary to weld up the screen header and the aperture left by the removal of the rear quarter panel and we fitted a very elemental flexible roof covering. The results of road testing this vehicle were sufficiently encouraging to result in the order to Michelotti.' Harris Mann confirms that neither he nor his colleagues in the Longbridge design studio were involved in the design of the TR7 convertible.

Alan Edis organized the necessary shipment to Turin in September 1975: 'It proved not to be as difficult as we had feared. The difference this made to the appearance was striking; so it did not take long for the real thing to take shape.' Tony Lee went out eight weeks later to Turin in order to collect Michelotti's handiwork, bringing it back at the end of November 1975:

> It was a green painted car and I remember I was asked by Customs if it had had any work done on it; to which of course I replied that it hadn't! However, I'd just driven it all the way from Turin with the windows down to try to get rid of the smell of the new paint.

Bryan Reynolds was in the Triumph Experimental Department when the Michelotti prototype arrived:

> It was a 'cut and shut' job and looked to me as though they had roughly sliced the roof and rear pillars off a fixed head donor car. Although it was a styled hood I do not believe that it was functional. I cannot be sure now but I think it was a rigid wire frame structure. Also I do not recall the Michelotti car having any structural modifications to the body structure fitted. In order to make the soft top work, we created the first functional hood frame in the Detail Shop at Fletch North from wooden patterns that I believe were manufactured at Canley.

After initial assessment in the UK, the Michelotti-built prototype was, Norman Rose recalls, shipped off to the USA for further appraisal: 'The decision to go ahead was given on 23 February 1976 and this happened to virtually coincide with the final cancellation of the SD2 project [*see* Chapter 3], thus freeing up enough labour for Triumph to do the job'.

The car looked fine, but suffered from atrocious scuttle shake. To cure this, Spen King instigated

A finite element diagram representing the structural analysis of the TR7 convertible bodyshell. (BL photo)

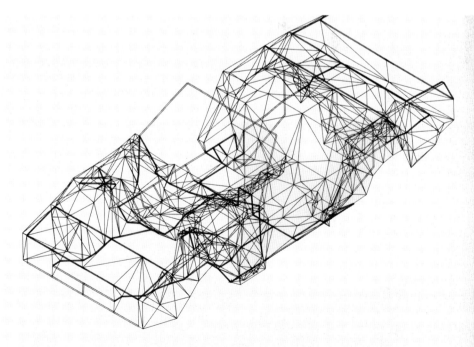

 THE TRIUMPH TR7 DROPHEAD NEG NO 301006
FINITE ELEMENT COMPUTER ANALYSIS DIAGRAM
For release March 2, 1980

suitable structural modifications and resurrected the pre-war invention of Scott Iverson, a pupil of the Danish scientist Niels Bohr. This was the so-called 'harmonic bumper', such as the type produced by Wilmot-Breeden, which used the principle of finely tuned weights at the vehicle's extremities to counteract scuttle shake. Harmonic bumpers had previously been seen on pre-war Rovers. The engineering of these bumpers into the open-top TR7 fell partially to one of the engineers at the MG plant at Abingdon, Denis Williams, who explains, 'this was during a slack period at MG, and we were acting as a sort of contract office for Triumph. The harmonic bumpers were pivoted at the centre line, with the heavy weights at each end.' As Steve Redway points out, 'even today when you look at a convertible side by side with a coupé, you'll notice that the convertible's front bumper visibly droops at the ends due to the central pivot point initiated for these cars'.

In addition to the harmonic bumpers, additional body reinforcements were introduced to compensate for the loss of structural strength due to the removal of the coupé roof, using state-of-the-art computer finite element analysis to optimize the changes needed. An additional box section was welded across the cockpit behind the seats, bracing the sills and 'B' posts, while the doors were fitted with additional tongue-and-groove latches to increase torsional rigidity. This was effective, albeit at some penalty in terms of overall rigidity, although the overall weight of the open car, at 2,348lb (1,067kg), was actually 9lb (4kg) less than that of the coupé. The folding hood was easy to stow, with simple catches fixing to the top of the windscreen frame, and at the rear the main rectangular clear plastic window could be zipped out to provide a generous throughput of fresh air even when the hood itself was erect. Either side of the main rear window, clear quarter windows, similar to those on the MGB roadster, allowed a high level of rear visibility when the hood was up.

George Spence was involved in designing the new fuel tank filler arrangements suitable for the TR7 convertible:

I was in 'Chassis Engineering', which by then was really 'Vehicle Engineering' on a car like the TR7, which didn't have a chassis as such. So our job was to sling it all together. The rear deck of the convertible was lowered to make it look better but this impinged on the fuel tank and the underframe was modified to make it possible to build coupés and convertibles together. The Californians had this vapour release nozzle to cater for vapour escaping – so you had this big thing on the petrol filler – so there was limited room below the deck to accommodate the vapour recovery fixings between the hood and the boot.

The programme (tight as ever) called for twenty-five pre-production bodies to be ready at Speke by January 1977, the intention being to allow volume build to start in May and an announcement in the USA in September. Norman Rose explains that the panels with the longest lead-in times were, unsurprisingly, the rear wing panels and the rear deck: 'The first twenty-five sets of these duly appeared in January 1977 from hand-cut blanks; drawings for these had been issued the previous March'. This was, of course, just days after the project 'green light' and Rose says that this short lead-in of nine months 'broke all records':

The original design programme began at the end of February 1976 and was completed – including all the body assemblies – by September. What did throw us a little was that there was a request from Speke to introduce the common underbody into the coupé first, and in effect give them time to iron out any problems on that before getting immersed in the specific problems of the convertible.

Nine bodies were built, using as many production parts as possible, and this meant that the first body was delivered by the end of June 1976 and the rest by September. This number was needed to ensure that all aspects of the safety testing could be carried out for the new variant. Thankfully, early concerns that the body structure might have been unacceptably weakened in terms of rear end and side impact tests soon proved unfounded, and of course the nose of the convertible was hardly different from the coupé. Various structural additions, including diagonal bracing of the radiator aperture, bracing of the front turrets to the dash, and beefing up and bracing of the sills allowed an improvement in torsional stiffness of the convertible by some 23 per cent over that of the first open prototype. By the early part of 1977, therefore, the TR7 convertible was almost ready for possible production.

Although the original plan was to build the TR7 convertible alongside the coupés at Speke, this swiftly changed as the TR7 story was swept up in the changes that led to the move to Canley (*see* Chapter 4). As a result, the first production TR7 convertibles started life at Pressed Steel Swindon's 'B' Building and finally emerged from the traditional Triumph home wearing the same laurel wreath badging as their coupé contemporaries. For reasons that will become apparent later, however, home market TR7 convertibles with the laurel wreath badges were a short-lived phenomenon.

Fun at the Launch

As ever, the most important market for the new TR7 convertible was deemed to be North America; with cutbacks in spending under the new regime, however, the actual press launch was less elaborate. Indeed Mike Cook recalls that, unusually, no official photographer was on hand and, as he and his colleagues were kept busy with organizing and managing the event, sadly no photographs are known to have been taken.

According to the irrepressible Mike Dale, the dealer launch had some memorable moments:

> The theme of the presentation was Directions '79 and was an all singing and dancing affair aimed at getting the dealers pumped once again. At the appropriate moment a female model was to drive the convertible TR7 onto the stage amid much fanfare. I was doing the talking at the podium and all went well until the lady tried to get out of the vehicle. I could see out of the corner of my eye that she was having trouble opening the door and, while I was ad libbing to give

An artist's cutaway view of the TR7 convertible.

> her time, I measured up the distance from the podium to the stage and decided I could jump it.
>
> Trying to make it sound as if it was all part of the show, I leaped onto the stage, grasped the door handle firmly and hissed in the lady's ear to push! She did and the door opened to great applause. I may never know whether the audience twigged anything but later I was presented with a cartoon made by one of the team which showed the scene with various salty comments made by colleagues as they saw the problem unfold.

The public debut of the TR7 convertible took place at the Los Angeles Auto Expo at the beginning of May 1979, the first mass-produced open sports car to be introduced into the United States for ten years (the last, according to the Leonia PR people, had been the 1970 model year Dodge Challenger). The 'port-of-entry' US price for the new open TR7 was quoted as $7,995, dearer than the contemporary coupé that remained on sale. BL spokesmen were keen to stress that, as with the original TR7 coupé, the new open TR7 would be built exclusively for the US market for some time, as it would be an important dollar earner for the company.

That assertion that the TR7 was a key source of dollar revenue would change from a blessing to a curse in the coming months: the British General Election also took place in May 1979, and brought with it a change of government that heralded the beginning of Margaret Thatcher's period as Prime Minister and a rise in the strength of the pound sterling. (For the consequences of this, *see* Chapter 9.)

Magazine Reports: North America

Road & Track heralded the arrival of the new open-topped TR7 with a preview report by 'Editor at Large' Thos L. Bryant in the June 1979 issue. Bryant had been part of a contingent of about two dozen international journalists invited to England for an introduction to the TR7 convertible and the TR8 coupé at the famous Donington race circuit – blanketed in snow at the time, judging by the photographs that accompanied his report. Bryant undoubtedly summed up the feelings of many journalists – not to mention Triumph enthusiasts – by stating that 'frankly we were getting rather exasperated about ever having a chance to see, let alone drive, the TR7 Convertible', adding perceptively that 'British Leyland Motors Inc., the US arm of the firm, was obviously getting just as impatient as we were'. On hand were three cars: a red TR7 convertible (EAC 595T, first registered 12 February 1979, and still in existence), a white left-hand-drive car (YRW 572S, present whereabouts unknown) and a TR8 coupé (YDU 617S; *see* Chapter 8).

Bryant confessed that he had been among those who had failed to warm to the looks of the original TR7 coupé, but admitted he was surprised at how much he liked the new open version: 'it simply looks right – it's what the car should have been all along, with a crisp, clean shape that evokes feelings of speed and sports car driving excitement'. The car that Bryant drove was a pre-production specimen with a satin-black rear panel of the type seen hitherto on Speke-built TR7 coupés: all production convertibles had a colour coordinated rear panel that matched the remainder of the bodywork. Bryant also pronounced himself pleased with the on-road experience:

> Driving the TR7 Convertible is virtually the same as driving the Coupé, except that now you can be out in the open, where every right-thinking sports car driver should want to be! The smooth wedge body and raked windshield reduce wind buffeting to a nearly undetectable level, even at highway speeds, and

A North American advertisement from November 1979 for the TR7 convertible by Jaguar Rover Triumph proclaims 'Triumph invites you to a new opening'.

the structural rigidity is immediately apparent when you hit the first bit of rough pavement – no squeaks or rattles.

It would be another three months before *Road & Track* reported in detail on the TR7 convertible, the September 1979 issue reaching the newsstands at roughly the same time as those from rival publications *Car and Driver*, *Motor Trend* and *Road Test*. In a report headed 'comfortable, practical and, best of all, entertaining', the testers began by confessing they had a soft spot for open cars, admitting that 'on a scale of one to ten, most of our staff would immediately give another two or three points to a two-seater sports car with a convertible top'.

By the time of the test, the TR7 was one of a dwindling number of open sports cars on the market; one of its key competitors was BL's

TR7 30th Anniversary Limited Edition

The first of the two factory-sponsored US limited edition versions of the TR7 convertible was unveiled in the summer of 1980 as the '30th Anniversary Limited Edition'. Quite what precisely this anniversary was intended to signify was unclear – even the promotional literature left this rather fundamental question unanswered. In 1950 a TRX prototype had been shown at Earl's Court (*see* Chapter 1), but it was another two years before a recognizable 'TR' sports car emerged. However, irrespective of the story behind it, the purpose of the 'anniversary' limited edition was clearly in the usual tradition of such specials, to generate some interest and showroom traffic, and bundle in a package of free incentives – in this case $900 worth of accessories – at a time when the dollar-sterling exchange rate was causing the TR7 list price to spiral upwards (the 1980 list price was $1,000 greater than that of the previous year). 'It's our birthday and you get the presents', proclaimed the publicity flyer. The accessories included an AM/FM stereo radio/cassette player, a leather-bound steering wheel ('made in France') and special wheel styling comprising polished alloy centre and rim trims, foglamps, floor mats and a smart chrome-plated luggage rack on the bootlid. The interior was graced with a rectangular brushed-alloy plaque with a '30th Anniversary' legend and a small Union Jack logo. Unlike some limited editions, this one did not come in a special colour scheme and so genuine specimens may be harder to identify, although a thin twin coachstripe ran along the side, following the upper wing line in a vain effort to disguise the swooping TR7 swage.

own MGB, which would shortly be given a death sentence, although this was not known to the magazine when it conducted its TR7 test. Unsurprisingly the *Road & Track* testers found that most of the things they liked and disliked about the fixed-head TR7 were replicated in the new open version, with the obvious exception of the styling, open top and all-round visibility, each of these being pronounced as much more to the magazine's liking. On the other hand, such negative aspects as the rough engine noise and flat mid-range performance were much as before.

Extensive on-road driving over mixed road surfaces showed that while, in their opinion, the rigidity of the new car was adequate, it was not outstanding, and the testers voiced the opinion that it could have been even better, given the fact that it was supposedly 'state of the art'. Part of the problem was undoubtedly the fact that the chunky hardtop coupé TR7 had such an impressively rigid structure, which open-top surgery was bound to diminish. Cowl shake, a common infliction with open sports cars, was notable by its absence, although the shift in weight distribution caused by the lack of roof and the harmonic bumper weights, coupled with the inevitable increase in body flexure, did mean that the magazine found rear-end shake could be induced on bumpier roads, no doubt a consequence of the fact that the forces transmitted through the coil springs had less body structure than on the coupé through which to dissipate.

Generally, *Road & Track* liked the fixtures and fittings, even if they felt 'there is little attempt to mask the extensive use of plastic' both inside and out. The convertible top was, they felt, a great deal better than those of most British sports cars, even if it was still not quite up to the standard of the best of the Italian opposition. 'All in all … it rates as a first class ragtop', they stated. The *Road & Track* test car had optional air-conditioning fitted, which they felt worked well enough, albeit at the expense of a noticeable drop in power and engine speed whenever the compressor kicked in. 'Various minor criticisms notwithstanding, we're quite impressed with the TR7 in convertible form', the magazine concluded, proclaiming the car as 'one of the most comfortable, practicable and entertaining sports cars on the market today.'

Over at rival publication *Car and Driver*, Larry Griffin oversaw the equivalent September 1979 report. In an upbeat write-up liberally illustrated with photographs featuring a fetching female blonde roller skater, intended to convey youthful lifestyle aspirations and raise heartbeats, the opening sub-heading described the open TR7 as 'a sunshine roadster skating through life with a bounce, a wiggle and a wink all of its own'. Griffin's report jauntily started by claiming that 'light-hearted ragtops throw an arm around the

THE 30TH ANNIVERSARY TRIUMPH TR7.
ITS HERITAGE IS PRICELESS. ITS OPTIONS ARE FREE.

'It's our birthday and you get the presents' was a subtle way to point out that the TR7 30th Anniversary limited edition was loaded with 'free incentives'. Inside the brochure, seen here, the theme continued: 'Its heritage is priceless. Its options are free.'

world and ask it in for a good time'. Continuing in a similar vein, Griffin went on to counter preconceptions that the TR7 convertible would be the usual rough-and-ready fare:

> Purists the world over are probably breathing a collective sigh of relief because of the new roadster: saved from the comfortable life, and not a moment too soon! Bad news, cretins. The TR7 roadster is as cushy and pleasing as the coupé, a far cry from the cantankerous open-air creations that still scuttle out the gates of many British and Italian factories.

Car and Driver liked the folding roof, in particular the massively improved rearward visibility, and the changed styling: 'the removal of the TR7's original lid makes us wish all the old boxtops could be trimmed off and sent in with 25 cents for a snap-on software conversion'. The interior also came in for praise from Griffin, especially the clear instrument layout (largely unchanged from the original TR7). Even so, in the 'counterpoint'

section at the end of the main report – where other members of the *Car and Driver* road test team provided snapshot impressions of the test car – Griffin's colleague Mike Knepper likened the quality of the interior of the TR7 convertible to a plastic snap-together model car kit: 'That's the TR7 roadster. A snap-fit sports car', he declared. Even if *Car and Driver*'s Editor David E. Davis Jnr was moved to declare the TR7 convertible as 'the best English car since the Jaguar XJ6L', and other testers were more enamoured of the car than Knepper, his comment that Triumph would need to 'clean up its act' if it hoped to lure away some Mazda RX-7 customers was a valid criticism.

Meanwhile at *Motor Trend*, the third of the trio of major US car magazines to carry a September 1979 issue road test, Bob Nagy defined the TR7 convertible as 'The wedge with an edge'. In general, Nagy was as charmed with the open TR7 as his magazine rivals, although he did have a passing concern at possible quality glitches: 'in what we can only assume to be a passing nod to Motherland, the speaker in the

Jaguar Rover Triumph proudly issued this reprint of four glowing TR7 Convertible road tests from Road & Track, Car and Driver, Motor Trend *and* Sports Car Graphic.

passenger's door also chose to go out on strike periodically and return to work for equally capricious reasons'. At a base price of $7,995, Nagy noted that the convertible commanded a $300 premium over the coupé (a reversal of normal British sports car policy) but he concluded the new model had been 'well worth the wait'.

Car and Driver magazine included the TR7 convertible in its 'Wine Country Safari' group-test for the May 1980 issue, which involved the onerous task of driving a convoy of European sports cars around California's Napa and Sonoma river valleys, sampling the best of the region's celebrated vineyards. In between the *dégustations*, Rich Ceppos and his colleagues reflected on the varied charms of their mounts: a Triumph Spitfire, MGB, Fiat X1/9 and the TR7.

By the time of this test it was common knowledge that the MGB and Spitfire were not long for this world, although for the time being at least

there seemed to be the possibility that the MGB might find a second wind through the Aston Martin Consortium bid to acquire the rights to build it. However, although the testers at *Car and Driver* confessed a certain soft spot for both the MGB and the Spitfire, they also felt that with the open TR7 on offer, the time finally had come to put the old-timers out to pasture.

While the testers' top ratings generally fell to the mid-engined Fiat, they felt several aspects of its British rival were particularly praiseworthy: 'the TR7's handsomely appointed cockpit, in contrast to the snug confines of the X1/9, is spacious enough for a pair of Steeler linemen', they felt, adding 'there is a velvetiness to the ride, and a general feeling of mass and solidity heretofore missing in British roadsters'. Steve Redway observes that much of this was due to the 55lb springs all round that gave the boulevard-cruising TR7 a very soft ride indeed.

Alongside the road testing, the public relations people at Leonia were working behind the scenes at 'product placement', and TR7 convertibles began to pop up in some popular television programmes. Viewers of the *Dallas* soap opera, starring Larry Hagman, might occasionally see the character of Lucy Ewing, played by actress Charlene Tilton, tooling sedately round the streets of Texas in an open-top TR7.

In Canada the sales and marketing effort for the TR7 convertible was subtly different from across the border; note the side stripes and alloy wheels featured in this JRT Canada brochure from 1980.

TR7 Spider

One of the more sought-after TR7 limited edition specials is the 'Spider', introduced in the North American market (and Germany) late in 1980 and produced through 1981. Exclusively available in black (although, contrary to popular American 'TR' folklore, not the only black factory TR7), what really set off the coachwork of this special was the retro-reflective red 3M tape treatment for the exterior decals, reinforced by a twin coach-stripe in the same finish; this was the inspiration of Alan Edis, who commissioned the creation through Michelotti. Standard-fit alloy wheels were basically the same (although differing in detail, being a brighter silver and bearing a special part number – RKC2111S) as the Dave Keepax-styled offerings fitted to the TR8. Inside, extra-thick pewter-coloured carpets were fitted and the distinctive silver and grey striped seat facing theme was borrowed from the contemporary UK-market MGB. Standard fit air-conditioning, AM/FM cassette radio and a three-spoke sports steering wheel completed the interior package.

On the way to developing the definitive livery for the TR7 Spider, it seems that ideas were being supplied – probably by Bruce McWilliams. (John Lloyd)

In the press release that accompanied the introduction of the TR7 Spider, Jaguar-Rover-Triumph Inc. explained that the spider name had first been used in the United States around a hundred years earlier for light horse-drawn traps, before the name was adopted by the Dutch (who changed the spelling to Spyder). The TR7 Spider was believed to be the first – possibly the only – instance of the spider name being attached to a British-built volume sports car. At a time when dealers were heavily discounting regular TR7s, the retail price of $10,585 ($11,010 in California) included roughly a $1,000 premium, but even so the TR7 Spider was a sales success. Sources vary on the number built as between 1,200 and 2,000 (when announced, the plan was to build 1,700 in 1980), although only a lengthy trawl through the surviving records at British Motor Heritage is likely one day to yield the precise answer. California-market Spiders with fuel-injection are a sub-set of the whole.

An even rarer car is a 'holy grail' of TR limited editions – the TR8 Spider. According to TR Drivers' Club TR8 Registrar Rex Holford, only one such car is known to exist and is believed to have been a one-off factory pre-production experiment; certainly no advertising or active marketing of such a variant ever took place.

David W. O'Neill is the lucky owner of this immaculate TR7 Spider – undoubtedly the most sought-after limited edition TR7 variant. (David W. O'Neill)

Magazine Reports: United Kingdom

Whereas North American customers had the opportunity to buy an open-top TR7 from the summer of 1979, it would be the best part of a year before their European counterparts would have the same privileges. That summer, however, the US sales and marketing team did lay on a brief test session at Summit Point track in Virginia for British newspaper journalists. The European debut came at the Brussels Motor Show in January 1980 and sales followed in March. *The Times* carried news of the new car's imminent arrival on 3 March 1980, reporting that 'BL expects the drophead will take about 35 per cent of TR7 sales in Britain'. UK prices of the open and fixed cars were given as £5,959 and £6,176, respectively.

As the open-topped car was introduced, some trim changes that had been previewed on the 'Premium' limited edition were standardized across the whole TR7 range, with a new improved interior trim (in a choice of navy or tan) and a dark grey fascia instead of black. A one-piece carpet of superior quality was also fitted and the dashboard featured improved

The TR7 Spider was marketed in North American and some European markets; it is quite collectible today and was the only black TR7 sold in the USA.

INTRODUCING THE TRIUMPH TR7 SPIDER

Black, beautiful, and bewitching.

The TR7 Spider is an elegant new version of the famous TR7 convertible. Quick in its reflexes, sleek in its lines and altogether entertaining to drive, the Spider is a special, limited edition with custom features. The TR7 Spider is immediately identifiable by its custom black paint, double red pin striping and hood badge and alloy wheels.

**Full of fun...
and elegantly equipped.**

Its interior, specially created for this limited edition, features black and grey upholstery, pewter-colored carpeting, black facia and instrumentation and a black padded competition-type steering wheel. In addition, the TR7 Spider is fitted out with air conditioning, AM FM stereo radio and cassette deck.

The Spider is captivating.

One test drive and you'll be caught! When *Road & Track* tested the TR7 convertible they said (among other favorable things) that it is "comfortable, practical and, best of all, entertaining." The car is quick to respond, with rack and pinion steering, five-speed stick shift and a positive combination of disc and drum brakes. The engine is a lively 1998cc four. The feel for the road is surefooted and positive, yet the ride is comfortable, due to a well-tuned suspension system that combines coil springs, MacPherson struts up front and anti-sway bars. The overall experience is pure pleasure.

To many eyes, the TR7 convertible is more balanced than the coupé – even if many 'Speke purists' may disagree! (Alisdair Cusick)

switch faces with clearer and brighter symbols, a new 'low coolant' warning lamp and indicator, and wiper stalks swapped over to match the European norm. Four new metallic paint finishes were introduced and a black plastic spoiler was fitted underneath the front bumper.

Just as in North America, British sports car fans took very well to the new open-top TR7, and sales of the hardtop coupé dropped dramatically, to the extent that behind the scenes Rover Triumph management began exploring dropping the fixed head entirely in favour of either a targa-top or a removable hardtop. Indeed the convertible was outselling the coupé at a rate of nine to one and as such the factory introduced the alloy wheels as standard on the coupé to try and boost sales. These wheels always remained an extra for the standard convertible.

Autocar carried a test of an Inca Yellow TR7 Drophead (as the model was referred to) registered JRW 595V for its 15 March 1980 issue, beating its rival *Motor* to the task. *Autocar*'s testers wondered what had happened to the promised Sprint-engined version, but deemed themselves reasonably satisfied with the new car's performance, obtained at the MIRA test circuit and including a top speed of 114mph (183.5km/h) and a 0–60mph time of 10.7 seconds. The test car had done only 1,400 miles (2,250km) when the magazine took it over, and the testers conceded that, had it been fully run in, the car could have proved faster.

Autocar praised the handling of the TR7 convertible, saying that it 'inspires confidence' and that the structure was more rigid than they might have expected. 'Much of the charm of the TR7's road behaviour derives from its impeccable steering', the magazine proclaimed, adding that 'control is absolutely precise, with response to the tiniest movement of the wheel, and yet no wheel shock is transmitted on poor roads'. The report concluded that 'there is indeed little to criticise in this new TR7 Drophead, and instead one is reassured to see that – at a not outrageous price – BL are still able to turn out a thoroughly modern, attractive and well-finished car.'

Motor eventually carried its full road test of the TR7 Drophead in the issue of 14 June 1980, the first that had been published in six weeks owing to a strike by journalists at IPC, publishers of the magazine. It seems strange nowadays to imagine that a weekly magazine could be effectively shut down for the best part of two months, but this elegantly illustrates the strike-torn situation that was still virtually the norm at the start of the 1980s. *Motor* was very taken with the new model (the test car was a brown Canley-built specimen, registered JRW 594V) and the the report's summary stated 'Triumph's new two-seater is a thoroughly enjoyable, well-developed and refined car with lively performance and reasonable economy; we liked it immensely'.

For the UK market, as *Motor* noted, the TR7 coupé was sold at a premium price (the reverse of the situation in the USA), partial justification for this being the standard fitment on the hardtop of a sunroof and alloy wheels (fitted as an optional extra to *Motor's* test car at a cost of £260.07). As mentioned above, the list price for the TR7 Drophead was £5,959 (with steel wheels), with the TR7 coupé priced at an extra £217. It is interesting to look at the contemporary prices of the rivals that *Motor* selected for comparison; the Fiat X1/9 was £5,533, the Lancia Beta Spider 2000 two-plus-two £6,789 and the VW Golf Cabriolet GLi (only recently launched, the first of a new wave of hatchback-based 'cabrios') was £6,540. British Leyland's other sports cars still on sale at the time were the Triumph Spitfire (£4,308) and the MGB (at £5,474, about £500 cheaper than the new TR7), while TVR offered its 3000 convertible at £8,730.

The rear view of the open TR7 is certainly less imposing than the quite brutal shape of the hardtop. This particular car belongs to TR Drivers' Club member Jim Johnson. (Alisdair Cusick)

The combination of an open top and light colour seating makes the open TR7 a more inviting place than the slightly claustrophobic interior of the earliest coupés. (Alisdair Cusick)

As with most other magazines, *Motor* noted the harshness of the engine in the upper reaches of its rev range, but at the same time suggested that this was perhaps less of an issue in the open-top TR7 than its closed coupé sister. *Motor* managed a top speed of 109.8mph (176.7km/h), a 0–60mph time of 9.6 seconds, 30–50mph in fourth gear of 7.1 seconds and an overall fuel consumption figure of 25.5mpg (11.1ltr/100km), which, as they noted, was better than the last MGB they had tested, way back in 1972 (106.2mph [170.9km/h]; 0–60mph 11.5 seconds; 30–50mph in fourth 9.3 seconds and 23.5mpg [12.04ltr/100km]). The magazine liked what they called the 'road manners' of the car, saying that 'the TR7's initial bias is towards safe, scrubby understeer especially on slower corners, though there is usually enough power in reserve to punch the tail out into controllable oversteer … although many will argue that the TR7's handling remains somewhat unsophisticated, it is nevertheless safe, enjoyable and entertaining'

One thing that *Motor* did not particularly like, in common with most other publications, was the braking:

Although the brakes on the test car always slowed the car strongly when called on to do so, they never *felt* particularly reassuring, especially after a series of hard applications when we noticed a slight trace of fade. The pedal itself has a rather dead feel and requires a hefty push to bring the car quickly to a halt.

The folding top was regarded rather more favourably, as was interior trim. Although the ride comfort was felt to be 'extremely good' for a sports car, *Motor* did feel that something had been lost in the conversion to an open body:

With its long-travel suspension, the TR7's ride is sportingly firm without being uncomfortable, though there is some low-speed harshness which deep ruts or potholes tend to magnify. There is also the occasional

---

Motor's Long-Term Test TR7 Convertible

Today, Howard Walker, a seasoned professional motoring journalist with decades of experience, writes not only for *Autocar* but also for many US publications, based at his home in Florida. In 1980, however, Walker was road test assistant on Britain's weekly *Motor* magazine and was given a dream allocation of a long-term test TR7 convertible. Over the following twelve months he posted a series of detailed reports that demonstrated above all that BL had finally nailed the quality problems that had plagued the original Speke-built cars. 'They had to break my fingers to hand over the keys the day our long-term test TR7 Convertible had to go back to BL', he told me:

I loved that car. With a passion. It was April 1, 1980 – yes, really – when *Motor* magazine's chocolate brown convertible arrived for a year's evaluation. I was the mag's 20-something news editor, single, with a Bee Gees hair do, and assigned the tough task of being its new keeper. I thought I'd died and gone to heaven. We'd run an original fixed head TR7 on long-term test and the thing proved to be an absolute dog. Horrid four-speed gearbox, Yugo build quality, the kind of ride that could loosen dentalwork. But our

convertible proved to be a gem. Yes, its 2-litre Dolomite-based four-banger wheezed like a Chelsea Pensioner, and 0-to-60 acceleration was best measured with an egg-timer. But it was a joy to drive thanks to its muscley mid-range torque, its precise, responsive steering and leech-like grip. And it made a terrific convertible. You sat low down in the cockpit with that big windscreen offering lots of protection from the elements. But if I remember right, the key to not being blown around was to have the driver's window down and the passenger side raised. In the end I put 20,000 miles on the TR's clock. And apart from a couple of broken hood press studs, a broken boot lid gas strut, a slight oil leak from a slack gearbox bolt, the car proved completely reliable. Of course, just when BL got everything right on the TR7, they stopped building it. Pity.

Howard Walker has fond memories of the TR7 he ran on behalf of Motor *magazine. (Howard Walker)*

---

feeling that the front end is somewhat under-damped, for it will wallow slightly on some surfaces. Despite its secure location, the live rear axle can hop around on broken surfaces, and mid-corner bumps occasionally cause the rear wheels to step out of line.

Most of the other features that drew praise or mild condemnation, such as the excellent heating and ventilation, and the poor visibility forwards of the leading edge of the bonnet, were factors common to the TR7 coupé, but *Motor* summed up by saying:

the transformation from ugly hardtop to attractive drophead has been achieved with considerable skill and is reflected in the excellent finish. As in the fixed head, the colour of the massive plastic fascia has been changed from oppressive black to dark grey, and there is new upholstery for the seats and door panels.

European sales of the new Canley-built TR7 convertible were just getting underway when, in traditional BL fashion, there was a fresh crisis and a change of plan.

Third Time Lucky? The Move to Solihull

It is fairly unusual for a production car to be uprooted and to move lock, stock and barrel from one factory to another. Doing this twice is almost unheard of, yet that was what happened to the (by now extended) TR7/TR8 family in 1980 when, in the wake of the TR7 convertible's debut, production moved from Canley to Solihull (for the TR8, *see* Chapter 8).

When Sir Michael Edwardes announced the sweeping BL cutbacks of September 1979 that would include the end of the MGB (*see* Chapter

For the UK market, Jaguar Rover Triumph resorted to this corny but eye-catching 'launch pad' advertisement theme.

10), he also announced that car production would cease at the Canley plant (thereby also pitching the forthcoming Honda 'Bounty' – the Triumph Acclaim – in the direction of a different home; *see* Chapter 9) while the TR7/TR8 family would be transferred to the Rover SD1 facility at Solihull.

There the sports cars would occupy that factory's chronically underutilized third line, which until the end of 1977 had been intended to take over Dolomite production from Canley.

In December 1979 the Solihull factory, which, like the Speke facility, had never been used to its full capacity, experienced a major shutdown as 4,000 workers were laid off for three weeks because of a glut of unsold Rovers. When they returned from their Christmas break, they also went onto a two-month period of short working while the TR7 jigs and fixtures were brought in. Bodyshells, produced as before at Pressed Steel Swindon's 'B' building, were sent to Solihull for painting before transfer next door to the assembly hall for final assembly.

Meanwhile, the Leonia office of Jaguar Rover Triumph announced the introduction of the 1980 model TR7 on 21 February 1980. A handful of changes included the grey dashboard, as previewed on the home-market TR7 Premium limited edition, a revised range of exterior colours and new navy or tan tartan seat trim, with matching door facings. For the California market, the TR7 appeared with Bosch fuel injection, and the recommended price was $9,235 'POE', with air-conditioning optional at $600 extra.

The change took place in an orderly fashion, with the first TR7s emerging from Solihull from 31 March 1980, just as UK sales of the new TR7 convertible were getting under way. There was an overlap until August, when the

TR7 convertibles – almost certainly 'Spiders' judging by the left-hand drive and black paint finish – pass down the line at Solihull in 1980. (Graham Robson)

Fuel-Injected TR7

To the more dedicated and knowledgeable North American TR enthusiast, the fact that European enthusiasts had been able to buy fuel-injected versions of the TR5 and TR6 has often been an understandable source of transatlantic envy. However, although the early mechanical Lucas fuel-injection systems had provided a route to greater power (even if with questionable reliability), the cost of meeting Federal emissions legislation was simpler to address using traditional carburettors. When the TR7 had arrived in the US marketplace with carburettors, a marketing opportunity was arguably lost, although, as we have seen, a great deal of work had been done on a fuel-injected 'Sprint' programme for both SD2 and the TR7. The more stringent emissions rules in California were typically a year in advance of those for the rest of the United States and this was demonstrated when the 1980 model year TR7 appeared with fuel injection for California but carburettors for the other states. All 1980 cars also received a Delco electronic ignition system–coil and distributor. In the view of US-based Triumph enthusiast Richard Truett, the cumulative effect of these changes was 'to wipe out at least 75 per cent of all the things that made the engine run poorly'.

The plan was for all 1981 model year cars across the USA to have fuel injection from the start, but the upheaval of the shift to Solihull and a logjam in US dealerships meant that production of the 1981 TR7 did not get under way until April 1981, halfway through the model year. The system itself was a Bosch L-Jetronic set-up and its adoption allowed much of the antediluvian paraphernalia, such as the recirculating air pump and EGR valve, to be dispensed with. While UK cars retained the traditional twin SU carburettors, cars for Canada had twin Zenith-Strombergs, which meant that for a while three different TR7 engine variants were being fitted on the line at Solihull. Fuel economy, performance and, by all accounts, reliability and engine smoothness all benefited, but it was another case of too little too late: May 1981 saw the announcement of the imminent end of TR7 and TR8 production. Richard Truett estimates that no more than 2,000 TR7s were built with fuel injection (of which 400 were TR7 Spider models), making it one of the rarer variants. Even it hadn't been killed off by Sir Michael Edwardes, the fuel-injected TR7 with the slant-four engine would still have been quite a rare car, since plans were in hand to replace the Triumph engine with the 'O' Series unit (*see* Chapter 9).

Truett bought a fuel-injected TR7 for his own use in 2003 and reported for the World Wide TR7/TR8 Owners' Club that the changes were a revelation:

> The EFi system did not bolster performance much. It was more or less used to bring the car into emissions compliance. But it brought a level of refinement unimaginable to those used to the carburettored version. The engine starts immediately and settles into a very smooth and consistent idle … [it] has Honda-like smoothness, but that wonderful whine from the cam chain can be heard when the revs approach 4,000 and power comes on strong, with no peaks or valleys.

Truett believes that if the TR7 EFi had been launched far earlier, as originally intended, it could have provided salvation:

> Had the TR7 survived, Triumph would have had to address the head gasket situation by using a better sealing gasket or redesigning the way the head attached to the block. That and a more robust water pump and timing chain system could have seen the TR7 engine through until the 'M' or 'K' series engine arrived.

Of course, if Triumph had their way we would originally have had the Triumph TR7 Sprint EFi, but that exciting prospect had been killed much earlier in the life of the Bullet (*see* Chapter 5).

last Canley-built cars were completed: BL and its North American dealer network still had bitter memories of the lengthy hiatus between Speke and Canley TR7 build and, by building the car simultaneously at Canley and Solihull, a more gradual handover was possible. Of course, this being BL, not everything was plain sailing: a strike by seventy workers at a BL gearbox

factory in Cardiff in February 1980 brought both Canley and Solihull to their knees for a short while.

BL took advantage of the changeover to make a few more relatively minor changes, the most obvious being to drop the slightly cumbersome laurel wreath transfer from the TR7 nose in favour of a neat, smaller round plastic badge with a chrome rim and the laurel wreath logo contained within it, set against a simple black background. Behind the scenes, further changes were being pencilled in. In due course some of these appeared on production cars, including new interior door handles and trim and colour detailing. However, these were relatively minor amendments to tide things over until the TR7 family could be given a more comprehensive upgrade, so long as sales revenue improved.

In the opinion of Peter Wilson, responsible for TR7 engineering liaison, the earlier Solihull TR7s were probably the best-built of the lot. This was because an orderly rundown at Canley also allowed a more gradual simultaneous ramp-up in the production at Solihull, with obvious build-quality benefits: 'There was time to train the operatives properly at Solihull because of the fact that cars were still being built in volume at Canley'. There were three tracks at Solihull and the original plan had been that one track would be for the 6-cylinder SD1, the second for the V8 SD1 and the third track for the Dolomite, which

was to have transferred to Solihull when it had first been planned to close Canley back in 1977. The Dolomite never came to Solihull, but instead the TR7 was introduced onto the 'spare' third track at Solihull. 'We started at around five cars per hour and gradually ramped this up to 18–20 cars per hour while Canley TR7 production was wound down', Wilson recalls. This was a promising start, but then came what Wilson regards as a typical blunder of inexperienced management:

> They decided to close the SD1 V8 track and move the SD1 6-cylinder cars onto the TR7 line and build the TR7 and SD1 6-cylinder cars together on the one track. However, the labour didn't know how to build the cars; they left the 6-cylinder SD1 labour on the old V8 SD1 line and the poor guys didn't have a clue. The build quality then plummeted to a new low level.

In the event, however, the move to Solihull would prove to be fairly short-lived, for the existence of the Triumph sports car was already hanging by a very thin thread.

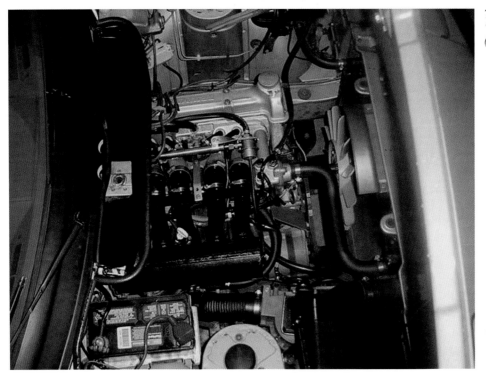

The production TR7 'EFi' engine bay. (Richard Truett)

8 The TR8

The Shape of Things to Come – With V8 Power

The fact that the Rover V8 engine would fit under the sloping bonnet of the TR7 was one of the worst-kept secrets in the British motor industry. Everyone knew that such a car was coming one day: the only question was when. Pre-production 'TR7 V8' road cars had been subjected to testing alongside the 2-litre cars from 1974, and the V8-engined cars soon usurped the 4-cylinder models wherever rules and competitive advantages allowed (*see* Chapter 6).

There was never much likelihood that Triumph's in-house V8 from the Stag would be chosen for the TR7 derivative, for by the time planning of the new model was under way Rover and Triumph were firmly wedded and it was obvious that the Rover unit would be chosen. Indeed there were attempts to shoehorn the Rover V8 into the existing Stag engine bay; Ian Elliott recalled seeing a styling mock-up in the design studios with a bonnet bulge aimed at accommodating the Rover V8's bulky carburettor intake set-up.

The name of the V8 model was almost as badly kept a secret as the car's very existence: the fact that the next available number in the hallowed TR series was 'eight' was hardly a coincidence, and during 1977 the Speke factory began building production-specification TR8 coupés for the intended US launch programme, although even then they were referred to as 'TR7 V8'. From the trickle of such cars produced, a handful were shipped over to the USA and were subjected to extensive photography as part of the creation of an advertising campaign that was still built upon the familiar 'things to come' theme, but simply added 'with V8'. A number of publicity brochures were produced that revealed the 'TR8' name; understandably these are highly coveted by Triumph literature collectors today.

The TR8 was initially developed primarily with the USA in mind and, as with the TR7, sales were scheduled exclusively for the US market before the car would be sold in the UK. For most

The 1978 model year TR8 interior as it would have appeared had the car been built at Speke and sold in the USA from late 1977 onwards.

Rover V8 Engine

The story has often been told of how the Buick engine was discovered almost by accident by one of the Rover directors, and how he negotiated with a sceptical GM management to buy the rights to an engine that they saw as obsolete. The Buick and related Oldsmobile engines had first appeared in a brace of modestly sized four-door saloons called the Buick Special and Oldsmobile F85, launched a year apart in 1961 and 1962 respectively. Both of these cars proved popular and sold reasonably well in their day, spawning two-door, convertible and even forced-induction versions that widened their appeal considerably. The tuning potential of the lightweight and compact engine was soon recognized, and the 'Aluminum Fireball V8' performed well in stock car races across the states. However, the engines were comparatively expensive in GM production terms and there were servicing problems, largely a consequence of ignorance by owners of the special care needed with aluminium engines.

By early 1964 J. Bruce McWilliams was the President of Rover's North American operation and he discussed with William Martin-Hurst, the British Managing Director of the Rover Company, the need for a new engine for the Rover car range, a problem already recognized by the company. The Rover 2000 had been successfully launched in 1963, with an all-new body and engine, but the larger Rover saloons still relied upon an ageing and heavy 3-litre straight six. Rover's main focus in the 1950s had been centred on the gas-turbine engine. An all-new larger capacity 6-cylinder in-line engine (based upon the Rover 2000 ohc 4-cylinder unit) was also developed, but was found to be too long and heavy for the Rover P6. McWilliams suggested adopting a suitable small American V8 engine, saving investment and benefiting from some degree of local familiarity in the US marketplace. Martin-Hurst was receptive to this idea. When he visited the USA to discuss the possibility of selling Rover engines to Mercury Marine, he was already primed to look out for a possible engine to fulfil Rover's future passenger car requirements. In Mercury Marine's experimental workshop there was an example of the Buick alloy engine, and Martin-Hurst was intrigued to learn more about this neat and compact unit. Checking its size he found that, despite its capacity of over 3.5 litres, it would easily have fitted in the existing engine bay of the Rover P6. Once he learnt that General Motors was abandoning the engine, Martin-Hurst contacted Ed Rollert of Buick to discuss the possibility of obtaining a licence to build the engine in Britain. The rest, as they say, is history; the Rover V8 engine was a great success and a natural for use in British Leyland's corporate sports car.

In 1977 BL prepared a run of sales and marketing literature, some of which escaped into the public domain. In the event, the TR8 would not go formally on sale until 1980.

Albert Tingey (left) examines the engine in a TR8 at a TR Drivers' Club event in 2005. (Roel van Es)

Threat to the V8: Fleet Fuel Consumption

By the time that British Leyland was thinking of sending cars to North America with the compact ex-Buick '215 cu-in' engine, corporate America was in the throes of yet another fuel crisis. The attention of Capitol Hill's legislators had widened from vehicle safety to encompass emissions and fuel consumption. President Gerald Ford's Energy Policy and Conservation Act (EPCA) of December 1975 set out a sliding scale of ever more stringent fuel consumption requirements that would be applied across a given manufacturer's fleet of vehicles. The next President, Jimmy Carter (from January 1977), saw no need to relax the requirements of the EPCA. In British Leyland's case, the relatively thirsty Jaguars were obviously a key part of sales strategy, and in order to provide a balanced average fleet fuel consumption figure it followed that the smaller sports cars would need to represent the parsimonious end of the spectrum. With the imminent demise of the MG Midget and Triumph Spitfire, all that JRT would be left with would be the MGB and TR7 (and, perhaps, a few Rovers).

In a paper Bruce McWilliams produced in early 1978, he estimated that 'fuel economy-wise, sports cars for the USA must average 30mpg by 1981 for fleet balancing and competitive reasons'. It is for this reason that question marks began to hang over the viability of the TR8 as a V8-powered car and why, for example, various studies either discounted the V8 or held up an alternative such as a turbocharged 'O' Series engine as a fall-back option. In 1978 GM was suggesting that, by 1985, the future of the V8-powered car in its line-up was looking doubtful – and this from a company whose output in 1978 was 81 per cent V8-powered. In the event, many of the strictures of the Act were progressively watered down and it was overtaken by other legislation in 1981 under President Reagan (sworn in to office in January 1981). But for a time in 1978/79 there was debate about whether or not the TR8 should be sold.

(left) Dave Keepax, in the foreground, was one of the Rover Triumph design staff responsible for the style of what would become the TR7/TR8 alloy wheel. (John Ashford)

(bottom left and below) Some of Dave Keepax's original artwork for the TR7/TR8 alloy wheel. (Dave Keepax)

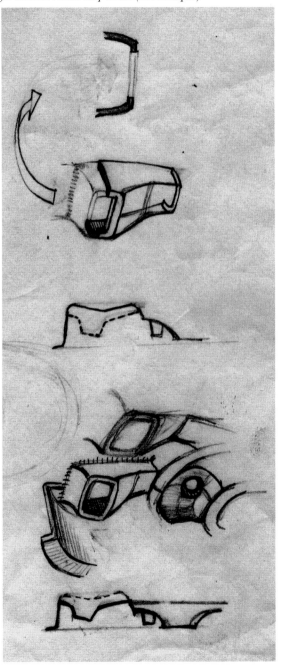

> ## Lucas and Bosch to the Rescue: The TR8 Fuel-Injection System

By the time that the TR8 was finally nearing production, it was obvious that the days of the traditional carburettor were numbered – for the North American market at least. Emissions standards were also becoming harder to meet in a few other markets too, such as Japan and Australia, and it was clear that eventually EEC standards would be likely to play 'catch up'. In developing a new fuel-injection system for their Rover V8, British Leyland naturally turned to their long-term partners at Lucas, but when it came to the new area of applying fuel injection and catalytic converters to the mix, Bosch in Germany arguably had more expertise. According to Albert Tingay, who was responsible at Lucas for developing the TR8 fuel-injection system, however, Bosch was unable to make the Rover V8 run well when cold using its system and was in any case unconvinced that it needed the bother of what would, in its terms, have been quite a low production volume:

> So it was Bosch who suggested to Rover that the work be given to Lucas, and so Rover's Jack Swaine came to us. Rover already had a P6 Rover 3500 which they'd been looking at and we said that we'd take the project on. Bosch agreed to allow us to use their components other than the electronic control unit, which would be Lucas's responsibility. We went to see Bosch in Germany and France, and they told us all about their petrol injection system. After that, we went back to Rover and as the P6 was by now a dead duck, with the SD1 on the drawing board, we went ahead with work on the project with a view to all V8 applications.

Once the system was at the prototype stage, BL carried out a back-to-back test between EFi and carburettors: 'the carbs beat the EFi power at first, but for overall driveability the fuel injection was better; you could pull off from rest in fifth gear with the EFi system'. Clearly Tingey remains proud of the work he did on the TR8 EFi in particular and he still owns one today: 'My car was a US-specification car I bought in Nevada. I use it quite a lot; we've taken it to Gibraltar, Sicily and we had a lovely drive down the Pyrenees for three weeks, ending up in the Alps.' Not bad for a thirty-year-old car and a septuagenarian driver.

of the United States, the TR8 would be equipped with twin Stromberg 175 CDSET carburettors, but the tougher emissions legislation that had to be observed for the crucially important Californian market dictated that TR8s sold there would be fitted with Bosch-Lucas L-Jetronic fuel injection from the outset. With a fuel-injected TR7 also on sale in California (and destined for other markets), it was apparent that Triumph sports cars could soon have been totally 'EFi'-equipped.

Interestingly the car with the tougher emissions task had the higher power output: the power figure quoted for the '49 state' carburettor-equipped TR8 was 133bhp (SAE), but for the fuel-injected California car the figure was 148bhp. The standard fuel-injected car was also some 12lb (5.4kg) lighter than the carburettor-equipped version, adding further to the performance advantage of the Californian market model, while fuel economy, measured through the standard EPA tests, was an impressive 18 per cent better on the freeways (and 14 per cent around town).

All TR8s benefited from a moderate brake upgrade, including a larger servo and thicker but still non-vented front disc brakes, while the rear axle final ratio was changed to 3.08:1 instead of the TR7's more usual 3.45:1 or 3.9:1. The battery was relocated from the engine compartment to the boot, as much for improved weight balance as the need to free up space under the bonnet.

The TR8 was closely aligned to the contemporary TR7, although a General Motors Saginaw power-steering pump and an Adwest steering rack featured (giving a snappy 2.8 turns lock-to-lock, versus the contemporary TR7's 3.88), along with a sporting, leather-trimmed 'Motolita' steering wheel of smaller diameter. Outside, the TR8 was distinguished from its lesser brethren by 'strobe' patterned TR8 badge transfers on nose and tail, a small 3.5-litre transfer on the front wings along with matching Triumph laurel leaf transfers. Alloy wheels, as designed by Dave Keepax, were standard fitment from the outset, and of course the twin exhaust pipes were an obvious giveaway.

One of the people who got an early flavour of the TR8 was Bob Burden, who claimed one of the pre-production Speke-built TR8 coupés, which he believes was the second one built, ACN2, as a company car:

> Aside from the styling ('the shape of things to come' looked a lot better coming than going in my opinion), I thought it was a very good car – gobs of performance, responsive and a bit demanding in a good way if you like the act of driving, comfortable, everything worked most of the time including the AC, and fun to drive. Aside from the fit and finish (mainly design and purchasing shortfalls), almost all of the positive automotive clichés applied and I would certainly rank it high in my personal list of daily drivers.

TR8 Press Reception in America

The first opportunity motoring writers had to try the TR8 was the invitation for overseas journalists to examine a pair of pre-production TR7 convertibles and a single TR8 coupé (*see* Chapter 7). The TR8 was a Canley-built manual specimen (judging by its 'laurel leaf' nose badge) with left-hand drive and bearing the registration number YDU 617S. A number of publications tried it and expressed great optimism, particularly for the promised open version. However, these reports were in June 1979; it would be some time before any TR8 would be subjected to serious road-testing.

The official international launch date of the TR8 took place on 13 April 1980, not long after that of the US-market version of the Rover 3500 'SD1' hatchback. With sales due to begin on 1 May, the recommended price from Jaguar Rover Triumph was $11,900 at the port of entry, with air conditioning – like the TR7 – a factory-fit option.

Despite the agonizing wait, once it did arrive in US showrooms the Triumph TR8, by now only available as an open model, was received with enormous enthusiasm by the American motoring press, who had become used to feeling exasperated at the gradual enfeebling of most European sports cars, seemingly immured to progress. Typical of the acclaim that this

apparently mould-breaking car received was Don Sherman's eulogy in the August 1980 issue of *Car and Driver*, which featured a Triton Green TR8 on the cover. Sherman's article was also graced with images that, like the cover, were by celebrated US photographer George Lepp.

Sherman, one of *Car and Driver*'s leading writers of the day and a noted Anglophile, had already sampled one of the first (and few) US-specification Rover SD1 V8 models for the magazine's May 1980 issue, and he had concluded that report by claiming the Rover was 'a car one

George Lepp was commissioned by Car and Driver *to take a stunning series of photographs of the Triton Green TR8 tested by the magazine for its August 1980 issue and featured on the front cover. (George Lepp)*

Don Sherman at the wheel of the TR8 he tested in California for Car and Driver. *'Nothing less than the reinvention of the sports car' was his memorable summation of the new Triumph. (George Lepp)*

savours with the hope that there will always be an England'. Three months later, with a session in the similarly powered TR8 freshly under his belt, Sherman made his enthusiasm for the new offering clear as he kicked off his report:

> Please be patient while your reporter sets the Olivetti for a full-tilt rave review. It's the Triumph TR8, here after one of the most protracted gestation periods in automotive history. Now that all the heavenly bodies are in alignment, the TR8 is too. And it's good: nothing less than the reinvention of the sports car, mate.

The good news continued throughout Sherman's report, but he justified his enthusiasm by claiming that the new V8-powered Triumph was good for a handful of fundamental reasons: 'the TR8 is an amalgam of three simple elements that have combined in one of those rare reactions where the end product far exceeds all expectations … the fairy princess has touched this car with her magic wand somewhere along the line'.

The three elements that made the TR8 such a great car for Sherman were the basic TR7 platform, the new convertible top and − last but by no means least − the V8 engine, which he felt gave the new car greater power but at the same time a degree of civilization that he found lacking in the TR7:

The TR8 is a joy to drive because it's fast without a fuss. There's a nice rumble to the dual pipes when you crank it up and back out of the garage, but hardly any commotion under the hood thereafter. Put it into gear, step on the pedal, and the TR8 goes.

The smooth, even power also brought other benefits: 'The V8 brings a balance to this sports car that it never had as a TR7. There's a little understeer while turning toward the apex of a bend, but you can trade this in for manageable drift angles just by stepping on the gas pedal.' Sherman concluded that there were just two things he would have liked changed: one was the noise from a poorly muffled anti-smog air-pump, while the other was the disappointing quality of the brakes. The latter was a frequent complaint among other contemporary TR8 testers and owners, and a common cause for aftermarket improvement, as Sherman suggested: 'The TR8 weighs almost 200 pounds more than a TR7, and really could use fourteen-inch wheels and some hellacious disc brakes all round'.

So praiseworthy was the article that an obviously delighted JRT reprinted it in the form of a brochure, with a front page based on that of the actual August 1980 *Car and Driver* cover, that was given away to potential customers. Sherman's memorable line 'nothing less than the reinvention of the sports car' was also picked up in subsequent corporate advertising.

Looking back on his report from the perspective of more than 25 years, Don Sherman remains enamoured today – although the perilous state of British Leyland that precipitated the TR8's demise is of course even clearer with the benefit of hindsight:

> The end was in view for British sports cars: MG Midgets delivered 50 horsepower, Spitfires 52, MGBs 67. The good stuff was Italian – X1/9, Fiat Spider 2000, Alfa Spider Veloce. There was no Corvette roadster in this period and that classic was in any case suffering from a lack of inspiration and new emissions controls.

Perhaps surprisingly, some of the other more recent sports car offerings of the day did not particularly excite Sherman and his colleagues: 'the Datsun 280ZX was fat by now, the Porsche 924 and even the Ferrari 308 were underwhelming', he considers. 'So we were hungry for encouraging sports car news and the TR8 convertible filled that need quite nicely.'

The testing took place in California, which, as Sherman rightly points out, was the ideal place to enjoy a rumbling roadster. Looking back, he sums up his reactions:

> Basically, this was a Corvette sired by British parents … as you can see from the photos, we whipped that test car thoroughly and it took the abuse well. In its day, the TR8 stood out from a dreary background with a rare combination of virtues – decent looks, reasonable price, and satisfying performance. The car's competition record also sparked interest and enhanced the pedigree.

Road & Track's June 1980 issue featured that magazine's TR8 road test, under the sub-heading 'Good news from the other side'. The report started by celebrating the news that the arrival of the TR8 heralded the return of the 'lusty-hearted convertible sports car', which, the magazine suggested, 'will outrun most every other sports sedan and sports car this side of $15,000'. Interestingly, the magazine had been advised there would only

be 2,500 TR8s built for the 1980 model year and that 10 per cent would be closed coupés, but the latter would not be sold in California.

Road & Track sampled both a California-specification fuel-injected car and a regular Federal '49-state' car with twin carburettors, and commented that there seemed to be hardly any difference between the two versions, both offering far more satisfying performance than the TR7, albeit at a considerable penalty in terms of fuel consumption. While the magazine thought the TR8's ride was good, the testers suggested that the suspension was softer than ideal, and wondered if in future a stiffer, more sporting set-up might be made available as an option. Even so, the TR8 did well in the traditional *Road & Track* slalom test. The brakes, however, came in for similar criticisms to those voiced by *Car and Driver*.

Alongside the *Road & Track* issue on the newsstands, the June 1980 *Motor Trend* report on the 'TR8 V-8' also gave the new open V8-powered TR a hearty welcome. 'Trust the British to step backwards in time and, paradoxically, reveal the future', suggested Fred Gregory in his report. In a review that largely echoed the findings of the other two major US car enthusiast magazines, Gregory said that the TR8 'feels like a sports car should', although he was concerned at the likely high retail price, nudging Corvette and Datsun 280ZX territory.

A fourth US magazine also raved about the TR8. Walt Woron, writing in *Road Test* for the July 1980 issue, dubbed the TR8 the 'best new sports car of 1980'. 'Yes, the body of the coupé is five years old' he admitted, but 'it was five years ahead of its time when it was first introduced. You only have to look at the wedge shapes coming out of Europe, Japan and Detroit to see that, Triumph pioneered it.' Woron also noted that the TR8 engine had its roots in a 1961 Buick, but justified this by exclaiming that 'if any car deserved to succeed because of its engine, it's the Triumph TR8'.

It was also apparent that the writer's enthusiasm for the TR8 was shared by some of the onlookers he met out on the test: 'at a gas station a young man steps out of his sedan, looks longingly at the dark green TR8 convertible on the other side of the island, sighs and murmurs to no one in particular, "now *that's* the kind of car I should be driving ...'". Generally, Woron and his colleagues characterized the TR8 as a sort of junior Corvette, and they even had little complaint about the brakes, although they confessed they would have preferred to have seen discs all round. All in all, the *Road Test* eulogy rounded off a fantastic set of debut reports for the TR8 in the key US enthusiast media. Surely nothing could go wrong?

TR8 Assessments in Europe

Like the TR7 before it, the production TR8 appeared in the North American market first, the intention being that European sales would

Triumph TR8 Convertible – US Specification 1980

Engine	
Cylinder arrangements	90-degree V8 with pushrod operated valves with hydraulic lifters
Bore/stroke	3.5/2.8in (88.9/71.1mm)
Displacement	215cu in (3528cc)
Compression ratio	8.1:1
Fuel intake	49 states: Twin Zenith 175 CDSET
	California: Lucas/Bosch Electronic Fuel Injection
Ignition	Electronic
Horsepower	49 states: 133bhp SAE/5,000rpm
	California: 148bhp SAE/5,000rpm
Torque	49 states: 174lb ft/3,000rpm
	California: 168lb ft/3,250rpm
Chassis	
Transmission	5-speed manual
Rear axle ratio	3.08:1
Suspension (front)	Independent MacPherson strut
Suspension (rear)	Live axle with sway bars
Wheels/tyres	13-inch diameter 5.5J cast alloy wheel with 185/70SR13 steel-belted radial
Braking system, front/ rear	9.7 inch diameter disc/9.0 inch diameter drum. Power-assisted
Steering	Rack-and-pinion power-assisted. 2.8 turns lock-to-lock
Dimensions and capacities	
Curb weight	49 states: 2,662lb (1,654kg)
	California: 2,650lb (1,647kg)
Wheelbase	85in (2,159mm)
Front track	55.5in (1,410mm)
Rear track	55.3in (1,405mm)
Overall length	165.5in (4,204mm)
Overall width	66.2in (1,681mm)
Overall height	49.5in (1,257mm) (hood [top] erected)
Ground clearance	3.6in (91mm)
Boot [trunk] capacity	9.7cu ft (0.27m3)
Turning circle	31.6ft (10m)
Fuel tank capacity	49 states: 14.4 US gal (12.0 Imp gal; 54.5ltr)
	California: 14.6 US gal (12.2 Imp gal; 55.3ltr)
EPA mpg 'Highway'/'City'	49 states: 22/14mpg
	California: 26/16mpg

follow up to a year behind. Most European car magazines, however, were reluctant to wait until they got an invitation from Jaguar Rover Triumph and so the majority tested US-specification cars to provide an advance view of what was being promised for the future. Australian motoring writer Peter Robinson, a frequent contributor at the time to *CAR* magazine, tagged along with the American and Canadian journalists in the spring of 1979 and his preview report appeared in the June 1979 issue of *CAR*.

Robinson expressed regret that the TR8 had little to distinguish it, in visual terms, beyond a small bonnet bulge and twin exhaust pipes, but he felt certain it would be seen as 'the logical successor to the 240Z two-seater, the Austin Healey 3000 and perhaps even the open E-Type Jaguar'. He reported that the test car (YDU 617S) had been rallied by Jeff Herbert, had been crashed at least twice (once in Germany) and had led a hard life as an American specification prototype: 'Despite this, and the fact that it had an air pump which whined and lowered the power output from the Rover 3500's British figures of 155bhp at 5,250rpm to just 133bhp at 5,000rpm with torque chopped from 240ft lb at 3,000rpm to 198lb ft at 2,500rpm, it drove like a five-speed rocket.' Robinson was impressed:

> The acceleration is hefty. Leyland talk about a standing mile of around 16 seconds, with 0–60mph in 8.4 seconds. Whether these times are for the American specification car or the further-off British version wasn't mentioned, but one suspects that they are probably for the American car. There is power everywhere in every gear and this accentuates the car's lift-off oversteer characteristics. It's fun, but it needs learning, and concentration.

Of course, Peter Robinson's preview – of a US specification pre-production prototype – was a long way from a thorough assessment of a road-going European-specification TR8, but it was inevitable that enthusiasts would have to play a waiting game. In the case of *CAR* readers, their next chance to read about the TR8 was in the December 1980 issue, when writer Nick Valery

reported on a drive (in another US-specification TR8, albeit a production one) along the west coast of the USA, unquestionably prime sports car country.

Valery was unconvinced about the styling, but the ability of the TR8 to act as a 'Q' car, looking like a humble TR7, appealed to him. 'Few of the muscle cars are much of a match for the beefy little Triumph with its five-speed box', he wrote, adding that a Porsche 911 driver was taken aback when the TR8 failed to run out of puff in the traffic lights grand prix: 'At the next set of lights his eyes are crawling all over the Triumph. Once bitten, twice shy: he stays in the next lane, respectfully behind.'

During his drive to Washington, Valery tested his charge to the full and was clearly impressed, describing it at one point 'as solid as a rock, as predictable as gravity'. Concluding his report with an optimistic ending, Valery said that when the TR8 was launched in the UK there would be 'nothing in its class to touch it, save perhaps the Porsche 924'. However he was concerned that it might be priced too high, noting that Americans paid 'only' $11,900 for their TR8s. Sadly, however, Valery and his colleagues would be denied the opportunity to sample a production TR8 on their home turf.

The Best TR Never Sold in Britain

George Spence was part of the Rover Triumph team charged with getting the European TR8 into production, a task which has bitter-sweet memories for him:

> My remit was the TR8 UK and the proposed updates for the 81 model year. The plan was that all changes and modifications had to go through a 'Modification Committee'. Kerry Cook, the Development Engineers and I were of the view that things should happen – things like improved front suspension bearings and so forth, which had become apparent as problems in service. The committee would save these things up for a model change – and there were about 150 on the list! We actually set out to build a car with all these changes made to it.

X898 resurfaces at a TR Drivers' Club event in 2005. (Roel van Es)

The TR8 X-Cars

Rex Holford, TR8 Registrar of the TR Drivers' Club, has a passion for the UK-specification TR8 and has made a study of the special 'X' coded prototypes. The following is a summary of the cars known to survive, derived from his records.

X898 – a coupé – is the earliest known example to survive. It is believed to have been built in 1976/7 with the very early (pre-1977) large fuel filler cap. This was fitted with an EFi engine and was subjected to testing by a TR Drivers' Club member who at the time worked for BL. Its colour is Triumph White.

X919 – the earliest known convertible – is believed to have been built in 1977/8 with left-hand drive and a fuel-injected engine and automatic transmission to USA specifications. Later modifications changed it to right-hand drive, with altered trim and modified engine. Its original colour was Triumph White.

X921 – a convertible – was built in 1979 to UK specifications, having a carburettored high compression engine and automatic transmission. It had evidence of temperature sensing equipment on the carburettors, inlet manifold and oil pump. Its colour was Carnelian Red.

X923 – another convertible – was also built in 1979 to UK specifications but had a five-speed manual gearbox. On the MIRA test track it recorded a flying quarter-mile of 130.43mph (209.9km/h), an all-time record for Triumph at the track at the time (although later beaten by a TR7 Turbo; *see* Chapter 9). Its colour was Platinum Silver.

X924 – a convertible – reverted to one of the older examples being built in 1977/8, probably in the same batch as X919. This was built as a TR7 and converted to V8 specification in 1978 with a manual gearbox originally to USA specification. Later a high compression engine UK spec was fitted. Its colour was Vermilion.

X925 – a convertible – was the last of the experimental cars and was built in right-hand-drive form to UK specifications with manual transmission. It was used to evaluate interior trim. Its colour was Silver Leaf with colour co-ordinated bumpers, brown interior, brown-tinted windows and modified centre console and glove pockets in the doors.

According to Holford, TR Drivers' Club members currently own all the above X-cars.

At the time, car industry unions were still very strong and George Spence and his colleagues found they were unable to get the parts they wanted from the production section in order to build a special car in the experimental department with all the changes:

> We had a list of the bits we wanted but the unions wouldn't let us have them. They knew that they were missing out on the opportunity to get paid to build it! So in the end we just put a bodyshell on the line and they put all the bits in, and then we took it off the end of the line and up to 'Fletch' to the experimental shop. So the union men were happy as they got paid for not building a car!

Spence recalls that this special car was very well built and after the project was cancelled he hoped to get hold of it at a knock-down price. However, the handful of 'TR8 UK' cars were all taken to British Car Auctions at Measham where they were sold at a closed auction that was by invitation only – to a trade audience. 'The one with the modifications which I had wanted went for around £10,000', Spence recalls ruefully.

TR8 Registrar Rex Holford suggests that this car may have been X925, which featured a number of experimental features, including brown velour interior, a modified centre console, different glovebox, suspension bushes and colour coordinated bumpers that match the car bodywork.

Someone else with memories of the right-hand-drive TR8 is Kevin Jones, who in 1980 was one of the last Triumph apprentices and in later years became better known as the public face of MG Rover press and publicity. 'I helped build the first RHD TR8', Jones recalls, adding with crystal-clear recollection that the metallic silver-grey car was given the registration number MHP 404V and was passed to Brian Fox, a BL Director. This car is still in existence, as are many of the very rare factory UK-specification TR8s; according to Rex Holford, this car has the special striped TR7 Spider seat facings.

When it eventually arrived, the TR8 came at a difficult point in Triumph's history and, as we shall see later, the whole sports car business was struggling under a number of sources of pressure; in the end, cancellation of the TR8 for the home market came as a Product Planning Letter (PPL) produced by Denis Chick, who in those days worked in Product Planning and, like Kevin Jones, went on to a senior role in corporate PR for the company:

> Sales of TR7 were dwindling, which meant that TR8 was already looking like a sales and profitability challenge. New investment was badly needed in a replacement for SD1 and the mid-range cars like Maestro/ Montego. It all added up to a PPL cancelling the TR8 for the UK and then, before long, the whole TR7/8 project in the US and Europe.

X925 – now registered as PVC 568W - is a silver TR8 convertible with colour-coordinated bumpers, a brown velour interior and an experimental centre console. (Roel van Es)

Compare these photographs of a factory prototype for a UK market TR8 with the photo of X925. The side tape stripe, different alloy wheels and unique tail lights (similar to but not the same as those fitted to the contemporary Rover SD1) do not feature on the surviving road-registered car, but the brown interior trim appears to be the same. (John Ashford)

Rare Breed: The Home-Market TR8

The Triumph TR8 is a relatively rare car worldwide; an estimated 2,634 were built in total, although the precise accuracy of this figure is uncertain. On the basis that the overall TR7 and TR8 build was of the order of 115,090, this means that the TR8 made up less than 2.3 per cent of the total. When it comes to the TR8 built for the home market, of course, the figure is even tinier; only twenty-five Drop Head Coupés are believed to have been built to UK specifications (a batch of sixty-three Fixed Head Coupés is believed to have been scheduled, but none is known to exist).

The key TR8 UK-specification cars are the two batches of nine Drop Head Convertibles built as pilot-build runs in 1980 and 1981. This extreme rarity of genuine TR8 convertibles means that there has been a strong temptation for the less scrupulous to pass off a TR7 V8 conversion as the real thing, or to modify a LHD car to RHD and claim it is one of the eighteen pilot-build. Fortunately there are experts in the various clubs who can help identify a genuine UK-spec TR8, including Rex Holford, the TR Drivers' Club TR8 Registrar, who helped produce a useful guide *Is it a TR8?*, which is available from the club.

Holford says that 'to date, 16 of the 18 UK-spec cars, plus a further 112 have been found'. The latter are a mixture of re-imported USA-spec cars, factory demonstrators, experimental cars, USA and UK specification cars that were retained by BL for test purposes and prototype cars. Among the UK cars are a number with special stories, such as Richard Pilmore's Platinum Silver experimental car (X923; registration KHP 574V), which took the MIRA test circuit speed record for a Triumph car, having achieved a flying quarter-mile speed of 130.43mph (209.9km/h) and a lap record of 127.53mph (205.23km/h) in August 1981. Unlike the North American specification cars, the UK-specification did without the constrictions of catalytic converters and benefited from a higher compression ratio engine, so performance was definitely better, with the power output up to 152bhp at 4,750rpm with twin Stromberg 175CD carburettors.

9 Rearguard Action: Boxer, Broadside and Others

We have already seen how the British Leyland merger had brought together MG and Triumph as slightly uncomfortable bedfellows. The situation hardly became any easier as the 1970s progressed. Satisfying marque loyalties could arguably have been addressed through thoughtful and strategic planning, but despite the various half-hearted efforts at this, management focus was usually diverted to much bigger issues than the matter of sports car policy.

An obvious obstacle to change was the decision to retain MG as part of the 'Austin Morris' instead of the 'Rover Triumph' division. Clearly the increasingly marginalized MG sports cars remained tied to Austin Morris by their components, although the MG Midget did receive a Triumph engine from 1974, and the various divisional restructurings could have made more of the old chains of command redundant if there had been the political and financial will. Of course, MG's Abingdon factory was on Cowley's doorstep and MG alliances had always leaned more closely towards the old 'BMC' camp than the 'Leyland' one, but by 1975 these old allegiances were becoming less and less relevant other than to traditionalists. Another factor was the almost mystical status that the MG factory itself had gained – fostered and encouraged by advertising and MG's own people – but it would take someone of Michael Edwardes's force of character to consider overturning this.

Rather belatedly, in the wake of the relaxations in planned Federal legislation, it was recognized that the customer for a 'traditional' style MG Midget, Triumph Spitfire or MGB was not necessarily going to opt for a 'modern' TR7, whether open or hardtop.

Sports Car Number One

In August 1978 Jaguar Rover Triumph produced a 'Product Plan' that set out the division's objectives for the next decade. By this time the MG Midget and Triumph Spitfire had already been targeted for euthanasia, but it was recognized that with their demise would also go a useful part of the company's North American business, even if entirely separate models to replace the outgoing ones would be a financial impossibility. Earlier in the year Bruce McWilliams had suggested a major reskin (even if were to be of the MGB) as a way forward and so, doubtless with a partial nod to this idea, the JRT team proposed 'SC1' ('Sports Car Number One') as a route to replacing all the small and medium sports cars, from Midget to TR8.

The idea was to introduce a 'light sports' version, powered by the 1.7-litre 'O' Series engine and using the MGB gearbox, to sell as a Midget/Spitfire/MGB replacement from the autumn of 1983, while the TR7 and TR8 would remain on sale for a further year. Then, it was suggested, the 'medium sports' version of SC1 would be introduced, marrying the 2.0-litre 'O' Series with the 77mm five-speed gearbox and the corresponding heavier duty back axle. According to the Product Plan, there would be a 'high level of common mechanical components and possible adoption of floor pressings from one of the current sports cars to minimize investment'.

An original design styling sketch by Dave Keepax for Triumph Broadside – the ultimate iteration of the TR7/TR8 programme. (Dave Keepax)

Thus SC1 could have offered a route to both an 'MGD' and a 'TR9'. To ensure sufficient distinction, there would be 'two open models with common sheet metal. Differential exterior style would be achieved by use of "bolt-on" plastic front and rear structures' as well as 'alternative trim levels to support engine and body variations'. The SC1 would have to be designed to meet EEC and North American safety, emission and fuel economy standards, but at the same time it was suggested that there could be exploration of 'alternative cost-reduced features for non-NAS models where safety legislation permits – e.g. bumpers, impact and occupant protection'. Interestingly, despite the imminent arrival of the TR8, the SC1 product proposal appears to have made no specific reference to the V8 engine as an option, almost certainly because of the fleet fuel consumption issues (*see* Chapter 8).

Alongside SC1, the product plan made reference to the succession of the Dolomite. It was suggested that a new Dolomite could be co-engineered with SC1, and went on to suggest that the Dolomite replacement (possibly 'son of SD2/TM1') would be even more crucial than SC1, although the product planners provided no detail to support their thinking. As far as I have been able to determine, no prototypes of SC1 were built: it remained an idea on paper, but would later be overtaken by the less ambitious 'Project Broadside' (*see* below) while the 'new Dolomite' would soon be replaced by a joint project with Honda that led to the Triumph Acclaim. From time to time, other ideas to improve the TR7 range were

considered and one of the more unusual ideas was a three-seater, undoubtedly modelled on the Matra-Simca Baghera and Murena sports cars. Stephen Ferrada - who joined Rover Triumph in 1974 but would move to Porsche in 1979 - recalls the work done on this: 'I do remember proposing a special three-seat-abreast version, rather like the Matra Bagheera. For my benefit a TR7 was converted to this layout with handbrake located between driver's seat and door, but the middle seat space which resulted would only have accommodated a child. Nothing came of it, but a good idea all the same!'

Project Boxer: The End of the MGB

Everyone knew it would come some day, but when the death sentence was finally passed on the MGB, and with it MG production at the famous factory at Abingdon, it sent echoes reverberating through the industry. There may have been financially more significant cutbacks during Sir Michael Edwardes's tenure at the helm of British Leyland – not least the closure of Speke – but, as he himself would later acknowledge, none made such emotional waves as the MG affair. Just as significant was the fact that in 1979 sales and support of the MGB remained a fundamental part of the business of British Leyland's North American dealer network.

Suddenly the loss of the MGB, admittedly a car that was becoming increasingly inconvenient to manufacture, meant that the economic viability of the US Jaguar Rover Triumph sales

Triumph's Trojan Horse: The Acclaim

British Leyland had been looking for cooperative partnerships with varying degrees of effectiveness and enthusiasm for quite some time when Michael Edwardes arrived on the scene. Renewed impetus came from the recognition that BL had a glaring gap in its forward programme and it became increasingly obvious that the only practical way to fill that hole would be through some kind of licensing deal. After a number of false starts, the best fit appeared to be with Honda (at that time similar in terms of car volumes to British Leyland) and so, after a brief courtship through diplomatic channels, a relationship was brokered with the promise of a new small/medium car for the British partner. However, rather than an entirely natural product of the marriage union, the first 'offspring' was something of an automotive stepchild in the form of a thinly disguised Honda saloon, which it was agreed would be badged as a Triumph and assembled at Canley.

Based on the Japanese-market Honda Ballade, itself a close relative of the Honda Civic, the new car was lightly re-engineered to suit European tastes and marketed as the Triumph Acclaim. As time passed and the engineering work (mostly production engineering in order to build the car) progressed, however, British Leyland's plans for Canley changed and the production plans for the Acclaim shifted to the former Morris factory at Cowley. Marketing people at British Leyland tried gamely to suggest that the 1.3-litre Honda-engined Acclaim was in some way a replacement for the Dolomite range, but apart from the fact that both cars were four-door saloons the connection was tenuous at best: there was certainly no Triumph Acclaim equivalent of the Dolomite Sprint. There is no doubt that the Acclaim would go on to be one of British Leyland's best-built and most highly regarded cars in terms of reliability and customer satisfaction, and it sowed the seed for a relationship with Honda that brought forth several projects closer to the spirit of 'partnership' than 'transplant', but in the end the reliable but rather dull car – replaced in 1984 by a small Rover – would prove to be a sad and limp finale for the Triumph marque.

network began to look shaky, except for those businesses able to rely upon the largely independent Jaguar family of models. JRT put on a brave face, however, and with the final arrival of the TR7 convertible and TR8 range it seemed to the outside world at least that salvation was in sight.

There is little doubt, however, that the simple fact that the MGB refused to lay down and die – partly through the efforts of the Aston Martin Lagonda Consortium to either buy MG outright or to build the MGB under licence – caused a great deal of grief in the BL camp. US dealers were rallying to the cause of the Consortium when BL would have preferred them simply to focus on the TR7 and TR8. BL certainly wanted to move on, and had tasked its Rover Triumph subsidiary with the task of creating an MG out of the TR7 gene pool; meanwhile the top-level BL talks with Aston Martin, who wanted exclusive access to the MG name, made this a Herculean task.

Just before Christmas 1979 *Motor* published a 'diary' of BL dates that suggested, among reasonably accurate if slightly optimistic dates for other models and facelifts, that at the beginning of 1981 the MGB would be phased out and a '2+2 TR-based MG model' would go into production. This was clearly harking back to the last MG-badged iteration of 'Lynx', but by this stage Lynx itself had been confined to history.

In January 1980 Rover Triumph produced a fresh Product Plan (not for public consumption at that stage), which included the following sports car proposals:

December 1980	MGB run out
Spring 1981	TR7/8 removable hardtop with heated rear window; introduction of 'Boxer', a new model based upon the TR7 convertible with the objective of replacing the MGB initially in the US market
Autumn 1981	2.0-litre 'O' series engine in TR7 and Boxer for 1982 Model Year, with twin-carburettors
Spring 1983	Model range replaced by 'Broadside'
Autumn 1984	Broadside electronic facelift: instrument pack
Autumn 1984	Rover 'Bravo'; four-door saloon to replace SD1 based on SD1 centre section, TR7 front suspension and SD1/Lynx back axle. 2.0 'O' series, 2.6-litre 6-cylinder and 4-cylinder turbo-diesel

Autumn 1985   Rover 'Bravo' five-door hatch or wagon, with V8 engine too

Autumn 1987   Run out Broadside. Dependent on the future opportunity of developing a new sports car in collaboration with Honda, together with a successful launch.

'Boxer', intended as a quick-fix replacement for the MGB, was conceived as a low-budget facelift of the TR7 in arguably the worst BL tradition of 'badge-engineering'. The Boxer project came about at the tail end of 1979, in the immediate aftermath of the announcement that the MGB was to be dropped. Recognizing the importance of the MG name, BL management had looked at the most expedient means of providing the US dealer network with a stopgap MG while something more permanent could be prepared.

The Boxer programme was given the tightest possible budget constraints: total tooling investment was to be no more than £1 million, manufacturing costs of the new model should not exceed a £50 premium compared to the Triumph TR7, and the car would have to be ready for introduction in October 1980, just in time for the 1981 model year and to allow a smooth handover from the outgoing MGB. The five participants in this competition were Triumph Engineering, BL Styling Services (under David Bache), the Michelotti studios (Edgardo Michelotti, son of founder Giovanni), Bob Jankel of Panther Westwinds and Cars and Concepts. By January 1980 all five were ready for review by BL management, and it was decided that the Cars and Concepts one created under Bruce McWilliams's watch should be investigated further.

Mike Dale was not a fan of the Boxer proposal:

> The idea was to badge engineer the TR7 as an MG with small cosmetic changes. I was totally opposed to this because I was a retail salesman when BMC started this trend and I had experienced trying to sell such a silly idea. However, the then international BL management under Tony Ball [BLEO – BL Europe and

The Jaguar Rover Triumph office at Leonia, New Jersey, was responsible for this version of the 'MG Boxer' proposal for an MG-badged derivative of the TR7, featuring forward-tilting Porsche 928 pop-up headlamps and a peculiar MG 'grille' on the nose panel. 'Rostyle' wheels mimicked those of the contemporary MGB; inside the cockpit the red line graphics on the instrument display would one day appear on the MG Metro and Maestro. The tail-lamps were as already proposed for the 1982 model year TR7. It was not one of Leonia's better efforts, but was constrained by budget. (J. Bruce McWilliams)

It is believed that this offering for the 'Boxer' design contest was the one produced by Cars and Concepts in the USA (note the New York licence plates). Although not visible in this view, the rear of this car carried 'MG D' badging. (J. Bruce McWilliams)

Overseas] thought it was going to save the world and flew out in the Concorde one Saturday to go past us to the Dealer Council to convince them I was wrong. The dealers gave him short shrift and the idea died.

Dale admits that he was 'not seen in a very cooperative light' over this and a number of other episodes at the time but:

> it was typical of the kind of thing we had to handle trying to make sense of what the UK was capable of accomplishing and the realities of the marketplace. At times I felt the only thing that kept me in my job was that I had a great relationship with the dealers and the Dealer Council in particular. I knew that successful marketing of any product is decided, in the end, by the strength of the dealer body selling it. Our dealer oriented attitudes provided BL with ten years in the US that the product didn't deserve, save Jaguar in the '80s and again in the '90s.

Alan Edis readily agrees that Boxer had 'no real credibility as an MG'.

Bruce McWilliams admits that his heart wasn't really in the Boxer project either: 'it was a totally ill-conceived plan operating on the notion that you could sell TR7s to MG buyers if you called the car an MG. Still, from my viewpoint, it was

an interesting opportunity to see to what extent a different model could be derived from only two panel changes.' The Leonia interpretation of Boxer – dubbed the 'MG Touring' by its creators – was clever in its use of Porsche 928 headlamps, which rested back in the nose of the car when switched off, remaining on view and providing a modest but clever differentiation from the TR7. The nose was also modified to accommodate a peculiar interpretation of an MG radiator grille, while at the back of the car Rover SD1-style tail-lights were fitted, part of a common facelift already being investigated for the TR7 in any case.

While this review was going on, however, the future of MG continued to be spun out with the long drawn-out saga of the – ultimately abortive – Aston Martin Lagonda talks to either buy or licence produce the MGB. With the Boxer and indeed the whole BL sports car programme remaining in a precarious position, the intervention of Aston Martin provided what would be a brief respite and before long the Boxer project was abandoned. Bruce McWilliams recalls that Jeff Herbert was tasked with pulling together the feasibility: 'the tooling bill came out within the million pound ceiling. But then, sales forecasts for the car were, understandably, gloomy, and that was the end of this bizarre excursion in product planning.'

Project Broadside: Last Ditch Effort

If 'Boxer' was a relatively hasty attempt to tackle the consequences of the loss of the MGB, the contemporary 'Broadside' project was a more considered attempt to move the TR7 family forward a step and to tackle the MG problem in a reasonably rational way.

The Broadside programme – referred to internally as project RT061 – was envisaged as providing both a new Triumph convertible (with optional hardtop) as well as an MG-badged 2+2 GT. The MGB GT had proved quite a popular car in the home market during its declining years, but even so the idea of seemingly abandoning the far more important US open MG market purely in favour of a Triumph smacks of commercial suicide. But then desperate times call for desperate measures ... the whole sports car programme was already resting on a knife edge.

As Product Planner with an oversight of Triumph, Alan Edis had often enjoyed the privilege of naming new projects, and in the case of Broadside he had a little in-joke, for the final four letters of 'Broadside' equate to a reversal of his surname. The Product Plan described Broadside as:

> a direct replacement for the TR7/8 model range and Boxer derivative. The vehicle will be based on the TR7/8 underbody (with longer wheelbase) and mechanicals utilizing some new panels previously developed for the discontinued Lynx programme. Engines 2.0 litre 'O' series and V8. Dependent upon Austin-Morris engine strategy, an opportunity exists to install a turbo-charged version of 'O' series from the introduction of Broadside.

Jeff Herbert confesses that, in a way, 'Broadside' became his pet project: 'the problems with the TR7 included its appearance – it had been such a radical departure at the time; Harris Mann's design was so far ahead of its day. If the TR7 had been well engineered and well built, it might have

Triumph Engineering also had a go at the 'Boxer' project; its effort was finished in a pale metallic green (a long-standing tradition with MG prototypes and record breakers) and a shallow, almost vestigial MG grille. There were changes to the 'wraparound' of the rear bumper and the treatment of the tail panel. Side stripes sought to disguise the characteristic side sweep. (J. Bruce McWilliams)

been more readily accepted in the marketplace.' Herbert explains that Broadside was intended to take some of the more desirable aspects of the aborted Triumph Lynx project and use them to improve upon the basic TR7 package:

> We tried to make the TR7 look better and to put in the basic engineering changes to put right the things that were wrong. And we wanted to minimize the controversial styling. The TR6 and MGB were still regarded as iconic sports cars. We look at wedge shapes nowadays and they look okay – but in those days it

'O' Series Engine

Throughout the existence of the TR7, the distinctive Triumph-engineered slant-four helped to define the car. However, with the erosion of Triumph's independent engineering base and the need to rationalize components, not least in the US market, the pressure to drop the slant-four in favour of Austin Morris's 'O' Series engine (also destined for the MGB) became irresistible. Not that Rover Triumph did not fight its corner: a slant-four was even tried in an MGB, although according to Triumph's Martin Smith,

> It was an extremely tight fit! It was one route that MG were keen to use, but the engine bay was very narrow in the B and the chassis rails were also narrow meaning the engine had to sit up quite high, not a problem for the height other than it raised the centre of gravity and made the transmission line through the tunnel high as well.

By the spring of 1981, with the discontinuation of the Triumph Dolomite, the TR7 had become the only car still using the slant-four Triumph unit (a similar situation to when the MGB had been the last to use the old BMC 'B' Series). Slant-four engine production was now down to an uneconomical 300 per week, and *The Times* suggested on 14 March 1981 that the 'O' Series engine might be destined for the TR7 as part of an economy drive to save the sports car. From the records compiled by TR Register member and enthusiast Derek Graham, it appears that at least twenty-six TR7 prototypes were fitted with 'O' Series units and at least one of these was a turbocharged unit, with which it is recorded that TR7 Commission Number ACW30210 (registered as KHP 537V) 'lapped at MIRA on the 27th April 1982 at 132.35mph [212.99km/h], with the flying quarter mile at 129.16mph [207.86km/h]' (thereby just eclipsing the TR8 record referred to in Chapter 8).

After the cancellation of the programme, many of the cars were scrapped or disposed of; the latter category were stripped of their experimental engine installations. A DVLA database search carried out by Derek Graham confirms rather intriguingly that some of the cars that had supposedly been scrapped are still road-registered, although it seems unlikely any now have an 'O' Series engine fitted. Perhaps it is unsurprising that the engineers at Canley were unconvinced of the merits of the 'O' Series engine, which of course hailed from Longbridge: Martin Smith, from the perspective of Canley's Engine Development section, says that his colleagues dubbed it the 'oh dearies'. One of their major concerns was the 'NVH' (Noise, Vibration and Harshness) of the two-valve per cylinder ('2V') 'O' Series, which Canley adjudged was unacceptable:

> This was in the TR7 – although in the MGB variant (which we at Triumph worked on in conjunction with a small team of engineers at Abingdon) it was just about bearable. Some of this was no doubt due to the MGB being a much heavier bodyshell, designed for an 'upright' L4 engine, and the TR7 being designed for the 'Slant-4' engine and of more modern bodyshell construction (i.e. thinner gauge sheet!). The most memorable aspect of this 'harshness' was the throttle pedal 'zing' felt through the throttle cable (we tried rubber mounting the throttle to reduce this), the gear lever 'zing' which was like gripping a vibrator, and finally the roughness felt through the heels of the feet from the bulkhead heel board.

According to Smith, there was a considerable debate about the virtues of the slant-four versus the 'O' Series:

> The 'O' was reputed (and here I did see the actual figures) to cost just £85 at the end of the engine production line, the Slant-4 PE124 8-valve was £170, whilst the Slant-4 PE124 16-valve was over £240. However, the £85 cost for the 'O' was based on a production level of 22,000 units per week – for it was intended to be fitted in Ital, Princess, LDV Sherpa, TR7, MGB, and finally the SD1. I don't think it ever reached more than 6,000 units a week, if that!

The headquarters of the Austin Morris division, the source of the 'O' Series, was Longbridge – known officially as 'Group 1 engines'. According to Smith, the Longbridge engineers had only run the 'O' on carburettors as that was all that was needed at the time for UK and European emissions:

We at Triumph, selling into the North American market, were more involved in the more stringent Federal and Californian emission regulations of the time, which required the use of an efficient fuel system control, hence the use of the Bosch Fuel Injection system on Federal TR7s. We were tasked with 'Federalizing' the 'O' Series for use in both TR7 and MGB. Due to logistics problems with working with Bosch the decision was made to revert back to a Lucas control system (as Lucas then had the patent rights to digital fuel injection and the emerging Lucas system, with both fuel and ignition control, was seen as the better alternative).

We soon established that the 'O' was very poor in its combustion characteristics, it was very reluctant to idle at less than about 900rpm (the 2-valve Slant-4 could run as low as 400rpm on fuel injection), had problems in running with a catalyst and the basic design of the engine, with its flat head and bowl in piston chamber, meant that there was very little movement of the charge in the cylinder and the pistons (being bowl in piston design) were very heavy, giving rise to high secondary order imbalances. The engine worked for Austin Morris as they ran with carburettors which were tuned well to the rich side and their cars were more 'used' to 'rough' engines with the mountings being designed differently. We tried lots of things to get the engine to idle smoothly, extended spark plug electrodes, swirl vanes in the inlet, changed injection timing, and plenty of camshaft profile changes and cam timing 'swings'.

Eventually, to prove to the powers that be that the engine was just not suitable for 'Federalizing' in its current form, we introduced 'squish' to the combustion chamber design. To do this we made a 'plate' about 12.7mm thick and interposed it between the head and block. AE supplied some 'O' pistons with flat tops, and the plate was given a 'bath tub' chamber (similar to the Spitfire L4 engine), a pretty basic chamber indeed! A longer cam belt (10 teeth more if I recall correctly) was all else that was needed. The result of this transformed the combustion – allowing the engine to idle well – but still with the even heavier pistons the secondary order 'shake' was worse than ever!

But the point had been proven and as a consequence I wrote an internal document arguing for the adoption of a new dohc 4-valve per cylinder head to allow the 'O' engine to meet the stringent North American EPA regulations, which was then sanctioned by the 'powers'. This was called the TR7 4 Valve 'O', and was later to become the M series which found life in the Rover 820. But that, as they say, is another and some would say an even sadder story still, as the original engine was completely re-vamped by Longbridge, losing a lot of the best features designed into it at Canley. Annoying, as we at Canley kept the engine 'alive' after the scrapping of TR7 as a 'skunk project' hiding the running and initial development from the bean counters!

Smith is certain that no TR7 was ever fitted with a running 4V 'O' Series because of the programme being cancelled: 'the only vehicles to run such an engine was firstly an Austin Ambassador and eventually a Rover SD1 which had previously housed a 2V O-Series turbo'. Having studied Derek Graham's records referred to above, Smith concludes: 'TR7 O-Series vehicles listed in the registry were noted as 4Vs for Federal 1983 Model Year, but these cars were engineless as the 2V units had been removed in anticipation of the 4V builds; this is one possibility why no O-Series TR7s exist today other than the Broadside prototype at Gaydon'.

The engine rationalization debate came to a head around 1980/81; according to Smith, by this stage the Slant-4 in TR7 was 'signed off' for Federal emissions until 1986, with the tighter Californian regulations 'signed off' until 1985. He says that he does not believe any other single manufacturer could claim this for their product at the time:

The other major factor in favour of the Slant-4 was the fuel economy was far superior to the 'O' Series (hardly surprising as the combustion was so much more efficient), and 'our' ally in all this debate was Jaguar who were worried about the proposed Federal CAFE (Corporate Average Fuel Economy) tax, the so-called 'Gas Guzzler Tax', and without Triumphs in the North American market with a fuel-efficient car Jaguar were going to be hit hard by this tax.

In the end, however, all this debate became sadly irrelevant.

This peculiar treatment – mostly mocked up with paper, tape and a spare MGB bumper badge – was supposedly a 'TR7A' facelift to correspond to the MG Boxer. (J. Bruce McWilliams)

was arguably too novel. It was the same sort of problem with the SD1 being a five-door hatchback – nowadays that is less unusual for a luxurious car.

According to Product Planner Tony Dyson,

Broadside was an amalgamation of Lynx front wings, Lynx doors and a TR7 chassis which we stretched by just four inches in order to match the doors. We made the car into both a convertible and a coupé, the latter with a sloping tailgate à la Lynx, and were able to squeeze in two rear plus two seats in the rear of the passenger compartment.

Norman Rose further recalls the difficulty of accommodating the conflicting requirements of rear seating and the location of the fuel tank, and the fact that the Broadside convertible would have had a 'T-Bar' roof, similar to that of the Triumph Stag, rather than the harmonic bumpers of the shorter TR7 convertible. Broadside itself was therefore a hybrid of TR7 and Lynx parts; whereas the Lynx would have been eleven inches longer in wheelbase than the TR7, the idea with Broadside was to use the new fluted doors already tooled-up for the Lynx but with a floorpan lengthened only four inches,

Stephen Ferrada of the Rover Triumph design office produced this styling sketch for Broadside in December 1978 that showed a neat detachable hardtop; a hardtop with heated rear window was already a part of the forward plan for the TR7/TR8. Ferrada later worked at Porsche and Daimler-Benz in Germany. (Norman Rose)

Dave Keepax was responsible for sketches and this subsequent scale model for 'Broadside', which dates from February 1979. (Dave Keepax)

thereby allowing both a better-balanced chassis (both visually and dynamically) as well as the possibility of two-plus-two seating.

Early sketches were produced by Stephen Ferrada showing an open version with the 'Bache' side flutes as well as a fundamentally identical alternative with a removable hardtop; even before the creation of the Broadside concept, Rover Triumph had been considering dropping the fixed head coupé in favour of a removable or semi-secure hardtop version of the open car.

The concept allowed for Broadside to appear in 1983 as a wholesale replacement for the TR7 range, at the same time allowing many fundamental engineering improvements to be made in the interests of greater product quality and service durability. As Jeff Herbert explains:

For example, the wiring looms on the TR7 and SD1 were like elephant trunks. Simple things had been missed at the outset, like engineering a channel so that the wiring loom could fit properly, rather than allowing it to sit under the carpet in such a way that after a few months of use there would be a broken wire – that sort of thing seems so obvious, but it wasn't done! Those kind of changes can be expensive to make later on – so you really ought to do them right the first time. Facelifts were a means to help achieve the necessary re-engineering – although some of the facelifts weren't taken forward as they proved to be just too expensive.

There was increasing interest by both British Leyland and its supplier partners, Lucas Industries, in electronic dashboard systems (which would eventually see the light of day in the

The original open version of 'Broadside' begins to take shape in 1979, using the basis of a 'cut and shut' Lynx bodyshell. (John Ashford).

infamous talking dashboard of the 1983 Austin Maestro) and so perhaps it is hardly surprising that Rover Triumph considered the possibility of an 'electronic dashboard' facelift for the Broadside range by 1984.

Rover Triumph built just two known running Broadside prototypes, both of which were cobbled from surviving Lynx prototypes. The metallic brown coupé and silver convertible survive in the Heritage Museum collection, and the museum graciously allowed both out into the fresh air to be photographed especially for this book. I am also grateful to Steve Redway and TR Register member Derek Graham, who have jointly made a detailed study of these cars; an excellent article written by Redway has appeared in *TR Action*.

The silver convertible (X917) features an 'O' Series engine (number 20H647AAHPP006) and was built first, in February/March 1979. Although many TR7 cars were fitted with 'O' Series engines, it is likely that this prototype is the only 'TR7' or derivative still running with its 'O' Series as fitted at the factory, for all other cars are believed to have had their engines removed prior to disposal. The brown coupé (X922) – complete with a V8 engine – was built in October/November 1979 and started life as the second-to-last Lynx (body number Lynx0017L), painted in the same colour as the sole surviving Lynx (X905; body Lynx0018L); there is plenty of evidence of this, such as the underlying green paint visible in places and the hand-beaten panelwork on the rear three-quarters.

Although the two prototypes give the impression of being definitive proposals, they were in fact viewed merely as concepts demonstrating what could be achieved with more imagination. Rover Triumph wanted outside design consultants to cast their eyes over the Broadside project. Accordingly, a Business and Product Planning document of November 1979, entitled 'Broadside Concept Styling Design Brief', described the background to the proposal: 'the Broadside concept is the outcome of a sports car replacement study initiated in 1978 … The development of the Broadside Concept has now reached the stage where detailed styling/design exercises are necessary.'

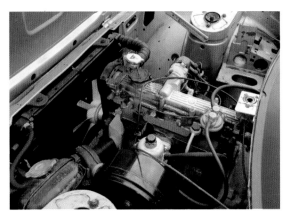

It is believed that the only surviving TR7 'O' Series installation is in fact the open Broadside prototype, which survives as part of the British Motor Heritage collection at Gaydon. (Alisdair Cusick)

The nose of the open 'Broadside' prototype is very similar to that of the production TR7, with the notable exception of the composite aluminium and plastic bumper unit. (Alisdair Cusick)

From the side, the open Broadside looks quite well balanced, and through the use of the Lynx side flute, loses the most controversial styling feature of the TR7. (Alisdair Cusick)

At the rear, the Broadside largely picked up on facelift proposals for the TR7 family that were already in the pipeline. (Alisdair Cusick)

It is perhaps a little too obvious from this angle that the Broadside coupé has been cut and shut from the rather more gracefully realized Lynx. (Alisdair Cusick)

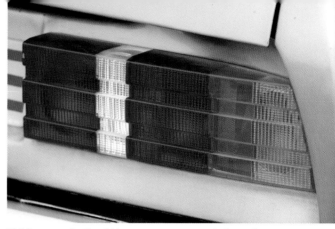

Shades of the late lamented Triumph Stag? The open-top Broadside eschewed the harmonic bumper solution in favour of the roof structure seen here. (Alisdair Cusick)

Tail-lamps on the Broadside prototypes were very similar to those on the contemporary Rover SD1. (Alisdair Cusick)

Whereas the open 'Broadside' prototype has an 'O' Series engine, the closed car has a 3.5-litre Rover V8, almost certainly inherited from the Lynx from which this car was cannibalized. (Alisdair Cusick)

From the front, the surviving Broadside coupé could almost be taken as a Lynx prototype, although the same composite bumpers as seen on the open car also feature. (Alisdair Cusick)

Light grey seats would become a hallmark of MG Metro, Maestro and Montego hatches and saloons in just a few years after the Broadside was built. (Alisdair Cusick)

The opening hatch of the Broadside coupé is a frameless glass unit with twin gas struts. (Alisdair Cusick)

The styling brief document made it clear that the coupé was seen as an 'MG' and the open car as a 'Triumph' with the minimum of other differentiating features (there was reference to the possibility of different grilles and maybe a reversion to fixed headlamps for one or both variants). According to Alan Edis, this was a conscious decision that built on the thinking at the time of Lynx:

> The coupé version was arguably a bit like the MGB GT in concept – it had a hatchback and 2+2 seating, and the MGB GT had become quite fashionable – particularly as a smart lady's car. The rear seats in the MGB GT were of no real value but at least they offered additional storage space.

Throughout the design brief document, there are references to the 'Styling Consultant' and the tight constraints he would face; it seems that only one 'consultant' entered the frame – and it was an old friend of Triumph's.

Broadside Mark II: Michelotti's Last Triumph

Michelotti's association with Triumph may have become severely diluted during the British Leyland years, but the styling company – with Giovanni by now ailing but assisted by his son Edgardo – still maintained connections with the old guard at Triumph. The work that Michelotti had done on the convertible TR7 prototype had probably rekindled awareness both of their capabilities and their enduring interest and affection for Triumph, and so the Italian company was asked to look at the Broadside project with a view to injecting a little more flair and updated thinking.

Although Edgardo managed the business, the senior stylist was Tateo Uchida, whose name appears on some contemporary correspondence with Norman Rose. Uchida also oversaw the contemporary styling of the Reliant Scimitar SS1 sports car, subsequently launched in October 1984 and bearing quite a strong resemblance to the final Broadside. Meanwhile, however, the Michelotti studio's efforts for Broadside resulted in a full-size 'softwood' model dating from February 1980 that, according to Norman Rose, was not turned into a running prototype. The front and rear of the car received a modest makeover, with body-colour bumpers that were faired in to the body shape. The bumper unit at the rear looks particularly redolent of the Reliant Scimitar SS1.

Just as these ideas were being formulated, however, the US market was suffering from one of its periodic recessions and this, coupled with the popularity in international finance circles of Margaret Thatcher's new Conservative government, and the successful exploitation of Britain's North Sea oil reserves, conspired to ensure that sales of the

Michelotti produced a considerable number of sketches related to the Broadside commission: these are just three of more than thirty produced in a similar vein, some with Triumph and some with MG badges. (John Lloyd)

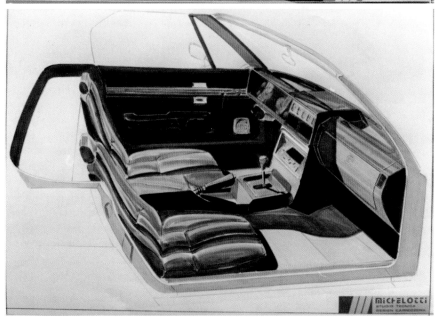

Norman Rose recorded the early stages of the construction of the full-size Michelotti Broadside, seen here at Orbassano. (Norman Rose)

TR7 and the highly rated TR8 fell way below projected targets. In a climate of cost-savings and production cutbacks, the status of BL's last medium-sized sports car programme became increasingly precarious.

By March 1980, when the TR7 convertible was at last on sale in the UK, BL and the Aston Martin Lagonda Consortium were still thrashing out terms for a deal over MG. A month later, TR7 and TR8 production began at Solihull – their third home – as production at Canley was ramped down towards an end for all car production at the historic Triumph plant (*see* Chapter 7). It appears that the Michelotti-styled Broadside Mark II was stored at Solihull for a number of years before being broken up.

Sports Cars at the End of the Road

By the summer of 1980, just a year into the first term of Mrs Thatcher's new Conservative government, BL found that it was shooting at moving targets. The seemingly inexorable climb of the pound sterling made a mockery of sales forecasts, as exports slumped, the price of imported raw materials rose and foreign rivals found it easier to sell their wares in BL's home market. BL was faced with some stark choices: to go cap in hand to an unsympathetic Industry Secretary, to retrench even more severely than previously planned, or even to close the whole business. It was obvious that the second option would need to be explored before contemplating either of the others.

July 1980 saw Sir Michael Edwardes initiate an exercise dubbed 'CORE' ('Concentration of Resource and Effort'), which mapped out a number of closures and programme curtailments aimed at keeping at least part of the business viable – pruning the business to a level below which it would no longer have been sustainable. Even before the 'CORE' team concluded its investigations, there were other implosions as, first, Rover Triumph was folded in to Austin Morris (meaning the departure of Jeff Herbert and the creation of what was called, for the time being, 'Light Medium Cars') and then the Aston Martin bid evaporated.

Just as the 'CORE' exercise was getting underway, Leonia initiated a sales promotion in the USA involving $1,000 rebates on Triumph TR7s (and £500 for Spitfires) in a programme that ran from 23 June to 30 September 1980. According to the *TSOA Newsletter*, this action helped to boost TR7 and Spitfire sales in July 1980 by 72 per cent over those for the previous July. It helped shift the stock from the showroom floor, but was it enough?

The Michelotti Broadside is wheeled out of the Michelotti premises into daylight. (Steve Redway)

By the autumn of 1980, BL's interim plans to retain the old MG factory as a CKD plant had been dropped: in October the last MGB went down the hand-propelled lines at Abingdon and in due course the factory site was redeveloped. Another sports car casualty was the Triumph Spitfire, which finally came to the end of the road and brought down the final curtain for the Triumph Herald chassis. The end of car building at Canley also led to the decision to switch the forthcoming Honda 'Bounty' (the Triumph Acclaim) from Canley to the former Morris works at Cowley.

By the winter of 1980, barring the limited edition run-out MGB and MGB GT models that BL had built, all hopes for the future of the sub-Jaguar BL sports cars rested with the TR7/8 family. At the same time BL was waiting to see if the outcome of its 'CORE' studies, including a bid to government for around £1 billion (30 per cent of which was intended solely for the 'LM' programme, including what would become the Maestro 'LM10' and Montego 'LM11'), would be supported by Industry Secretary Sir Keith Joseph and Mrs Thatcher.

Writing in *The Observer* in late January 1981, just before the announcement, Steve Vines said

Michelotti's own detail shots of their Broadside. (Steve Redway)

Rover Bravo: Rover Triumph's Last Gasp

Just as Broadside was intended to offer succession to the TR7/TR8 family (and a route to a new MG sports car), so 'Bravo' was conceived as a way to build on the Rover SD1 franchise, integrating the SD1 with the building blocks of the Broadside and realizing some of the economies of scale long dreamt of within Rover Triumph, but never achieved. The basic concept of Bravo was to carve a new Rover range out of SD1, offering a comparatively conventional four-door saloon and a five-door estate or 'wagon'. The idea in essence was to marry the front structure and suspension of the TR7 with a mid-section derived from SD1, coupled with a rear end and axle that were an amalgam of SD1 and Triumph Lynx parts.

In the 1980 Rover Triumph Product Plan, the four-door (project code RT-020) was sketched in for a late 1984 European launch, with the five-door scheduled to join it a year later to tie in with a phase-out of SD1. At launch, the proposed engine choice was to be the 2-litre 'O' Series (with the possibility of a subsequent turbocharged version), a new 2.6-litre Rover V6 (not the existing Rover straight six, but a new cut-down version of the V8, which would later feed in to the MG Metro 6R4 story – something for another book!) and an unspecified bought-in diesel engine. The five-door (project RT-023) was briefly conceived as a hatchback like SD1, but this was switched to a more conventional estate car configuration, also bringing in the V8 engine and a US launch as SD1 was dropped. The dotted line projected optimistically into the future included a tentative facelift for 1987, but the notes alongside these projects in the Product Plan carried a telling comment that they were as yet unapproved. As will later become apparent, they never would be approved, and the rear-wheel-drive Rover and Triumph ranges would eventually reach termination.

The Michelotti Broadside in finished form, probably photographed soon after completion in March or April 1980, and bearing quite a strong resemblance to the company's near-contemporary Reliant Scimitar SS1. (Steve Redway)

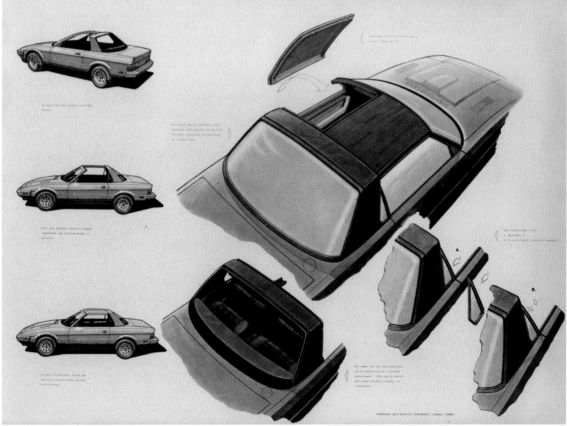

In the wake of the Michelotti-built prototype, Rover Triumph carried on – for a short time – to plan for the possible succession of the TR7/ TR8 family with a sports car based on 'Broadside'. These sketches, dating from July 1980, are by Dave Keepax. (Dave Keepax)

that 'rationalisation of model types and production is the main aim of the plan. BL is heading towards a situation in which it will build its Metro-to-Rover range on three basic frames with a high degree of component interchangeability.' Vines described the crucial role that the new Austin Metro would have, to be followed by the LM programme, but already the message for TR7 supporters was stark:

> Only the Jaguar will survive as a distinctive vehicle with few shared parts. The days of a distinctive Triumph car are numbered. The Triumph marque will shortly appear on the Acclaim, BL's joint venture with Honda. This is essentially a Japanese car assembled in Britain, providing what one major BL dealer describes as a 'vital stop-gap until we get the new medium-sized car ranges'. The Triumph badge may well disappear from some of the sports car range as BL is keen to revive the currently 'resting' MG marque.

It would, however, be about eighteen months before the MG badge returned – on a Metro.

Meanwhile, while Jaguar would clearly be given a special role (with a £150 million bid towards the XJ40 programme, leading subsequently to privatization in 1984), Rover's independence would be broken, its future pencilled in as an offshoot of the LM programme for 1985 (in the event, the large Rover would be linked to Honda, in the form of the 'Project XX' Rover 800). The *Observer* article noted that 'tentative plans for a new Rover code-named "Bravo" were scrapped recently and the improved specification of the current SD1 Rover range should keep buyers happy for another five years'.

In February 1981 the government gave BL most of what it had asked for, promising an injection of £990 million over three years and a review before contemplating the last tranche of money requested. By the beginning of the following month, however, *The Guardian* was reporting that 'Sir Michael Edwardes, British Leyland's chairman, said last night that BL Cars could ask for a further 20,000 redundancies by the end of next year. He said that the State-owned firm may still have to go back to the Government for more funds unless Sterling falls sufficiently in value'.

Soon after, on 14 March 1981, *The Times* carried the news 'Future of BL's TR7 sports car in doubt'. Clifford Webb, writing for the paper, said,

> BL is reviewing the future of the TR7, its only surviving sports car … the main problem is the strength of the pound. The TR7's losses have been cut back in recent weeks by the comparative strength of the dollar, but BL is still believed to be losing several hundred pounds on every car sold across the Atlantic.

A BL spokesman was at pains to stress that 'no decision has been made', but he admitted that the TR7 was under review along with other export projects. It was also in this article, as mentioned earlier, that there was a suggestion that BL might introduce the 'O' Series as a means of cutting TR7 costs.

This rather natty looking concept, clearly based on the work on Broadside, features MG badges on one side and Triumph ones on the other. But by the late summer of 1980 it was probably too late to save the TR7 programme. (John Ashford)

The fact was that BL's exports remained in serious difficulties in spring 1981. The popularity in financial circles of the Conservative government and the successful exploitation of North Sea oil meant that the pound continued to be strong relative to the dollar. To reinforce the point, Edwardes announced in the third week of March that BL had lost £387 million before tax in 1980 and he lay much of the blame for this simply on the strength of sterling.

A week later, BL belatedly announced the introduction of the 1981 model year TR7 range, which now featured a higher fifth gear (0.74:1 in place of 0.83:1, providing 21.8mph [35.1km/h] per 1,000rpm in fifth gear). Other changes included quartz halogen headlamps for those markets where they were permitted, six new paint colours, a new steering wheel, new hood and tonneau colour options (colour-coordinated to the interior trim) and intermittent windscreen wiper function, as well as new door lock buttons and bootlid locks. More interesting for North American enthusiasts was the universal adoption for the USA of fuel injection and, also on US-bound models, some new chrome-trimmed plastic wheel trims on those cars not already fitted with alloy wheels. Recommended retail price for the TR7 was set at $10,995.

On 18 April 1981 the *Financial Times* reported that 'BL has warned union leaders that production of the TR7 sports car might be suspended indefinitely from September'. The paper added that suppliers had been informed by BL that the uncertain market for sports cars meant that the company was not forecasting sales beyond August 1981. Less than a fortnight later, BL was claiming that Jaguar was losing something like £2 million per month, a fact compounded, no doubt, by the continuing cost of running the entire Leonia operation. It was confirmed that production of the TR7 would be suspended, owing to poor sales versus costs, while a different set of exchange rate problems – that of sterling versus European currencies – was having a damaging effect on sales of the Rover SD1, by now sharing production facilities with the TR7 and TR8.

Then on Tuesday 12 May 1981, a date almost as infamous in Triumph history as Monday 10 September 1979 had become for MG enthusiasts, BL announced that the flagship Rover SD1 factory at Solihull, built on a 'greenfield' site the previous decade, would be closed and that Rover SD1 production would be transferred to the former Morris plant at Cowley. Of main interest to Triumph fans, however, was the announcement that sports car production would not be following the Rover to Cowley: the TR7 would be wound down by October, and it seemed that the small BL sports car was, for the time being, well and truly dead.

A small glimmer of hope in May came in the statement by Ray Horrocks that, if TR7 sales in the USA improved dramatically during the summer, it might yet be possible to stay the execution and, as he told *Motor*, 'the Solihull plant could be reactivated for vehicle production'. However this proved to be a forlorn hope, for the sales never came in anything like the volume required. Meanwhile, engineering and development teams had continued to work away at various quality improvements, some of which were at a fairly advanced stage. Peter Wilson cites a solution to the headlamp pod corrosion problems as an example: 'We planned to use a plastic pod instead of the alloy one – in fact we had a solution that was just about production-ready, but in the end it was too late as the car was cancelled'.

George Spence says that the decision to pull the plug on the TR7/TR8 came at one of the quarterly Product Planning meetings:

> Harold Musgrove usually took the chair at these PP meetings and everybody would have had their say. The production plan was an issue: body production for the TR7 range became an embarrassment for them; they simply didn't want to build it and the volumes were low, so Sales & Marketing were pretty cool on it too.

David Nicholas of Pressed Steel feels that there was more to it than this: 'We'd have been able to revise production down to a trickle if need be;

we were very flexible in body production terms.' However, the fact remains that the axe had fallen on the TR7.

The day after the decision had been made to cancel TR7, George Spence was in the office of his line manager to discuss what they would be doing as a consequence:

> The guy I worked for at that time was Brian Cooke – he had come from Vauxhall where he'd been one of the last of the 'real' engineers there, once everything went over to rebadged Opels. He was a very nice, gentle guy and I only ever saw him lose his temper once. I was in his office the day after the TR7 was cancelled, when someone from Product Planning came into his office with an idea they'd costed to build 500 limited editions – a fantastic idea; but as he said, if only he'd had that information the day before, complete with their projected sales, the outcome at the PP meeting might have been different – he was absolutely furious!

So former Prime Minister Callaghan's comments to Michael Edwardes in the wake of the Speke closure announcement in spring 1978 – not to mention the threats posed at the time by the company in the transition after closure – had finally come to pass, albeit three years down the road. Boxer, Bravo and Broadside had all failed to protect any semblance of independence for Rover Triumph. The Triumph Acclaim, launched as the TR7 slipped from production (the last TR was built on 5 October), would prove to be a sad end to a once prosperous marque. Ray Horrocks tried to be positive, telling *Motor* that 'while BL has no immediate

A sad day, as the last TR7 goes down the line: there was little ceremony. (Graham Hood)

plans for a new sports car, the company certainly hopes to re-enter the market as soon as cash is available to finance the development of a two-seater based on volume production components'. As we now know, it would be many years before such a promise could be fulfilled – and it would not be with a Triumph.

The DeLorean Connection

Perhaps the strangest story of the final death throes of the TR7/TR8 family is the one that links it with the similarly timed misfortunes of DeLorean Motor Cars Limited, a connection that, as far as I am aware, has hitherto never appeared in print. The story begins during the period immediately following the announcement by BL in mid-1981 that production of the TR7 family would cease with the end of the model year. At the time John DeLorean's dream car, the DMC-12, was still being built at the specially constructed 'greenfield' site at Dunmurry, near Belfast, in Northern Ireland. Behind the public smiles, however, internally it was increasingly obvious to some that not all was well with the stainless-steel sports car business.

This is not the place to go into detail about the woes of the DeLorean venture, but just as BL was bringing down the curtain on the last of its mass-produced sports cars, some of the people associated with DeLorean and the company's wider interests were looking at ways to rescue the franchise. Experienced industry man Barrie Wills had come to DeLorean from Reliant (and before that Leyland Bus and Jaguar) and, with his connections and skill at managing automotive operations, he was drawn to the opportunities that seemed to stem from BL's problems.

Wills and a small team of DeLorean insiders in Dunmurry took a look at the TR8 roadster and planned to change as little of it as they could, in a similarly cost-conscious vein to JRT's in-house effort. One change proposed was to remove the sloping side-crease, and Wills had the feasibility of this planned and costed by the German August Laepple die-making company in Heilbronn (which had a well-established

Irish-based subsidiary): 'Laepple were ready to modify the dies in Heilbronn and stamp the new and unmodified panels at their Carlow plant in Eire'. There remained little scope for many other changes, but the team did their best to make a difference, as Wills recalls: 'We styled a new front and rear bumper, effectively – all on a limited budget'. All the Triumph badges were removed, and Wills says that he did a royalty deal in principle with Geoffrey Healey (the son of the late Donald) to take a licence for the 'Healey' name (but not, you will note, Austin Healey), 'but we never got around to agreeing the per unit value of the royalty'.

According to Wills, the business plan, which involved the creation of what was effectively a 'Healey TR8', was described in 1982 by the joint receiver, the late Sir Kenneth Cork (of Cork Gully, who had been appointed by DeLorean's secured creditor, the British Government), as 'the only viable plan to save DeLorean'. Wills and his colleagues developed this plan along with a few others and a number of trusted suppliers during the DeLorean receivership in 1982.

Of course, in order for the proposal to work, BL had to play ball. Will recalls meeting BL's top management to see if they would be prepared to cooperate:

We had several meetings in Portman Square [BL's London offices at that time] … I can remember one wonderful meeting with Mark Snowdon and one of BL's senior finance guys. Harold Musgrove wasn't present this time, but it was quite late – about six o'clock in the evening. I noticed, while we were talking, that there was a door in the corner of the office – which was more like a conference room – and that this was slightly ajar. The chair that I'd got had casters on it, so I pushed the chair back a little and sort of peered round – and around the corner of the door, I could just see Harold there – he was seated on a chair with his back to the door, his ear to the crack and listening in! I never let on to Mark or the finance guy that I knew Harold was there – but I don't know to this day if he simply didn't trust them to handle the deal alone!

Perhaps the strangest part of the whole TR7 story – and one never previously told: the 'DeLorean' connection might have spawned this Healey-badged TR8. (Barrie Wills)

Evidently Wills and his team made a convincing business case, for the BL team was persuaded to agree a deal in principle, and so there was suddenly a chance that the TR7/8 family might have survived, albeit in a different guise. BL was very strict about keeping the story under wraps, which probably explains why it has never come to light until now: 'They were paranoid about any publicity, in the wake of the MG Abingdon scenes [at the announcement that MG would be closed] when there had been marching in the streets – they'd just got over that – and so we had to "swear on the Bible", basically, to keep everything confidential.' The deal was possible only because it was done on the basis of a nominal royalty: 'there was to be no capital payment – no guaranteed up-front sum; you've got to remember the fact that British Leyland was nationalized, so to a degree we always assumed that it was a government thing in as much that together we were assisting the saving of jobs in Northern Ireland'.

The business plan was based on a much-reduced DeLorean volume of around 7,000 cars per annum of the face-lifted 'Healey' V8-engined TR8, mainly for the USA: 'BL stipulated that we couldn't call it Triumph and we couldn't call it a TR – so we had to call it something else – hence the 'Healey' brand name – and it had to look different'.

One fundamental problem that the DMC team faced in their grand plan to transplant the TR8 to Northern Ireland was the fact that they had no paint shop [the DeLorean body skin panels were stainless steel]. Barrie Wills explains how a solution presented itself just across the border in the Irish Republic:

This was in the era when Eire was phasing itself out of the initial EU membership deal that gave it a period of time during which it could progressively close down numerous 'CKD' [Completely Knocked Down] assembly plants. The country had about a seven- to eight-year window of phase-out of protected CKD, and it happened to coincide with the timing of our plan. There was a beautiful Nissan assembly plant in Dublin owned by a wealthy Arab family called Al-Habtain, who are still big importers and distributors

of cars in the Middle East: very wealthy people. And they were potentially one of our funders. But the prime investors were to be Hill Samuel and ICFC, what is now '3i' – they bought [into] the business plan.

At this time, all the DeLorean stainless-steel body panels were stamped by the Irish subsidiary of Laepple. According to Wills, the Irish government had assisted the funding of all the presses that were installed there,

but they don't like to talk about it! ... So we planned to move all the dies from Swindon [Pressed Steel Fisher] and Laepple Carlow were going to produce all the stampings, the stampings would then be shipped to the Nissan assembly plant in Dublin – where we'd have ownership of a very good 'body-in-white' facility – for which we'd have converted all the jigs and fixtures to suit. They'd got a first-class paint shop – as you could imagine with Nissan – and we were going to assemble and paint the bodies there, put them on the railway line and 'solve' the Northern Ireland problem instantly by introducing massive trade between the south and north simply by moving the painted body shells up the railway. If you look at photographs of the DeLorean assembly plant at Dunmurry, the railway line ran right next to it – alongside of the plant – and the government had already agreed the principle of putting a rucksack rail siding in so that we could eventually bring the bodies and the engines in that way – it was all planned.

Next, the DMC team 'recruited' key players in the Irish component industry. Dunlop had a tyre plant nearby and there were about seven or eight quite major component suppliers in Ireland, including Goodyear's industrial rubber mouldings plant and Tenneco, all of whom were signed up in principle to supply the venture. In Wills's own words, everything was

hunky-dory ... And we got to the point with Hill Samuel where they'd got a draft press release ready, announcing what was going to happen. The only question outstanding was what we were going to call the company.

I can remember on one occasion towards the end of the negotiations leaving Sir Kenneth Cork's office at Cork Gully [predecessor to Cooper & Lybrand's, which later became PWC's insolvency division]. It was then in Gresham Street, in the City – and I walked with one of my colleagues round the corner to a nice little bar, where we sat from about eight o'clock until throwing out time – and got progressively smashed – while we brainstormed names for the company. By the time that we'd got properly smashed, the favourite was Johnnie Walker Cars! It had been a toss-up between 'Johnnie Walker Cars' and 'Martini Cars'! But once sober we decided eventually that we would call it the 'Dunmurry Motor Company' – retaining the 'DMC' of DeLorean Motor Cars.

But within less than a week the much-read 'City Slicker' column in the satirical magazine *Private Eye* published the first major 'dirt' in the UK about John DeLorean. 'Within 24 hours of that article appearing, Hill Samuel and 3i got very nervous!', Wills remembers.

Cork was distraught – as he had taken our plan to James Prior – who, as Secretary of State for Northern Ireland, took it in turn to Cabinet. We didn't have enough money of our own. We were dependent on other people's money, but we were told by Hill Samuel not to worry – they said to leave it to them, that they would get the money to fund the plan, in other words, the definitive business plan that would be substantial enough to [in turn] pay them to raise the money.

There was a sticking point in that Hill Samuel had a tiered fee structure for raising the money: one was for governments, the second was for large corporations, the third was for medium-sized corporations and the last was for Small and Medium Enterprises (SMEs). Wills explains the problem:

They didn't know in which category we were. Were we 'government', medium sized or an SME? … So then Prior took it to Cabinet and – through Cork - told us 'don't worry guys – Sir Kenneth and I will fix

it for you'. But what scuppered it – well, you know what his [Prior's] relationship was supposed to be like with Margaret Thatcher? Cork later told me that Prior apparently didn't do his homework properly, and that Thatcher threw it out of cabinet – 'Tell the receivers to do their job,' it was alleged she said. 'If these "investors" haven't even got enough money for their fund-raising exercise, how on earth were they ever going to fund the whole project?' Some thought she wanted it to go away, of course – after all, many thought she wanted the whole DeLorean thing buried, as we were a nuisance. And so we lost our funders; and it all came to nothing.

Tail End of the Wedge

The end for the TR7 and TR8 was more of a whimper than a grand finale, and with its passing came the end of the British volume sports car – for the time being at least. The significance of this was not lost on journalists like Csaba Csere of *Car and Driver*, who wrote a brief obituary for the magazine's October 1981 issue, under the heading 'The sun finally sets on the British sports car'.

Csere said that the death was 'not unexpected. The Triumph's British brothers have been dropping like flies for years. But considering Britain's once exalted position in the sports car market, the end of the era still comes as a shock.' When sports cars worked as well as the TR7 convertible, Csere suggested,

they're a dream. If we lived in California, we couldn't imagine being without one. If you're of like mind, and the British flavour of roadster is more to your taste than the Italian kind, this is your last chance. Besides, it's an opportunity to own the last car of an era while it's still fully contemporary. That's a situation only the British could create.

Less than eight years later, Csaba Csere and fellow open sports car fans would have a new icon to admire, but of course the Mazda Miata didn't hail from Italy.

10 Strange Fruit: Aftermarket Conversions

The Drive to Improve and Modify

The TR7 promised from the very beginning the possibility of a more exciting V8-powered version, although this enticing derivative was pushed ever further into the future until, in the end, it never went on sale in its home market. Although there have been a number of dedicated enthusiasts who have created their own Triumph TR7 Sprint, thereby fulfilling another broken Triumph promise, by far the most popular conversion always was – and remains – the substitution of a Rover V8 engine for the humble two-litre Triumph four.

The quality of conversions has understandably varied from the better-than-factory to the frankly lethal, but with the existence of a legion of dedicated TR experts and specialists (*see* Chapter 11) there is no longer any excuse, if ever there had been one, for a poorly executed conversion. It is outside the scope of this book to delve into the detail of how to go about building your own TR7 V8 – Roger Williams has written an excellent book on that subject – but if you do want to go down that road, please work with the specialists who have established the best route to get to your chosen destination.

If the TR7 V8 has been a fairly cheap way for British Triumph fans to acquire their own home-brewed 'TVR substitute', for many American enthusiasts, the TR8 – and the more numerous TR7 V8 conversions – have long offered an off-the-wall alternative to conventional domestic sporting cars: an enticing left-of-field mixture of European chassis and an exotic but nevertheless mechanically simple alloy V8. *Car and Driver's* Patrick Bedard shares a poignant memory of a late colleague who clearly managed to fit the bill:

> In the nineties we had a young tech editor named Don Schroeder at *Car and Driver*, a gifted driver and passionate left-winger. He had a TR8 with a Lingenfelter-modified engine, his choice of a keeper car to love and infuse with dollars. He was killed while testing an amped-up Benz at a God-forsaken tyre-test track in Ft Stockton, Texas, a half-dozen years ago. Best I can tell, he owned the TR8 because of what the press said about it in earlier times, and because it had the right stuff (read a V8), and because he didn't care what anybody thought.

While people are still custom-building their own special TR7 variants, over the years there have been a number of series-built offerings developed by specialists, and some of these are described in the following section.

Del Lines and the Atlantic Garage

Whilst a few specialists in the field of TR7 V8 conversions have come and gone in the blink of an eye, and a few have offered little more than a rudimentary engineering service, one of the better known and regarded practitioners in the 1970s and 1980s was Ian 'Del' Lines, who ran the Ian Lines Atlantic Garage in Weston-super-Mare, on the west coast of England. Setting up in 1970, Del soon specialized in Triumphs and during the late 1970s focused on the TR7 V8 and Rover SD1 sector of the market. Lines's business extended way beyond the rudimentary function of engine transplants, however, and he offered customers everything from engine upgrades to disc conversions to address one of the TR7/8's noted weaknesses.

'We originally started to build new cars at the rate of one per month, to clients' specifications', Lines told me, adding that he completed, 'around twenty-six this way until Type Approval stopped us. After that, we did twenty-five or twenty-six conversions including quite a few TR7 rebuilds'.

Steve Redway, who made a study of the Del Lines cars, suggests the story really started around 1973 when Lines was converting Triumph 2000 to V8 power, of which he completed some forty-eight specimens:

> Getting under BL's skin in the local area, as new factory 2000 estate sales slumped, Del thought nothing of borrowing the odd BL logo too! … He followed this with a supercharged 150mph Stag and then went on to build eleven TR7 rally cars for private entrants. He was quite successful on the local rally scene too and amazingly he was contracted to build two for BL themselves as rally 'recce' cars in the 1979 1000 Lakes for Lampinen, the San Remo rally for Eklund, the Manx for J.Allan and finally a car for Makinen as well that year.

Lines himself told me that these rally cars were 'a mixture of four or five TR7 Sprints and the rest

Although the UK factory was more reticent, the North American distributors made much of the range of bold striping kits on offer through Triumph dealerships, such as these offerings from 1977.

Eddie Moore bought this specially finished TR7 from Millar Brothers in 1977. (Eddie Moore)

Jeff Poole's special patriotically liveried TR7. (Jeff Poole).

V8s'. Naturally, Redway points out, this activity meant that word soon got around that here was a TR7 man who indeed knew his stuff:

> Soon he was building road-going TR7 V8s from brand new bodyshells for anyone who could afford them. Altogether through 1979 to 1981 Del Lines made forty-three new TR7s, the bulk of them featuring V8 power plus other suspension and braking modifications – and at £7,000 a time they were great value. Many of these still exist, which is a reflection of

the quality of his workmanship and can be identified by unique VIN number plates with DL plus three numbers.

The pinnacle of Lines's TR7 V8 projects surely has to be his take on the Le Mans car (*see* Chapter 6). Lines's effort combined his engineering talents with the bodywork expertise of Dave Bennett, also based in Weston, and Lines even went to Janspeed to pick Jan Odor's brains about how best to set the car up. There was talk of a limited run of replicas, but undoubtedly high costs and the uncertain reputation of the TR7 at the time conspired against the 'TRS'. After BL killed off the TR7, Lines was briefly uncertain about the future, although he went on to specialize in rally versions of the SD1 Rover.

The Atlantic Garage closed its doors in 1985, and nowadays Lines is based in Spain, although he maintains active interests in Triumph and Rover SD1 affairs.

The Premier Motors 'TR7S'

The fact that the TR7 Sprint never made it to production did not stop at least one enterprising Leyland dealer, Premier Motors of Romford, Essex, from seeking to meet the latent demand for such a car. *Motor* had already observed, during its road test of the standard TR7 in 1976, that the Dolomite Sprint engine could 'transform the performance', and just a year later the magazine took the chance to road test one man's attempt to meet the challenge. Gerry Honeyman, Sales Manager at Premier Motors, set out to create a 'super' version of the TR7, which he dubbed the 'TR7S'.

The prototype was a standard TR7 coupé (SLA 925R) to which Premier had initially fitted US-market side stripes and Wolfrace alloy wheels. Taking the upgrades a step further, the company cleverly married a Dolomite Sprint cylinder head and ancillaries with standard SU HS6 carburettors, the end result remarkably still eligible for the Leyland 'Supercover' warranty terms offered to standard cars. *Motor* got to test the TR7S for their issue of 18 June 1977 (alongside the Coombs overdrive car) and they expressed their disappointment that the performance gains were not as great as they had expected. The magazine achieved a 0–60mph time of 8.6 seconds (0.2 second slower than a Dolomite Sprint and just one second faster than the standard TR7) and a best top speed of 116.9mph/188.1km/h (112.5mph/181.0km/h for the standard TR7).

Motor analysed the results and reasoned that part of the problem was the fact that the Sprint engine 'only has a marginal advantage in torque … 122.1lb ft versus 118.7 … and it develops it 1,000rpm higher'. In conclusion, *Motor* felt that the TR7S was a nice idea but not particularly good value for money: 'to put the TR7S properly in perspective, it's only necessary to quote the price: £630' (more than twice the price of the Coombs overdrive conversion, described below). In conclusion, 'the TR7S is an interesting development, but only in so far as it disposes of a myth. For real production power wait for the V8'. Of course, as we now know, that would be a rather long wait.

The Coombs Overdrive Conversion

When the TR7 was first launched, it came with the rather uninspiring four-speed gearbox as standard. The supply problems with the new five-speed gearbox proved frustrating, and the existence of an overdrive option in the similarly engined Dolomite only added to the frustration. Leyland engineers suggested to anyone who asked that squeezing the Laycock de Normanville overdrive unit, an electrically operated device that effectively added two ratios to the four of the standard car, was difficult if not impossible to achieve. Either the team at Leyland dealers Coombs of Guildford were not listening, or they took this as a challenge, but either way they created an interesting conversion that *Motor* tested alongside the 'TR7S' described above.

The conversion was fairly simple, as *Motor* explained:

> no cutting and shutting of the bodywork is necessitated. No trick adaptor plates are required either, for the overdrive was designed to fit the single-rail gearbox.

Changes are limited to the revision of the gearbox mounting, output shaft, linkage and the gearlever, which is a shortened Dolomite one with the overdrive switch mounted in its tip. Finally, the gearbox-mounted bracket for the exhaust has to be resited.

Motor liked the use of the traditional switch set in the top of the gearknob (as seen on the Dolomite and contemporary MGB): 'The one on the Coombs vehicle operated a commendably smooth unit. Even full-throttle changes were accomplished with little more than a slight jerk, while part-throttle ones were very smooth.' *Motor* concluded that the Coombs conversion effectively added to the normal TR7 option catalogue: 'in our opinion the Coombs overdrive conversion is a valuable addition to this list, particularly while the dearth of official five-speed cars continues. The cost of converting an existing car is £416.26 including VAT. For those ordering cars direct from Coombs there is a special price of £302.44.'

Crayford TR7 Tracer Estate

Crayford Engineering was well known in the late 1960s and early 1970s for conversions on a range of British saloons, in particular Fords but also a smattering of BMC products. By 1976 the company had shown a hatchback conversion of the Leyland Princess and had developed a business converting Mercedes saloons to estate cars. It was with this in mind that Page Motors of Epsom, Surrey, hatched a plan to create a TR7 estate car in a similar vein to the Reliant Scimitar GTE.

Without the scope of a major change of the kind promised by the factory's ultimately abortive Lynx project, the use of mostly standard panels challenged the designer's ability to make a good-looking TR7 estate car, and the result was certainly 'challenging' in appearance, albeit quite a practical proposition for a small sporting estate car with room for extra luggage. Inside the cockpit, room was found to make a '2+2' arrangement that could certainly have widened the car's potential appeal.

However, there was only one taker, registered in August 1977 as TPE 944S. It now resides in

Page Motors of Epsom commissioned the TR7 Tracer from Crayford Conversions. (Mike Collins)

The TR7 Tracer (unique, although that had not been the intention) under construction at Crayford's Caterham premises in 1977. (Mike Collins)

Switzerland in the care of second owner Mike Collins, who believes that the rumour that two cars were built is unfounded:

> I'm not sure where the two car story started, but according to the builder only one car was commissioned. The car was originally yellow with a black vinyl roof, green check interior and four-speed box. After an accident in the mid-80s the previous owner changed the colour to Red with a Red vinyl roof.

Collins plans to return the car back to the original colour scheme when he rebuilds it:

> In order to make it a four-seater, two petrol tanks were made and these were put in each rear wing at the back (like the Jaguar XJ6 of the 1970s). The rear seat back tilts forward like a true estate to give you a big load area. The rest of the car was left as standard by Crayford apart from some Wolfrace wheels.

Collins is convinced that the cost of the conversion put off people from ordering any cars from Crayford: 'I have been told that the conversion cost the same as the car price again. It simply did not make sense to spend that much money.' So the TR7 Tracer remained a one-off.

Interestingly enough, Collins likens the TR7 Tracer to the Volvo 480ES estate car: 'If you look at the styling today it looks like the Volvo 480 two-door coupé from the 1990s, and of course the original TR7 looks like the first generation Toyota MR2 from the side – i.e. low nose, high boot, it just goes to show how good the Triumph designers were all those years ago'. Ian Elliott says that David Bache of BL Design once claimed to have had a hand in the styling of this car; maybe the Volvo was the TR7 estate by another father?

Coca Cola TR7

One of the more distinctive, and rarest, of the TR7 specials is the Coca Cola/Levis car owned by Chris Turner, who, as well as allowing us to photograph his car, related its fascinating history. In mid-1978 a company called Star Vans of Luton

Possibly the only surviving Coca Cola/Levis TR7 (of three built) is now owned by arch-TR7 enthusiast Chris Turner. (Alisdair Cusick)

On the bootlid, small 'Coca Cola' and 'Levis' badges were added alongside the usual 'TR7' logo. (Alisdair Cusick)

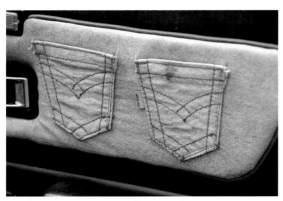

These are Levis door pockets, of course. (Alisdair Cusick)

was commissioned to convert a small number of TR7 coupés for joint promotional purposes by Coca Cola and Levi Strauss:

> The cars were to be given away as 1st prize together with £500 spending money in a competition called 'all summer long'. I always thought there were nine cars built (three for each competition) but I am now convinced there were only three in all. There were three competitions in all the first ending on 1 July, the second on 19 August and the third on 18 November.

The distinctive red and white 'Coca Cola' exterior livery is self-evident, but in addition, denim material was used to trim the interior, including the door panels, which feature 'jeans' pockets on them.

Grinnall TR8

Among the many fans of improved and seriously modified TR7s, the Grinnall probably stands head and shoulders above most of the rest. I am indebted to Steve Redway, who has researched these distinctive cars, as well as Mark Grinnall, who started the business of creating bespoke TR7 V8 conversions. Stourport-based Grinnall was always a motorcycling enthusiast at heart. As he explained to Steve Redway, when he wanted to make his own TR7 go faster in 1982, he employed a large V8, plus good-looking modifications that caught the eye.

Within a few years, Grinnall Cars was formed. Rather than focusing on the provision of new TRs to discerning enthusiasts, it concentrated instead on converting tired customers' cars to their own particular choice using Grinnall's catalogue of modifications. There were three distinctive body styles. Although Grinnall denied, in an interview with Redway for *TR Action*, having seen or been influenced by Harris Mann's sketches showing how the designer had thought the TR7 should develop, there was in Redway's view a case of like-minded thinking.

The Grinnall repertoire covered complete strip downs, V8 engine conversions, full suspension and braking modifications, 2+2 conversions, drive train modifications, colour co-ordinating and leather interiors for around 350 owners. The bulk of the conversions were to V8 3.5 to 4.0 and 4.2 litre specifications but some 2-litre Grinnalls exist, as does the very exciting one-off Jaguar 5.3-litre V12 car, albeit now without that original engine.

Unlike others, the Grinnall TRs were distinctive with full body modifications, their wide arches and side skirts influencing others and setting Grinnall apart. The final cars, known as the Ramestien body shape, were just what the TR9 should have been, in Steve Redway's view. In both convertible and fixed head formats these used a few new bodyshells with the moulded body shape far ahead of any other TR ever seen before or, for that matter, since.

Grinnall TR7 V8 conversions were sometimes quite subtle; the extent of the alterations depended upon the customer's tastes and the depth of his or her pocket. (David Knowles)

After the TR7 business, Mark Grinnall moved on to his distinctive bespoke creation, the Grinnall Scorpion. While he no longer converts TRs, he looks back with fondness to that stage of his business. Steve Redway says that the Grinnall TRs are still the most sought of all TR7 derivatives: 'some would say they're the most sought after of all TRs!' The TR Register maintains a detailed register of the Grinnalls.

Sheaffer TRZ

Towards the end of the TR7 production life, the famous Sheaffer pen company acquired a TR7 and had it specially customized by Wood & Pickett, the coachbuilders probably best known at the time for their luxurious Mini 1275GT conversions. The exterior of the car, dubbed the 'TRZ' to correspond with the name of a new pen range, was relatively unchanged, other than eighteen-spoke Wolfrace alloy wheels and special silver and black paintwork with bold 'TRZ' graphics picked out in red. Inside, however, there was a thorough makeover, with silver Dralon seat facings, an onboard computer with a digital locking system in place of a conventional door key (the height of futurism in 1981!) and a state-of-the-art Blaupunkt Berlin stereo system. The competition involved guessing the precise mileage taken on a journey in the car, described step by step. The winner was the entry nearest to the actual recorded mileage.

June Dean, who is is now Sales & Marketing Projects Manager at Sheaffer Pens' UK office, recalls the promotion: 'The car was taken everywhere by a low-loader; I remember Harrods,

The Sheaffer TRZ was a one-off special designed to promote a new type of pen. It is not known if the car has survived. (William Kimberley)

Rackhams of Birmingham and Kendall of Manchester being part of the tour'. Sadly no records from the promotional activities survive at Sheaffer, and the car's whereabouts are unknown.

IAD TRX

At the end of the 1970s a new British design studio was formed under the direction of Ian Shute. Keen to show the world the talents it could offer, International Automotive Design (IAD) decided to redesign a British sports car and exhibit it at the 1980 NEC Motor Show at Birmingham. With the recent erosion of choice caused by BL's retrenchment from the sports car market, the choice of base model was down to a choice of one – and so IAD's 'TRX' (reviving the

project name of the very first 'TR'; *see* Chapter 1) was heavily based on the TR7.

IAD did its best to transform the TR7 into a two-plus-two hatchback coupé, retaining most of the basic structure but transforming the exterior and interior style using new panels. No doubt BL was moderately interested, in light of the 'Broadside' project, and indeed BL cooperated with IAD even if there was never any hint that the one-off show car would form the basis of a production run. The car was quite well received and was obviously a good showcase for IAD's talents: the company would later be heavily involved in the genesis of what became the Mazda Miata/MX-5.

The TRX has survived and is now owned by Rolls Royce specialist, Harvey Wash.

The 'TRX' show car was a means for International Automotive Design to show off its prototype building talents. (IAD)

The TR40 was not to everyone's taste – but it was rather well executed.

Poor Man's Ferrari: The TR40

Over the years, the attraction of kit cars has tended to wax and wane according to fashion and the state of the economy; when money is tight the attraction of building a lookalike of some highly expensive exotic is fairly obvious. In the USA quite a business would develop in 'converting' humble Datsuns and Pontiacs to represent Ferraris, but in the United Kingdom one of the more memorable efforts was the Eurosport TR40. This well-engineered kit was intended to give some of the aura of a Ferrari F40 to a TR7, which on paper sounds a pretty peculiar idea. However, the end result, although not to everyone's taste, was quite a well-proportioned effort.

Eurosport UK had started producing kits for the Fiat X1/9 but they next turned their attention to the TR7. A one-piece glass-fibre nosecone with integral spoiler and wheel arches gives the typical Ferrari look, with fixed headlamps (sourced from the Triumph Acclaim, but set behind Perspex panels). The standard steel TR7 bonnet was retained, albeit with special capping pieces either side to marry up with the wings, while at the rear end a new tail panel featured a quartet of round lamps intended to look like a Ferrari but sourced from a French commercial vehicle. The choice of engine was, of course, down to the individual, but to maintain any shred of credibility a tuned V8 would surely have been the minimum choice.

Inevitably the TR40 is quite a rare animal, as each one was strongly dependent upon the budget and skills of its owner, but it nevertheless has a small but dedicated following. In recent years the moulds have been in the possession of Rimmer Brothers, who no doubt can offer the parts for any 'Triumph Ferrari' wannabees.

Influences Today: The German Wedge

As a final ironic postscript on the avant-garde wedge styling of the TR7, it is interesting to note how the kind of themes that seemed so daring in the mid-1970s are being rediscovered in the 'noughties'. If you doubt my sanity, take a look at the side view of the 2006 Mercedes SLK roadster, or even the 2008 Dodge Demon concept, and tell me you cannot see some Darwinian TR7-esque styling traits. The difference of course is that the Mercedes mystique (and price tag), coupled with the increasing rarity of the TR7, means that the chance of an SLK and a TR7 (or indeed a Dodge Demon, which reverses the side slope feature) being parked side by side in the golf club car park are fairly remote. But it does make you think: maybe that Harris Mann fellow had something after all?

Harris Mann did not play any part in styling the Mercedes Benz SLK – or did he? (Daimler Chrysler)

11 TR7 and TR8 Today: Clubs and Specialists

Anyone who buys a TR7 or TR8 will soon find themselves in need of support from one or more of the numerous specialists who deal in the marque. They should also consider joining at least one of the many Triumph clubs in existence. Indeed, if you have yet to buy the TR7 or TR8 of your dreams, then you really should join a club and make the acquaintance of one or more of the specialists with whom you will hopefully forge productive relationships. Both types of outlet will be able to advise on the selection of the right car to buy and of modifications that are feasible and worthwhile, as well as providing the sort of first-hand knowledge that even the best books cannot offer.

Triumph Clubs

Starting with the UK clubs, you should first consider whether you want to join a traditional

A TR Drivers' Club rally in the spring of 2007. Both the TR Drivers' Club and TR Register hold major events in the UK each year. (David Knowles)

subscription-based club. Such establishments can usually offer not only spare parts, links to insurers and in-house magazines but also social events such as rallies and valuable registers of historic information. Clubs can often help the novice enthusiast to avoid being duped; the possibility of a TR7 V8 conversion being passed off as a 'genuine' TR8 is an obvious and all too frequent hazard. There are two principal clubs of this type in the UK: the long-established TR Register and the younger TR Drivers' Club. Each has its particular advocates and many TR enthusiasts choose to be members of both clubs; certainly a number of the people who helped me with this book were members of both, and proved to be equally knowledgeable and enthusiastic, irrespective of their primary allegiance.

Beyond the traditional clubs, classic car enthusiasts nowadays have a growing choice of internet-based sites that vary from the freely available fact-packed offerings of a single dedicated enthusiast to professional sites providing a wealth of information, including downloadable video clips, in return for a membership fee. Many of these sites also offer member forums, bulletin boards or chat-rooms; in an age of instant information these can, for example, offer a rapid route to solving a problem or sharing a solution. One of the best internet-based TR7/8 clubs is the excellent World Wide TR7 TR8 Owners Club (http://www.tr7-tr8.com), which is affiliated to the TR Register and run by Richard Connew. As well as clubs and websites, there are independent specialist magazines, including the UK's *Triumph World*, probably the only Triumph monthly sold through newsagents.

In the rest of the world, there are local Triumph TR clubs as well as TR7 or TR8 'Chapters' within other clubs, many also affiliated to UK clubs. The longest established in the USA is the Vintage Triumph Register, which, as the name implies, covers the whole panoply of Triumphs. The 'VTR' is fortunate to have Mike Cook as Editor of the club magazine, which started life in 1957 as a factory publication and continued as an independent entity after JRT suspended support for it with the end of TR7 production. Across

North America there are many locally based groups in most states – Georgia and Florida are just two examples with their own Triumph groups – and some of these have their own dedicated TR7 chapters.

Special mention should also be made of the highly regarded TR8 CAR Club of America, another internet-based organization offering access to a variety of excellent information relevant to this particular model, which of course is relatively rare in other markets.

The Triumph Specialists

Alongside the clubs, there are specialists – big and small – who can cater for just about every possible need of the TR7 or TR8 owner. Indeed, Triumph TR owners are nearly as fortunate as MG, Mini and Jaguar enthusiasts in being able to find most of the parts they could possibly want or need.

The bigger and more established UK specialists – people like Rimmer Brothers, Moss, TR Bitz and Revington TR – have been around for a long time. They are also sufficiently well-financed, organized and connected that many of the parts for these cars that might otherwise have become NLA ('no longer available') have often either been re-sourced or even recreated from scratch. With some classic cars – including the TR6, MGB and Mini – it is possible to buy complete bodyshells, sourced from British Motor Heritage and built using the original factory tooling. Sadly this recourse is not open to TR7 or TR8 owners, due to the scrapping of critical tooling, but thankfully most of the service-critical parts can be obtained, and some specialists even offer reconditioned bodyshells.

Alongside the major suppliers, most of whom have their own websites and massive catalogues (often in printed form or as downloads from their websites), there are also many smaller companies who specialize in particular services desired by TR7 or TR8 customers. The continuing popularity of performance upgrades means that there are a number of companies that offer such services as V8 conversions or the parts needed to

Tim Lanocha and Bruce Quackenbush are partners in Lanocha Racing, which is one of the leading US exponents of the TR7 V8 conversion. (Bruce Quackenbush)

undertake them. In the UK such companies as S+S Preparations and Revington TR are keen exponents of performance improvements.

In North America, there are similar well-established companies, the obvious examples being Moss, The Roadster Factory and Victoria British, all of which offer fantastic catalogues and comprehensive stocks. Equipped with one or more of their catalogues, a copy of the official workshop manual and parts catalogues, you will be in a position to plan restoration or improvement of your TR7 or TR8, and it is worth noting that some of these suppliers offer special discount schemes for customers who commit to them when embarking on a major project.

More is Never Enough

Whereas the TR8 is such a rare animal in the UK that just about any TR7 V8 conversion is a

Lanocha Racing is able to build bespoke replicas of the famous Group 44 Inc. racing TR8, such as the prototype, dubbed 'Bulittt'. (Bruce Quackenbush)

novelty, in North America the situation is subtly different. The TR8 was sold (albeit still in fairly small numbers) and so for many enthusiasts the idea of a V8-engined TR7 is merely the starting point. For some enthusiasts in the V8 arena, 'more is never enough' and there are a number of specialists able to cater for just about every whim.

Tim Lanocha of Lanocha Racing, Jarrettsville, Maryland, is a true acolyte of the TR8 who has built some of the fastest-accelerating TR8 drag racers around, as well as replicas of the Bob Tullius Group 44 Inc. TR8. Tullius's crew chief Lanky Foushee has even been advising the Lanocha group on the mechanical aspects of the car, as well as the moulding of the glass-fibre panels. Lanocha's business partner Bruce Quackenbush explains: 'these special panels haven't been reproduced in over twenty years and, where possible, are made from the original moulds or moulds made from panels

off a genuine IMSA Triumph TR8 Competition Car'. The result is a car that Lanocha Racing has dubbed 'A Triumph With No Rules'. The company's impressive demonstrator – dubbed 'Bulittt' (yes, that's three 't's) as a clever dual reference to the TR7 project code and the famous Steve McQueen film character – has a claimed power output of 800bhp, which Lanocha believes is the highest output of any roadgoing TR.

Lanocha is a serious exponent of improvement of the Rover V8, using techniques that have served him well and allow him to service not only Triumphs but Range Rovers too. 'What I have done is really nothing new in relation to small block Chevys, Fords, etc., but the Rover people are still promoting Weber carbs and dual point distributors. I believe in a balanced ensemble, not just internal race balancing but balancing the overall package', he explains on the company website.

The cockpit of 'Bulittt' is a businesslike environment. (Bruce Quackenbush)

A friendly rival of Lanocha Racing is Woody Cooper of the WedgeShop in Raynam, Massachusetts, whose own TR8 is often pitted against Lanocha's at drag racing events. Woody explains he was drawn to the TR8,

> because of the power that it had, which was something I had always grown up with. However the TR8 actually handled and went around a corner as well, which is what really drew me in. One of the great things about the TR8 is that for every small improvement you make it is extremely noticeable. This applies to both power and handling aspects of the car. Even though most of the cars are around thirty-two years old, the look still fits in with most modern sports cars and is still capable of competing with them in every facet of driving.

Woody's business, The WedgeShop, was started in 1990:

> I started due to the interest of other TR8 owners in the area that could not find anyone else to help them perform upgrades to their cars. Our specialty has always been in improving the performance handling and braking on the TR8. We do offer a full line of parts and accessories for both the TR7 and TR8 as well as technical support. We just recently expanded to a website which is still up and coming and will soon include a full parts list and technical sections.

Woody Cooper of the WedgeShop also builds TR7 V8 conversions, such as his own car, 'Bad 8'… (Woody Cooper)

… seen creating smoke from a tarmac-rippling standing start. (Woody Cooper)

Appendices

Triumph Bullet prototypes: the 'TR7 Style' Bullet as listed in the 'X' Register

Project Number	Model	Registration No.	Date in Register (if given)	Details in register	Notes
X827	Bullet	PVC 212L	02/10/1972	1st prototype (white, right-hand drive)	This is believed to be the first 'TR7' style Bullet
X828	Bullet	FWK 788L	10/11/1972	2nd prototype (white; pave car)	Note added says '1977 tune and master carbs'. See photographs. Photos show this car to be LHD
X830	Bullet	not recorded	15/01/1973	Auto general development vehicle (1976)	Probably the 3rd prototype although not described as such
X831	Bullet 'C'	not recorded	15/01/1973	Prototype Bosch PI	Possibly a motor sports application
X834	Bullet	TLB 253M	—	4th prototype (automatic)	Notes say 'written off/for sale' and 'side intrusion test'. This black car, along with TLB 254M, was used for cold-weather testing in Ontario
X838	T2000 Bullet	SHP 431N	c. 1974	1975 Model Year Bullet Federal Certification Test = 4V PI Bosch	Note the reference to 4-valve fuel injection
X839	T2000 Bullet	not recorded	—	Correlation vehicle	
X840	Bullet	TLB 254M	—	Bosch No. 2 prototype	Note says 'master carbs 1977'. Photos show this black car being used for cold-weather tests in Canada alongside TLB 253M
X841	T2000 Bullet	HWK 457L	—	1976 Bosch 4V PI Development vehicle	
X842	T2000 Bullet	not recorded	—	1976 Federal	Note says 'not mileage'
X843	Bullet	UXC 582M	—	[illegible]	Note says 'for sale'
X845	Bullet/ Innsbruck	OVC 311M	—	[illegible]	Note says 'Swiss test car'
X846	Bullet/ Innsbruck	not recorded	—		Note says 'was 50,000 reactor. Cannibalised for components'
X847	Bullet/ Innsbruck	not recorded	—	Carb development vehicle	
X848	Bullet/ Innsbruck	OKV 547M	—	Zenith [carbs]	Note says 'despatched USA'
X849	Bullet/ Innsbruck	not recorded	—	1975 auto mileage Federal certification vehicle (auto)	Note says 'destroyed'
X850	Bullet/ Innsbruck	not recorded	—	1975 mileage Federal certification vehicle	Note says 'for disposal when agreed with design department'

Project Number	Model	Registration No.	Date in Register (if given)	Details in register	Notes
X851	Bullet/ Innsbruck	not recorded	—	1975 auto mileage Federal certification vehicle (auto)	Note says 'group co-ordination vehicle'
X852	Bullet/ Innsbruck	not recorded	—	1975 Federal 4,000 (auto)	Note says 'not started mileage'
X853	Bullet/ Innsbruck	not recorded	—	Bodyshell only	Notes say 'cancelled' and 'destroyed'
X854	Bullet/ Innsbruck	not recorded	—	1975 50,000 mile catalyst certification vehicle	Note says 'approximately 37,500 completed'
X855	Bullet/ Innsbruck	not recorded	—	1975 50,000 mile catalyst certification vehicle	Note says 'not started mileage'
X856	Bullet/ Innsbruck	not recorded	—	Cancelled	
X857	Bullet/ Innsbruck	GWK 357M	06/11/1974	Development car	Notes say 'SD1 development' and 'MIRA'
X858	Bullet	not recorded	—	V8 general development (red)	Notes say 'pave car' (1977). It is possible, but by no means certain, that this is the first TR7 V8
X859	Bullet	not recorded	—	V8 general development	No notes

This table collated with grateful acknowledgement to Richard Brotherton of BMIHT. Note that references to 'Bullet/Innsbruck' are not TR7 as such, but instead Triumph 2000 test vehicles with prototype TR7 slant-four engines. Note also that the existence of photographs of a convoy of test vehicles in Wales, including FWK 788L (X828) and at least one V8-engined car, has led to popular speculation that TR7 V8 test vehicles were on the road as early as 1972 or 1973. However, the photographs are dated 1974; the V8 development programme was secondary to the slant-four programme and it was entirely logical that serious work on the 'TR7 V8' should not begin until the TR7 was nearing launch and the '77mm' gearbox was available in prototype form. X858 (the first 'TR7' listed as a V8) appears to date from around November 1974. A substantial part of the 'X' Register documentation appears to have been lost and so information about many later 'X' number prototypes may be missing from the table. Where known, some have been referred to in the main text and are listed below.

Later 'X' Cars, Including TR7 'O' Series, TR8, Lynx and Broadside

X882 Lynx		one of 15 built	MYX 411P
X891 Lynx		was EFi, one of 15 built	WHY 952R
X898 TR8		FHC USA Spec	
X905 Lynx		last remaining of 15 built	BHP 2T
X917 Broadside		2+2 'O' Series	
X918 TR7		FHC 'O' Series, DEV1 development prototype	JVC 840V
X919 TR8		DHC USA/UK Spec	
X921 TR8		DHC UK Spec	
X922 Broadside GT		V8 Spec	
X923 TR8		DHC UK Spec	
X925 TR8		DHC UK Spec	

TR7 and TR8 Chassis Number Series

Cars Built at Speke, January 1975–May 1978

North American TR7 Coupé 1975 and 1976 Model Years
ACL/1 (January 1975) to ACL/7248 (September 1975) 1975 Model Year
ACL/10001 (September 1975) to ACL/34099 (October 1976) 1976 Model Year

Home Market, Europe and 'Rest of World' Markets TR7 Coupés, 1976–78
ACG/1 (June 1975) to ACG/4688 (October 1976). NB only 50 cars were built in 1975
ACG/10001 (October 1976) to ACG/23406 (June 1977)
ACG/25001 (June 1977) to ACG/27053 (August 1977)
ACG/35001 (August 1977) to ACG/37661 (May 1978). NB despite claims to the contrary, BMIHT advises that there was no series starting ACG/30001

North American TR7 Coupé 1977 and 1978 Model Years
ACW/1 (September 1976) to ACW/17115 (June 1977) 1977 Model Year
ACW/30001 (June 1977) to ACW/33051 (August 1977) 1978 Model Year
ACW/40001 (August 1977) to ACW/44328 (May 1978)

TR7 Sprint Coupé (never released on general sale)
ACH/1 (February 1977) to ACH/700 (October 1977). NB not all numbers in this sequence were allocated

TR7 V8 Coupé for North America (never released on general sale)
ACN/1 (February 1977) to ACN/1116 (October 1977). NB not all numbers in this sequence were allocated

TR7 Convertible for North America (never released on general sale):
ACT/1 (April 1978) to ACT/110 (May 1978). NB not all numbers in this sequence were allocated. Just nine prototypes are referred to by Norman Rose (*see* Chapter 7)

Cars Built at Canley, October 1978–October 1979

TR7 Coupé for North America
TCW/100001 (October 1978) to TCW/115604 (October 1979)

TR7 Coupé for Home Market, Europe and 'Rest of World' Markets
TCW/100001 (October 1978) to TCW/115604 (October 1979)
NB North American and other market cars in the above sequences shared the same commission number series.

TR7 Convertibles for North America
TCT/100001 (January 1979) to TCT/105825 (June 1979) 1979 Model Year
TCT/110001 (June 1979) to TCT/115897 (October 1979) 1980 Model Year
NB 1979 models possessed a unique commission number sequence, but 1980 models shared the same commission number series with the 'TCG' and 'TCW' coupés.

TR8 Coupés for North America
TCN/150001 to approximately TCN/150198 1978 Model Year
TCN/160001 to approximately TCN/160142 1979 Model Year
BMIHT records that some cars were renumbered from the 150000 series to the 160000 series. It is also doubtful that all numbers in these sequences were allocated.

TR8 Convertibles for North America
TCV/200001 upwards for the 1979 Model Year (unclear as to precise numbers built)

Canley-built Cars with 'VIN' Prefix Numbers, 1979–80
- Prefixes have eight characters starting with 'TP' and ending with 'AT'
- The number sequence is 200001 (October 1979) to 215080 (August 1980)
- A single batch of '1981' Model Year models were built at Canley in May–June 1980, bearing numbers in the sequence 402001 to 402026

Solihull-built Cars, 1980–81
- Solihull-built Cars with 'VIN' Prefix Numbers, 1980–81
- Prefixes have eight characters starting with 'TP' and ending with 'AA'
- TR7 and TR8 models shared the same number sequence
- From May 1981, the '1981' models had an additional three-letter 'SAT' prefix in front of the eight-character prefix
- North American export models possessed different style prefixes to meet Federal legislative requirements
- 1980 Models: 400001 (April 1980) to 401918 (September 1980) (these were mostly US Limited Edition models)
- 1981 Models: 402027 (September 1980) to 405636 (May 1981)
- '1981 ½' Models: 406001 (May 1981) to 408534 (October 1981)

The last TR7 to leave the factory was SATTPADJ7AA-408402 on 16 July 1982
The last TR7 to be built was SATTPADJ7AA-408534, which was despatched on 26 October 1981 and left the factory on 16 November 1981

I am indebted to Richard Brotherton for his assistance with the compilation of the above data. The British Motor Industry Heritage Trust holds the surviving TR7 and TR8 production records and should be your first port of call in checking the history of your car, from which it will usually be possible to establish key data from the time of its manufacture.

Acknowledgements

In most written endeavours there are people to whom an author owes a debt of gratitude, and this book is certainly no exception. I must pay special tribute to photographer Alisdair Cusick, TR7 owners (and TR Drivers' Club members) Chris Turner and his son Robert, and to Jim Johnson, who braved a windswept Gaydon for the photoshoot specially commissioned for the book. Their cars grace the front cover and the interior of the book. Thanks are also due to Rachel Andrews and her colleagues at the Heritage Motor Museum for their help in allowing us the rare opportunity to photograph the surviving Lynx and Broadside prototypes outside the museum, as well as to designers Harris Mann (TR7) and John Ashford (Lynx) who came along for the photoshoot and added a personal touch to the day, which was appreciated by all concerned. Behind the scenes I have also been most fortunate to tap into the fantastic wealth of knowledge and research accumulated by members of the Triumph clubs, in particular Steve Redway (Editor of *TR Action*) and Derek Graham, both of the TR Register and who have studied and reported on the Lynx and Broadside stories in considerable detail, as well as Rex Holford and Roel van Es of the TR Drivers' Club, who are supremely knowledgeable about the rare home-market TR8s. Along with many of the engineering, design and management people who were crucial to the genesis and evolution of the TR7 family – not least Tony Lee, Mick Bunker and Norman Rose – I have been most fortunate to hear the sales and marketing stories and motor sports stories from both the home market and the all-important North American sectors. Too often we Brits forget the enormous significance of the most important marketplace for our favourite sports cars, and it is Mike Dale, Mike Cook, Bruce McWilliams and Bob Burden who not only sold the cars when they were new but have also added the benefit of their experience and expertise to help me tell their crucial part of the story. Sadly Bruce died just as this book was being completed. Similarly Bob Tullius, John Buffum, Bill Price and many others have helped with the motor sports side of the story. I am also indebted to relatives of some of those who once carried the torch for Triumph but are no longer able to speak for themselves: Martin Lloyd and Cliff Young are both proud sons who have helped my efforts to do justice to their fathers' work. I have tried to ensure the list below is comprehensive, but any omissions are unwitting and unintended.

Keith Adams, automotive journalist; Brian Anderson, Triumph Engineering: Principal Development Engineer, TR7; Rachel Andrews, BMIHT PR; John Ashford, Triumph Styling; Gillian Bardsley, archivist, BMIHT; Andre Bassick, Bassick Photography; Tony Beadle, former editor, *Triumph World* magazine; Pat Bedard, *Car and Driver* magazine; Professor Huw Beynon, Cardiff University School of Social Sciences; Richard Brotherton, BMIHT Archives; John Buffum, TR7 and TR8 Pro Rally; Peter Bulkowski, Canadian TR8 racer; Mick Bunker, Triumph Engineering: Project Manager, TR7; Bob Burden, BL Leonia/JRT; Mike Carver, Product Planning and later Corporate Planning; Bob Chater, Triumph Research & Development, Canley; Denis Chick, Product Planning and later BL PR; Mike Collins, owner of the TR7 Tracer estate car; Michael, Cook, BL Leonia/JRT; Woody Cooper, proprietor WedgeShop (US TR7 V8 specialists); Steve Cropley, Editor-at-Large, *Autocar* and seasoned motoring journalist; Chris Cunnington, TR Register; Alisdair, Cusick, photographer; Michael Dale, former VP, JRT; June Dean, Sheaffer Pens; John Dugdale, BL Leonia/JRT; Tony Dyson, Triumph Product Planning; Alan Edis, Product Planning and later senior management; Sir Michael Edwardes, Chief Executive, BL 1977–82; Ian Elliott, BL PR; Wayne Ellwood, photographer at Sebring, 1980, and other races; Stephen Ferrada, Rover Triumph Designer; Derek Graham, TR Register; Mark Grinnall, Grinnall Cars; Malcolm Harbour, Product Planning and later senior management; Ian Harrower, ADA Engineering – TR8 Le Mans; Ken Hazelhurst, Maintenance Fitter at Speke No.2 factory, 1969–78; Dr Jeffrey Herbert, Managing Director Rover Triumph 1977–81; Joe Herson, US JRT dealer; Rex Holford, TR Drivers' Club; Ray Horrocks, BL Managing Director; Joe Huffaker Jnr, Huffaker Engineering, California; Jim Johnson, TR Drivers' Club and TR7 Sprint enthusiast; Kevin Jones, former Triumph apprentice and BL PR; Kas Kastner, former Triumph Competitions manager in the USA; David Keepax, Triumph Styling; Ron Kielbiski, photographer; William, Kimberley, automotive journalist; Spen King, Technical Director Triumph 1968–72; Tim Lanocha, Lanocha Racing; Tony Lee, Triumph Engineering; Ian 'Del' Lines, Former TR7 V8 conversion specialist; John Lloyd, Triumph Engineering: Technical Director; Martin Lloyd, son of John Lloyd; Harris Mann, Longbridge Styling; Bruce McWilliams, former VP, JRT; Edgardo Michelotti, Michelotti Studio; Eddie Moore, former Millars 'Jubilee' TR7 owner; Michael Mönstermann, Triumph enthusiast and e-Bayer; John Mueller, son of the late Lee Mueller, distinguished SCCA racer; Dave Nicholas, Senior Engineer, Pressed Steel (Body & Pressings); John Olliver, former 'Henlys' salesman; Richard Pilmore, TR8 owner; Jeff Poole, TR7 Enthusiast; Jon Pressnell, motoring writer and historian; Bill Price, former Manager of Leyland ST; Alec Pringle, TR Register (and support to Le Mans TR7 team); Bruce Quackenbush, Lanocha Racing; Bruce Qvale, former TR7 and TR8 racer; Kjell Qvale, President BMCD (USA West Coast BL distributors); Steve Redway, TR Register; Bryan Reynolds, Triumph experimental fitter/tester at Canley; Geoffrey Robinson MP, BL senior management 1970–75; Graham Robson, Triumph historian; Norman Rose, Triumph Engineering; SCCA, Sports Car Club of America; Michael Scheper, German TR Register Archivist; Karin Schlesiger, archivist, Wilhelm Karmann GmbH; Don Sherman, *Car and Driver* magazine; Dennis Simmanaitis, Engineering Editor, *Road & Track* magazine; Ken Slagle, former TR7 and TR8 builder and racer; Martin Smith, Rover Triumph Engineering; George Spence, Rover Triumph Engineering; John Srugis, Detroit Triumph club; Albert Tingey, Lucas Engineering, responsible for TR8 EFi; Ian Tinsey, TR Drivers' Club; Richard Truett, US-based automotive writer and Triumph enthusiast; Bob Tullius, Group 44 Inc.; Chris Turner, TR Drivers' Club member (owner of the 'Coca Cola' TR7); Robert Turner, TR Drivers' Club and owner of TR7 Sprint; Roel van Es, TR Drivers' Club and TR8 expert; Howard Walker, former *Motor* staff member; Harvey Wash, owner of the IAD 'TRX'; Dr Timothy Whisler, industrial historian and author of a number of books about the British car industry; Denis Williams, MG, Abingdon (and detailer of TR7 convertible bumpers); Barrie Wills, formerly with De Lorean; Peter Wilson, Rover Triumph Engineering; and Cliff Young, son of Rover Triumph Projects Director Fred Young.

Index